RESOLVING MARITAL CONFLICTS

Resolving Marital Conflicts

A Psychodynamic Perspective

Herbert S. Strean, D.S.W.

Distinguished Professor
Rutgers University

A WILEY-INTERSCIENCE PUBLICATION

JOHN WILEY & SONS

New York · Chichester · Brisbane · Toronto · Singapore

Library of Congress Cataloging in Publication Data:

Strean, Herbert S.
  Resolving marital conflicts.

  (Wiley series on personality processes)
  "A Wiley-Interscience publication."
  Includes index.
  1. Marital psychotherapy.   2. Marriage counseling.
I. Title.   II. Series.

RC488.5.S773   1985   616.89′156   85-13616
ISBN 0-471-82504-2

Printed in the United States of America

10 9 8 7 6 5 4 3 2 1

To
Marcia,
with
love

Series Preface

This series of books is addressed to behavioral scientists interested in the nature of human personality. Its scope should prove pertinent to personality theorists and researchers as well as to clinicians concerned with applying an understanding of personality processes to the amelioration of emotional difficulties in living. To this end, the series provides a scholarly integration of theoretical formulations, empirical data, and practical recommendations.

Six major aspects of studying and learning about human personality can be designated: personality theory, personality structure and dynamics, personality development, personality assessment, personality change, and personality adjustment. In exploring these aspects of personality, the books in the series discuss a number of distinct but related subject areas: the nature and implications of various theories of personality; personality characteristics that account for consistencies and variations in human behavior; the emergence of personality processes in children and adolescents; the use of interviewing and testing procedures to evaluate individual differences in personality; efforts to modify personality styles through psychotherapy, counseling, behavior therapy, and other methods of influence; and patterns of abnormal personality functioning that impair individual competence.

IRVING B. WEINER

University of Denver
Denver, Colorado

Preface

Marriage counseling has become a booming industry. If a prospective client picks up the yellow pages of a telephone book and looks under "marriage counselor," he or she is quite likely to feel overwhelmed. In the marketplace of "marriage savers" (L. Koch and J. Koch, 1976) are practitioners who utilize many different perspectives: gestalt therapy, transactional analysis, bioenergetics, psychodrama, behavior modification, encounter groups, family therapy, sexual therapy, pastoral counseling, marriage encounters, and feminist therapy to name just a few. Practitioners who counsel individuals experiencing marital conflict are known by such diverse titles as trainers, facilitators, group leaders, therapists, counselors, swamis, and advocates. Some are psychologists, others are psychiatrists; many are social workers and a few are psychoanalysts. Also in the marketplace are clergymen, teachers, physicians, lawyers, and members from many other professions and vocations. To complicate matters still further, "marriage savers" do long-term therapy, short-term treatment, conjoint counseling, and a host of other treatment modalities.

If the prospective client is overwhelmed by the differing perspectives, practices, and procedures falling under the rubric of marriage counseling, he or she is not alone. Many marriage counselors, particularly those beginning a practice, also experience confusion. During the past 25 years, while supervising and teaching practitioners and graduate students, I have heard many of them share their bewilderment. They often expressed the need for a book that would serve as a guide through the labyrinth of diagnosing and treating marital conflicts. This book provides such a guide for the many students and practitioners who are positively motivated to help unhappy spouses but who have been unsure about what they are doing, why they are doing it, and where they are going.

My goal in this book is to make the underlying rationale of marriage counseling as explicit as possible. By synthesizing concepts from psychoanalysis and ego psychology and by utilizing some notions from system theory and role theory, I have attempted to provide the basic diagnostic and therapeutic skills necessary for the helping professional to assist husbands and wives in resolving their marital conflicts. I have learned that clearly defined interventive goals and disciplined use of a professional relationship are more important than any cluster of techniques. If students and practitioners can acquire a grasp of dynamic principles, they will be better able to adapt their activities to the client and his or her conflicts, rather than slavishly follow some prescribed procedure.

Regardless of the setting in which the therapist practices, and regardless of his or her theoretical predilections and therapeutic biases, I believe that the principles and case vignettes described and discussed in this book will help the marriage counselor in a major way as he or she assists husbands and wives in the resolution of their marital conflicts.

In this text I have tried to illuminate every diagnostic and therapeutic principle with a case example. The dozens of individuals described in these illustrations are very real men and women; some identifying facts have been altered to respect confidentiality. Most of the case examples are derived from my own work, but clients of students, supervisees, and colleagues also appear.

A few words of caution: Many clinicians see married couples and unmarried couples in the same light. The reader is advised that although many of the principles discussed in this book apply to unmarried couples, some do not.

I would like to thank the many students, practitioners, clients, teachers, and colleagues who have contributed ideas and case examples to this book. I am especially grateful to Herb Reich, Editor, at John Wiley & Sons, for his splendid cooperation. I would also like to acknowledge my profound gratitude to Mrs. Phyllis Burton, who has been typing my manuscripts and supporting my writing efforts for over 15 years. Finally, I would like to thank my wife, Marcia, and our sons, Richard and Billy, who have had to cope with my professional preoccupations while they would have liked me at times to be more involved with other concerns.

HERBERT S. STREAN

Teaneck, New Jersey
September 1985

Introduction

In working with conflicted husbands and wives over three decades, I have tried a variety of approaches in my own work with them as well as in my supervision and teaching of marriage counseling. From my successes and failures, several important diagnostic and therapeutic principles have evolved which appear to be quite effective when utilized in marital treatment. Perhaps the most important principle is that every chronic marital complaint is an unconscious wish. I have observed over the years that the very complaints that husbands and wives bring to therapy are the characteristics in the spouse that they unconsciously desire. For example, the woman who constantly complains that her husband is too passive and too weak unconsciously wants such a husband. If she were with an active, assertive man, she would feel very threatened. Consequently, she stays with her passive, weak man and complains about him for years, not consciously realizing that this arrangement protects her and gratifies her. Similarly, the man who constantly complains that his wife is cold and ungiving unconsciously desires such a wife. His relationship with her, although manifestly dissatisfying, protects him—a warm, giving, erotic wife would terrify him. Therefore, it is important in assisting such a man therapeutically to help him eventually see why he unconsciously wants a cold and ungiving wife.

If therapists recognize that every chronic marital complaint is really an unconscious wish, they will be able to avoid many therapeutic impasses with their clients. When therapists accept the fact that husbands and wives, in many ways, write their own marital scripts, they are not so prone to manipulate them and advise them. Instead, they will try to help their clients understand themselves better. Therapists who truly believe that a spouse wants what he or she complains about can begin to recognize the futility of prescribing divorce, separation, or some other form of behavioral change. Such suggestions are futile because clients sooner or later will have to sabotage prescriptions of their therapists if those prescriptions are directed against what they unconsciously wish. For example, if a passive man unconsciously wants his wife to dominate and derogate him, then all the advice in the world to assert himself more, no matter how sage and well-spoken, will fall on deaf ears.

Over the years I have become convinced that in order to do marital therapy well, it is necessary to relate to the client's unconscious desires, unconscious superego commands, and unconscious defenses. When the unconscious is brought to bear in the clinician's diagnostic and therapeutic planning, many treatment failures can be avoided. For example, it is important for clinicians to recognize that many unhappy spouses stay together simply because they both have an unconscious wish to fight and hurt one another. When a husband and wife are in a power struggle and are unconsciously interested in sustaining their battles, advice on how to get along better will be resisted strenuously. Furthermore, if the husband and wife are unconsciously interested in fighting, they will find many reasons to avoid a separation or a divorce. If a battling couple is persuaded to divorce and their wish to fight is not discussed and resolved, husband and wife will continue their battles even if they both remarry.

When marriage counselors ask themselves what is unconsciously motivating their clients, they begin to empathize more with hostile and distant spouses. They realize that for these people intimacy and closeness conjure up associations which are painful and anxiety provoking. Frequently, when a spouse cannot tolerate intimacy, he or she has unconsciously made the marital partner a parent and feels like an overwhelmed child next to the partner. If therapists make room for unconscious motivation in their assessments and treatment, they begin to realize that provocative behavior with the spouse might be a way to seek punishment and avoid pleasure. It can also be utilized to sustain old family battles and to express feelings of low self-esteem.

Another crucial dynamic principle in diagnosing and treating marital conflicts is the importance of relating to "the child" in the adult husband and in the adult wife. When the therapist recognizes that within every husband is a little boy and within every wife is a little girl, marital conflicts again become more understandable to the practitioner. For example, when the practitioner recognizes that a sexually impotent husband is unconsciously arranging for his wife to be his mother, the husband's impotence is better understood, because sex to him is equivalent to forbidden incest. Similarly, when the therapist realizes that the frigid wife is acting out rivalry and envy toward her husband whom she has made her older brother, her sexual conflicts become easier to comprehend. Furthermore, many, if not most, unhappy spouses unconsciously turn their marital partners into punitive parents; that is, they project their own stern superegos on to their marital partners and frequently anticipate punishment from them.

When practitioners want to help husbands and wives resolve marital conflicts—in addition to focusing on their incompatible role expectations, discordant communication processes, and improper reinforcement patterns—it is equally imperative to show them how they are unconsciously helping to sustain and reinforce the very problems they say they want to extinguish.

Another dynamic principle which has evolved from my clinical work with individuals in unhappy marriages is the recognition that only happy people can have happy marriages. I believe that a marriage never made an unhappy individual happy. I also believe that a marriage cannot make a happy individual unhappy. While spouses will contend that the opposite is true, and in some cases will get their therapists to concur with them, it is the thesis of this book that immature individuals choose one another to be their marital partners. Their mutual unhappiness started long before they ever met.

As the theoretical discussions and case examples in this book will attest, perennial marital conflicts may be viewed as neurotic symptoms. Individuals seem to have the uncanny ability to find marital partners who buttress and fortify their neuroses. The masochist chooses a sadist, the alcoholic marries a spouse who will unconsciously collude with him to maintain the alcoholism, and the guilt-ridden, self-effacing individual will find a spouse who will berate and demean him. Although they are the last to agree, marital partners are usually at the same level of maturity, have complementary neurotic problems, and share many similar childish fantasies.

Clinicians of different persuasions have found that the most curative factor in counseling and psychotherapy is the client–therapist relationship. Also, if therapists believe in the unconscious and are not too influenced by countertransference problems, they observe over and over again how clients recapitulate their chronic interpersonal problems in the relationship with their therapists. Through case examples in the treatment sections of this book, we will attempt to show how the client's chronic complaints constantly emerge in the transference relationship with the therapist. Providing that the therapist does not take sides in the client's marital disputes and neither prescribes nor advises but quietly listens, clarifies, and interprets psychic conflict, the client's complaints about the spouse will become his or her complaints about the therapist. The man who berates his wife for being "a cold fish" will inevitably experience the therapist as a cold fish, providing, of course, that the therapist does not praise nor criticize the client. Similarly, the wife who feels that her husband pressures her too much will feel that her therapist does the same thing. The sexual, interpersonal, and other problems that the client believes are imposed upon him or her by the spouse are the very problems that the client will believe are imposed by the therapist in the therapist–client relationship. As clients begin to perceive that they experience their therapists the same way they experience their spouses, they also begin to have some internal conviction about writing their own marital scripts whereby their conscious complaints about their spouses are, indeed, unconscious wishes.

In helping clients resolve their marital conflicts it is important to show them how their fantasies, dreams, and history are part and parcel of their marital conflicts and how these are expressed in the transference relationship with their therapists. When clients attain more insight into their psyches, they begin to realize that marital conflicts are quite similar, if not identical, to neurotic symptoms which protect people from danger and also gratify their childish wishes.

In sum, the marital counseling that is discussed in this text is a therapy designed to show clients how they arrange for their own displeasure in their marriages. Just as many individuals wake up from nightmares and feel horrified by them but do not want to acknowledge that they themselves arranged these nightmares, most people do not want to see how they have arranged for their marital nightmares to occur.

It is helpful in counseling unhappy marital partners to have some grasp of the institution of marriage both historically and sociologically. In Chapter 1 we will attempt to show how roles, values, and customs have changed dramatically over the years. What is au courant for marriage for many of our clients may be quite different for many therapists. In examining the institution of marriage historically and sociologically, therapists can become more aware of their own biases and values, particularly as they are different from and similar to those of their clients.

Most clients and some therapists believe that choosing a mate is a free and rational decision that evolves from shared interests and mutual values. In Chapter 2 we will attempt to demonstrate that mate selection is essentially a subjective, non-rational phenomenon. Because mate selection so frequently emanates from unrealistic childish fantasies, these fantasies often have to be carefully examined in the client's therapy because they obviously interfere with his or her marital harmony.

In selecting a mate and relating to him or her in marriage, virtually all human beings recapitulate their own idiosyncratic histories. As already implied, husbands and wives make each other parents, siblings, grandparents, ids, egos, and superegos. Consequently, to help clients in resolving their marital conflicts, it is crucial to investigate their histories. In Chapter 3 we will try to explicate how the client's psychosexual development relates to his or her marital conflicts.

In Chapter 4 we will try to explain how conflict in marriage evolves, is sustained, and is very difficult to give up. In this chapter and in succeeding ones we will make use of actual case illustrations to demonstrate how marital conflicts are usually neurotic conflicts that would be present in virtually any marriage in which the client found himself or herself. Chapter 5 will be an attempt to pinpoint the major therapeutic principles involved in marital counseling. In this chapter we will discuss how pertinent data should be gathered, how to conduct a helping interview, how to make a comprehensive psychosocial assessment, how to choose the appropriate treatment modality, and how to work with transference, resistance, and countertransference.

In Chapters 6 through 10 we will discuss the dynamics and treatment of spouses who appear very frequently in the offices of marriage counselors: the symbiotic spouse, the sadomasochistic spouse, the spouse with sexual conflicts and/or problems with sexual identity, and the spouse who has unrealistic romantic expectations about marriage. In the final chapter we will attempt to describe a mature spouse and to define the mature marriage.

Contents

CHAPTER 1

The Institution of Marriage—Then and Now

Since the beginning of recorded time marriage has been an essential institution in virtually every known society. Eve had her Adam, Abraham his Sarah, queens their kings, and emperors their empresses. While the institution of marriage has varied in its forms and practices from place to place and from one historical period to another, it always appears to be in existence in every society, if not indispensable to every known human culture. Even when marriage is questioned and many individuals wonder if it is a viable institution, as is currently the case in United States, the numbers of people getting married do not decrease (Grunebaum and Christ, 1976; Hunt, 1974).

Despite its ubiquity, there has never been a Golden Age of marriage gleaming at us from far back in the historical past (Demos, 1976). Adam and Eve, not able to fuse their tender feelings with their erotic ones, were in serious trouble despite their clear symbiotic attachment. From the Bible, we know that Father Abraham was so preoccupied with his relationship to God that he seemed to have neglected his wife Sarah. The hatred that kings, queens, emperors, and empresses felt toward one another often led to violence and murder. Even in our current age of scientific sophistication, psychological know-how, and equality of the sexes, violence among marital partners is pervasive. The battered wife now has a counterpart, the battered husband. In *Wife Beating: The Silent Crisis,* Langley and Levy (1977) reported that one-fifth of the married women in America beat their husbands, although few of the men admit it.

Despite shifting roles, arrangements, and attitudes over the centuries it is virtually impossible to point to a historical era or a human society where the majority of husbands and wives consistently loved one another and consistently enjoyed their marital relationships. Let us take a brief journey and examine the facts of marital life among several cultures over the ages.

1

A BRIEF HISTORICAL REVIEW OF MARRIAGE

As already indicated, biblical characters in the Old Testament are not known for their wedded bliss. From the beginning of Christianity, sex between marital partners was something *not* to be enjoyed, perhaps even something to be abhorred. In his *First Epistle to the Corinthians,* Saint Paul declared, "I would that all men were even as I myself [celibate], . . . and I say therefore to the unmarried and widows, it is good for them if they abide even as I. But if they cannot contain, let them marry: for it is better to marry than to burn." In the third century A.D. Clement of Alexandria argued that married coitus remained sinless only if delight was restrained and confined, and in the fifth century Saint Jerome asserted that "he who ardently loves his own wife is an adulterer." By the seventh century it was established church dogma that passionate feelings between husband and wife were incompatible with the spiritual side of marriage (Hunt, 1959).

Written remnants from early civilizations, particularly Babylonia, Egypt, and Judea, reveal that marriage in these cultures was little more than an institution by which to subjugate women (Barker, 1984). A woman was property, possessed first by her father, then by her husband, and finally by her son. The husband often acquired the wife through purchase, capture, or contract when she was an economic asset. When she was not, her father essentially sold her to a man through a dowry. Only the husband was permitted to divorce in these societies, and his only obligation was to repay any dowry he had received. Marriage in this kind of atmosphere was, therefore, far from euphoric (Barker, 1984; Durant, 1935).

When equality between the sexes became valued, as it was in ancient Rome, the results still were not favorable for the institution of marriage. Divorce became extremely popular, family life decayed, and—in part because of the dissolution of family life—the Empire fell apart. Caesar Augustus instituted the "Julian Laws" which outlawed adultery and emphasized family togetherness, but his efforts were in vain. The Romans were inclined to let their hedonistic interests prevail over their willingness to conform to Augustus' new rules. Even Augustus' daughter and granddaughter rebelled against his edicts and were banished from Rome because of their disregard for the laws of the land (Barker, 1984; Humphrey, 1975).

The ancient Greeks were one of the first societies to experiment with "open marriage." Some of the highest ranking women of ancient Greece were the hetaerae, highly educated women who functioned as intellectual companions as well as mistresses. Many of the hetaerae owned their own homes and enjoyed considerable social status. According to Hunt (1959) many had a social status much higher than that of a legitimate wife. Concomitant with open marriage, sanctioned adultery, and the championing of hedonism, homosexuality became very popular in ancient Greece. Pederasty was an accepted practice and was regulated by law. However, the homosexual practices had a tendency to disrupt family life. Usually the homosexual relationship was between an older man and a boy and the Greeks regarded it as an important factor in the development and education of their wellborn youths. Such relationships were conducted in a formal manner, requiring the consent and approval of the boy's father. Following this approval, a public announcement was made of the intention to have the boy live with an older man as his lover. Family life became disrupted inasmuch as the parents were no longer held responsible for the boy because his lover became his guardian and teacher (Licht, 1932; Vangaard, 1972). From these and other reports marriage among the ancient Greeks was far from enjoyable and fulfilling.

A philosophical approach that has influenced marital interaction throughout the ages to this day is romantic love. Developed in the twelfth century among the nobility of France, romantic love is characterized by total fealty to and enormous idealization of the beloved. Of extreme importance, asexuality is considered necessary for romantic love to endure. The romantic lover, although always holding his beloved on a pedestal, refrained from even kissing her (Montagu, 1956). Contemporary marriage counselors recognize the influence of romantic love on their clientele when they frequently hear from husbands and wives: "I like him (her) as a companion. He (she) is a very nice person, but when sex rears its ugly head, our relationship deteriorates." Basic changes in romantic love did not take place until the Reformation when Martin Luther approved of marriage for the priesthood and condemned celibacy, stating that the best way to deal with erotic wishes in marriage was "to indulge in moderate enjoyment" (Vangaard, 1972).

The inability of the majority of husbands and wives to fuse tender and erotic feelings, to be warm companions and mutually satisfying lovers, to minimize hatred and to accentuate love, to avoid power struggles, to share and to remain monogamous, seems to be a poignant fact about human civilization. Even in America in the late eighteenth and nineteenth centuries the wife was to be asexual: "ethereal, passive, and far above having any lustful or passionate feelings" (Hunt, 1974, p. 176). As late as the early twentieth century, Havelock Ellis (1907) quoted Dr. William Hammond, the surgeon general of the United States at the time, as saying in a popular medical textbook that it was doubtful that most women enjoyed marriage and that maybe one-tenth of them enjoyed sexual relations with their husbands.

During the last few decades of the twentieth century, values, ideals, and espoused norms have shifted. A strong attempt to liberate and legitimate human enjoyment has been made. The notion that men and women, married and unmarried, have a right to self-fulfillment is rarely disputed. Our media declare that sex is not sinful and that interpersonal and sexual pleasure for both sexes is highly desirable. Freud, the Women's Movement, the Human Potential Movement, and a host of other movements, though not without their differences, do concur that all men and women have a right to enhance themselves as much as possible, providing they don't infringe on the rights of others (DeBurger, 1977; Grunebaum and Christ, 1976; Hunt, 1974). Recognizing this powerful shift in values and verbalized norms, we can explore what the current state of marriage is in the 1980s.

MARRIAGE IN THE 1980s

Perhaps one of the most salient characteristics of marriage in the latter part of this century, particularly in America, is that it has assumed so many different forms. Today we have "conventional" marriages, "open" marriages, unmarried couples living together, bisexual marriages, homosexual marriages, transsexual marriages, and celibate marriages. There are at least 100,000 married couples in the United States who consistently swap mates (Koch and Koch, 1976). Most researchers have concurred that about 50 percent of married men and women have extramarital affairs at some time during their marriages (Hunt, 1969; Strean, 1980).

How terribly difficult it is for the contemporary marriage counselor to do clinical work with confidence and relaxation. He or she must empathize with a rich diversity of clients who have many different life-styles and who flirt with many alternatives to traditional marriage. It is often a burdensome task for clinicians to remain therapeutically neutral as clients discuss various forms of marital interaction that are inimical to the clinicians' life-styles. Not only must marital counselors keep an open mind about such issues as divorce, separation, and open marriage, but they also have to come to grips with their own feelings about infidelity, homosexuality, celibacy, bisexuality, and a range of other behaviors. Today American marriage is a scene which displays a welter of conflicting norms, values, attitudes, and behaviors, and it behooves the therapist to be sensitive to this.

Contemporary marriage is, indeed, a very confused scene. On one hand there are widespread and persisting expectations that marriage should provide a major source of satisfaction for the individual. On the other hand, many critics are claiming that marriage is constricting to personality development, emotionally crippling to one or both partners, and a setting for mutual exploitation (De Burger, 1978). Some groups in the women's movement argue that a woman who commits herself to one man is collaborating in her own oppression (Durbin, 1977) and that traditional marriage is a form of serfdom or slavery (Smith and Smith, 1974). Many writers emphasize that masturbation or lesbianism are acceptable routes to sexual gratification for women (Hite, 1976) and that these means are superior to heterosexual intercourse. The comedian Groucho Marx said, "Marriage is a great institution but only if you want to live in an institution!" while the popular writer Jane Howard observed that marriage has become "a chancy, grim, modern experiment instead of an ancient institution" (1978).

Clients who visit the contemporary marriage counselor are very busy experimenting with different roles, practices, and rituals. Some of these roles and practices—such as "open marriage"—have already been tried in previous eras and in other societies without too much success. In any event our current generation of married men and women do not appear to be healthier and happier than their forebears. Among the married, regardless of the form the marriage takes, suicide rates are high, alcoholism is pervasive, violence and abuse are not infrequent, and anxiety is rampant (Serban, 1981). However, among the unmarried (the divorced, the widowed, and the single) all of these indices of interpersonal conflict and psychological stress are even higher. The unmarried die sooner than the married, and among the unmarried, heart disease is almost double the rate for the married (Lynch, 1977). Segraves (1982) has documented that the highest admission rates to mental hospitals are among single, divorced, and separated people. These unattached individuals are also overrepresented in out-patient psychiatric facilities as well. In the Midtown Manhattan Study it was pointed out that "the divorced of both sexes have the highest mental morbidity rates and . . . the differences between the married and divorced in both Impaired and Well frequencies are well within the limits of statistical confidence" (Srole et al., 1962, p. 185).

If being married is unhappy and unfulfilling for many husbands and wives and if unmarried life is lonely and distressful for singles, then one begins to think of the cultural context in which these events take place. As Ashley Montagu pointed out, "Neurotic interaction takes place essentially between individuals but the nature of the individuals and of the marriage itself cannot be thoroughly understood without some understanding of their cultural and societal context" (Montagu, 1956, pp. 3–4).

When sociologists and other social scientists reflected on marital unhappiness among our forefathers, they talked about unsophisticated and primitive technological, economic, political, educational, and communicative arrangements as major etiological factors causing distress. If survival was a dominant preoccupation, it was virtually impossible to think much about enhancing the interpersonal relationship of marriage. If so many chores had to be performed by husband and wife, they had little time for one another. If men and women were controlled by magical thinking and rigid religious rituals, they could not permit themselves to be spontaneous and loving. But, in the twentieth century, these factors have all changed. Today's husband and wife reap the benefits of the industrial revolution; they enjoy the conveniences of transportation and communication, they are the possessors of scientific psychological knowledge, and they have much time for leisure (Kirkpatrick, 1977).

What is transpiring in our current culture that may offer some understanding about why marriage is in serious trouble? Several writers have offered some interesting hypotheses. Many of them have agreed (De Burger, 1978; Fine, 1981; Grunebaum and Christ, 1976; Hendin, 1975; Montagu, 1956) that ours is a hedonistic society where sexual aggrandizement is extolled and narcissism is championed. In the popular media we are advised to be our own best friend, to promote our own self-interests, and to gratify our own impulses as much as possible. Books that are best-sellers are called "self-help" books. Few, if any, stress how to empathize and love; most offer suggestions about how to manipulate others. Television commercials pose magical solutions to gratify the viewers' grandiose wishes. For example, one prescribes, "Men, men, use this after-shave lotion and she'll be yours!" Another one exhorts, "Women, use this soap and he'll be entranced by you!" The hedonistic view which pervades our culture leads almost inevitably to some degree of disappointment and disillusionment with marriage. When spouses want instant gratification, when they want what they want when they want it, they are going to feel angry and exasperated with their marital partners who do not gratify their omnipotent and narcissistic yearnings. Testimony to the low level of frustration tolerance and fury of spouses is the popularity of newspaper columns full of vitriolic complaints from husbands and wives who feel deprived and unfulfilled.

Herbert Hendin (1975), a psychoanalyst who has studied the impact of cultural forces on individual behavior, dubbed our current era "The Age of Sensation." According to Hendin, individuals in our society are so exclusively concerned with their own desires that they find it too burdensome to love another human being. He contends that the high rate of divorce, separation, and feuding among married couples reflects the societal trend toward replacing commitment, involvement, and tenderness with self-aggrandizement, exploitation, and titillation. Another psychoanalyst, Reuben Fine (1981; 1982; 1985), referred to our society as "a hate culture" and pointed out that most individuals harbor a great deal of distrust and suspicion in their interpersonal relationships. Competition is more valued than cooperation and self-centeredness is more emphasized than genuine concern for others. In a hate culture, marital interaction reflects what is dominant in the society: frustration, anger, competition, and self-centeredness.

Another dimension of our current culture is the blurring of gender roles. As opposed to other societies and to earlier times in our own culture, there is neither a clear-cut division of labor nor clear-cut prescriptions for the roles of husband and wife. Approximately 50 percent of married women are now working. Many of them are in positions which previous generations of men thought were theirs, exclusively. When husbands and wives are unsure of their appropriate roles, competition and power struggles become more prominent in their transactions. The proliferation and popularity of books about how to fight in marriage (Bach, 1969) are testimony to the fact that the norms presumed to govern marital behavior are vague in the minds of most married individuals.

The social mobility that is characteristic of our contemporary society is another source of tension in marriage. Frequently in our culture, individuals marry outside their social class and/or ethnic group. Many marriage counselors hear their clients talking about how difficult and sometimes impossible it is for them to adapt to the rituals and customs of the spouse's group. Even spouses of the same socioeconomic or religious group may find themselves rising to another level and the disparity between their aspirations may drive them apart (Montagu, 1956).

Another issue which affects marriage in our culture is longevity. A model of marriage based on lifelong total fidelity seemed appropriate when people shared 20 years of married life with each other; this model may not work for marriages that can stretch on for 50 years. This may explain in part what Brody and Osborne (1980) call "the twenty year phenomenon." Many married people, they believe, cannot tolerate one another for more than two decades and want something better before it gets too late.

As we review marriage among our forebears and observe it today, the institution has not fared well and is not faring well. It would appear that at the present point in the evolution of human civilization neuroses are universal. There seem to be neurotic ingredients in every human personality regardless of the human being's prior socialization experiences. With the exception of a few, neurotic processes in "normal" individuals seem to play a distorting role in marital choices and in marital interactions. These neurotic processes are intensified and reinforced by the romantic complex, which rationalizes a neurotic state of infatuation. Unfortunately, the subsequent fate of marriages depends in many ways on the neurotic attraction which brought the couples together. As we have learned from our brief journey through history, there is nothing new about this problem; it has been in existence for centuries. However, because of the many marriages which were terminated by early deaths, the problem was shrouded in secrecy. It is now exposed by the steady lengthening of life expectancy. Apparently, longevity has now exposed for study the fact that the human race never has been mature enough for enduring and satisfying marriages and that the sources of marital discord are ubiquitous (Kubie, 1956).

If, as some authorities claim, about 80 percent of the current American population is emotionally disturbed with 25 percent markedly so (Fine, 1981; Rennie, 1962), and if the percentage of disturbance is higher in non-American societies (Leighton, 1963), is there any way of improving the amount of pleasure and fulfillment in married life and of eliminating some of the prevalent discontent?

THE AGE OF AWARENESS

If the task of any science is to describe reality, then all the mental health disciplines prior to Freud have failed, inasmuch as they have overlooked the deep conflicts which exist in any normal individual. It would appear that ours is really the age of awareness of emotional disturbance and is not only the age of anxiety or the age of narcissism (Fine, 1972; 1974; 1981).

If persistent marital dissatisfaction is symptomatic of the neurotic difficulties that are so prevalent in our society and in other societies, then the major means of improving marriages will be by effecting inner psychological changes of individuals. This is an extremely ambitious task but one that holds much promise. There is some documentation to support the notion. For example, Stern and Stern (1981) claim that in those societies where psychotherapy is popular, individuals are happier and married life is more fulfilling.

Many laymen and some professionals erroneously assume that a person in distress about his or her conflicts who seeks psychotherapy is less mature than the person who wishes to ignore psychic conflicts. To face the fact that one has emotional conflicts that interfere with marital happiness (or happiness in general) is a sign of good reality-testing and of mature courage. Distress about a problem is healthier than lack of distress and married (and unmarried) individuals who repudiate their need for psychotherapy are frequently using denial and/or repression.

When educators, politicians, and other social change agents recognize that psychotherapy is a remarkably effective method of changing human beings if performed by well-trained and well-analyzed practitioners (Fine, 1981; Kernberg, 1972; Meltzoff and Kornreich, 1970), provisions will be made to ensure that psychotherapy is available for the many who need it. Psychotherapy, which compares favorably with other means of changing human beings, can become a means of improving the institution of marriage in our society.

One of the problems in ensuring that most married individuals receive psychotherapy is that too many therapists and laymen are influenced by the medical model, which views human beings as sick and nonsick and cured or noncured. As Harry Stack Sullivan said, "We are all more human than otherwise" (Sullivan, 1947). We all have problems in adapting and in liking ourselves, and our human existence can be improved immeasurably through psychotherapy.

Marital counseling or any other form of psychotherapy should not, we believe, attempt to cure sick individuals. Rather, clinicians should attempt to help clients move toward what Reuben Fine (1981, 1982) calls the "analytic ideal." This hypothesis states that men and women can achieve much happiness if they love, have sexual and other pleasures, feel a range of human feelings, are guided by reason, have a role in the family and the social structure, have good self-images, communicate, are creative, work, and are free from psychiatric symptomatology.

CHAPTER 2

On Choosing a Mate

Why do people fall in love and get married? This question has preoccupied and perplexed poets, philosophers, clergymen, sociologists, psychologists, and many others, for countless centuries. For some the query has seemed so difficult to answer that they have attributed the phenomenon to divine inspiration or to some other supernatural force. Others, such as sociologists—who have done the most research on the subject—have contended that the answer is really quite simple. According to them all that has to be done is to determine such sociocultural characteristics as age, race, and religion of the people involved (Reiss, 1973).

On one hand, the ancient Roman philosophers described falling in love as a form of madness: *Amare et sapere deis non conceditur* ("the ability to keep one's wits when in love is not granted even to the gods"). On the other hand, social scientists have stressed the initial importance of such variables as socioeconomic status, propinquity, race, previous marital status, age, and educational level. They have also pointed out that these variables are not independent of each other but tend to interact. Thus propinquity may, in part, result from the fact that individuals with similar cultural backgrounds tend to live close to one another (Eckland, 1968).

While no one doubts the saliency of demographic and other sociocultural factors in the choice of a mate, the researcher of the marital choice phenomenon has to go beyond external factors and consider such intervening variables as unconscious wishes, ego ideals, life histories, life-styles, and philosophical orientations of would-be marital pairs. Indeed, when sociologists do go beyond superficial questionnaires and begin to interview individuals directly, the reasons for marital choices become a little more revealing. Pietropinto and Simenauer (1979) asked more than 3,800 representative subjects why they married; 48 percent of them gave as their principal reasons "warm and loving feelings coupled with physical attractiveness," while 25 percent of the respondents stressed "having a companion." Roper polls, which also involve direct interviewing, have come up with similar findings (Barker, 1984).

FALLING IN LOVE

Although most individuals, particularly in this day and age, point out that they chose their mates because they loved them and wanted companionship, they give insufficient consideration to answering the question of the well-known song, "What is this thing called love?" One of the most famous lovers in history, Romeo, described love as "A madness most discreet, a choking gall, and a preserving sweet." Unlike social scientists, Romeo was not concerned with such factors as propinquity and educational level. He experienced love as an intense, enveloping, ambivalent psychological state. The philosopher, George Santayana, described the process of falling in love and wanting to marry as that "deep and dumb instinctive affinity." In *Marriage and Morals* (1929), another philosopher, Bertrand Russell, pointed out that falling in love and getting married occur when people realize that they have finally found a means of escape from the loneliness which afflicts them throughout their lives. It should be noted, however, that for Russell the extinction of his loneliness through marriage did not endure for too long. He was married four times.

Psychologists and psychoanalysts have examined the falling-in-love process and many of them have stressed unconscious factors in mate choice. The psychologist, Carl Jung, believed that the search for a mate was completely unconscious: "You see that girl . . . and instantly you get the seizure; you are caught. And afterward you may discover that it was a mistake" (Evans, 1964). Ralph Linton (1936), an anthropologist interested in psychological motivation, described the "ecstasy and madness" of the person in love and compared the state to an epileptic fit. A contemporary psychologist, Dorothy Tennov (1979), used the term "limerence" to apply to the passionate, intense emotions that are experienced by the person in love. Limerence, according to the author, is a sudden knowing that only one person can satisfy your passionate desires. It is intensified through adversity, is "an aching in the chest when uncertainty is strong," and is the source of both the greatest happiness and the greatest despair.

Psychologists are not the only ones to aver that falling in love is a very subjective, nonrational, unconscious process. Even some sociologists have noted its peculiar characteristics. For example, Bernard (1972) found that only 3 percent of women felt free to marry—or even to date—shorter men, and only 3 percent of men felt free to marry or date a taller woman. Here we have an illustration of a subjective reaction to physical status. Despite the fact that our culture emphasizes equality between the sexes, Bernard found from her research that the vast majority of men and women wanted the husband to dominate when it came to decision making—another neurotic attitude.

Freud and several other psychoanalysts have examined the falling-in-love process. From a psychoanalytic perspective, one of the features of romantic love is that the lovers project their "ego ideal"—that is, their concept of the perfect person and what they wish they themselves could be—onto the loved one. The qualities ascribed to a loved one during the intense experience of romantic love are almost always far beyond the real qualities the loved one possesses. "Being in love," according to the psychoanalyst Reuben Fine (1975), has many unrealistic qualities and is obsessional and egocentric. Freud (1939) likened the romantic lover to the fond parent who projects his own ideal onto his child in order to substitute for the lost narcissism of childhood. He pointed out that what the lover wishes he could have been, he fantasizes his beloved as being. Freud concluded that falling in love is an irrational, immature, and unrealistic response based on the reawakening of family romances of childhood. The loved one is made into a parental figure and becomes the recipient of fantasies that emanate from the lover's childhood.

In the "honeymoon" stage of a romance the lover, having overidealized the partner, is emotionally convinced that the best person on earth has been found and that together they have found Paradise in something akin to the Garden of Eden. The lover lives only for giving to the beloved because he or she believes that the partner is doing the very same thing (Ables, 1977). The essence of falling in love is exclusivity—the feeling that one is fulfilling the partner's needs so completely that he or she does not and could not have any romantic interest in anyone else (Freud, 1914). Says the songster wistfully, "If you were the only girl in the world and I was the only boy!"

Freud, himself, was a very romantic lover. During courtship he likened Martha "to the fairy princess from whose lips fell roses and pearls, with, however, the doubt whether kindness or good sense came more often from Martha's lips" (Jones, 1953, p. 103).

One of the reasons that clinicians see many individuals in marital conflict during the first year or two of marriage (Paolino and McCrady, 1978) is that romantic love can never endure indefinitely. Reality asserts itself and lovers cannot depend on each other for everything. As husband and wife begin to perceive the real characteristics of one another, an inevitable disillusionment process occurs. Demands of living intrude and each partner gives less and focuses on his or her own needs more. As Ables (1977) pointed out, it is "the coincidence of giving less and expecting more" that punctures the romantic ideal and sparks many conflicts between spouses.

Because romantic love is only a temporary state many husbands and wives begin to hate one another quite early in their marriages. They feel deprived and frustrated because the omnipotent, grandiose ecstatic feeling of the courtship and honeymoon no longer exists and they are sure it is the spouse's fault (Sapirstein, 1948). From a psychoanalytic perspective the myth that romantic love can endure forever emanates from a fantasy that there really is an omnipotent, omniscient, perfect parent somewhere who can supply eternal bliss. A young husband who was married less than a year said to his therapist, "I feel miserable. I thought my wife would take care of me, dote on me, and meet all my needs. Instead, she wants so much for herself!" This is the plight of many newly married husbands and wives. It is well illustrated by Arthur Miller (1964) in the play *After the Fall,* when he has the wife say, "If you really loved me, you would do much more." The husband answers, "No one loves that much, except maybe God."

In his paper on narcissism, Freud (1914) concluded that the choice of a marital partner is either anaclitically or narcissistically based. The person who makes an anaclitic choice is oriented primarily toward nurturance and protection, and is focused primarily on the gratification of dependency wishes. As mentioned earlier in this chapter, a narcissistic choice is made by a person who sees himself or herself as the object. The person who is chosen either represents the ideal self or a projected ego ideal, or is chosen in an attempt to recapture a past self, a projected past object, or a person who was once part of the self. The chosen partner may represent a part of the self, for example, "my wife is my penis" (Stein, 1956). This is often expressed in discussions of the spouse as "my better half" (Paolino and McCrady, 1978).

A fairly common motivation in choosing a marital partner is the fantasy that the partner can protect one against vulnerabilities. For example, if an individual feels rebellious toward parents and other authorities, the partner is chosen so that he or she can buttress fantasies and strengthen defenses. One client found himself constantly humming the refrain, "You and me against the world!" In his therapy it was ascertained that he saw the world as an embodiment of his "cruel and sadistic" parents and felt that his wife could join him in exterminating other people. Dicks (1963) termed this phenomenon a "joint resistance" in that both partners resist facing the reality of the world and the reality of one another. Instead they become conspirators in a futile battle with fantasized enemies.

It is possible to glean from this brief review that the falling-in-love process is a highly subjective, nonrational, frequently neurotic, and sometimes psychotic process. Few marital partners see one another as they are and form a reciprocal relationship based on reality. Mature love—

which is based on devotion and attachment to somebody who cannot offer grandiosity but can offer warmth and companionship instead—is rare. Rather, most marital partners have immature love relationships and have fallen in love in a neurotic way. It will be helpful to take a look at the various forms of immature love inasmuch as clinicians must daily help married men and women resolve them (Fine, 1975).

IMMATURE FORMS OF LOVE

Clinging Love

In clinging love, the individual is always submissive to the loved one, saying overtly or by implication, "I will do anything for you; just love me in return." Lacking self-confidence the clinger is very ingratiating, flattering, and never feels worthy of very much. He can attract a partner who enjoys being idealized, but the relationship deteriorates soon after the marriage. The clinger never gratifies his own childish fantasy of having an omnipotent parent who is always available, and the clinger's partner soon feels contemptuous of her "better-half's" obsequious and servile attitude.

Alan and Barbara A. met at college. Alan felt that Barbara was the most beautiful woman in the world and constantly wined her, dined her, bought her expensive gifts, and flattered her excessively. Barbara very much enjoyed Alan's devotion and attention and demonstrated her gratitude by complimenting Alan a great deal by telling him what a great man he was. They both agreed that their relationship was "perfect" and made plans to live together. In the process Alan found it very difficult to accept Barbara's own ideas, particularly when she disagreed with him. He experienced her disagreements as rejections and began to withdraw from her and not give so much of himself. Barbara felt less appreciated and she began to withdraw from Alan and criticize him. The "perfect" relationship deteriorated before the couple had a chance to live together.

Sadistic Love

Basically, the sadistic person is one who feels very weak but compensates for and denies his vulnerability by choosing a partner whom he can derogate and demean. In effect, he places the partner in the position that he most fears. The feeling of weakness that the sadistic individual is trying to defend against emanates from his position as a child where he felt small and weak next to his parents. Consequently, he does to his partner what he felt what was done to him and says to himself, "I'll show you what it feels like to feel small and be dominated and demeaned."

Usually the partner that the sadistic person chooses is masochistic— often the clinging vine type that we just discussed. The masochistic lover vicariously identifies with the sadistic partner's seeming strength and is initially pleased to be associated with somebody so powerful. However, because both partners always identify with one another, the sadistic partner begins to feel guilty for his transgressions and seeks punishment and the masochistic partner begins to feel rage for being humiliated. After a short while the two partners switch roles with the masochist becoming the sadist and vice versa. The sadomasochistic marriage is one that confronts clinicians constantly.

Charlie and Daisy B. were a couple in their thirties who met in a political organization in which Charlie was the president. Daisy admired him for his "strength," "virility," and "assertiveness" and told her therapist that the main reason she married Charlie was to "absorb his strength." Charlie told his therapist how much he initially loved Daisy's "warm receptivity." Not too long after they were married, Daisy began to resent Charlie's abusiveness and contempt. She couldn't tolerate his constantly ordering her around and began to retaliate by ordering Charlie around. At first Charlie would apologize for his "insensitivity" to Daisy and try to make amends. After a while, however, he began to feel like Daisy's "servant" and started to abuse her again. The couple found themselves on a perpetual symbolic seesaw, each constantly struggling for power and each feeling guilty of having power.

Rescuing Love

Rescuing love is usually found among men but is also observed in women. In his *Contributions to the Psychology of Love* (1910) Freud described a form of love in which the man wishes to rescue the woman from her unhappy lot. Consequently, he chooses a woman who seems quite unhappy and he wants to save and strengthen her. This behavior derives from the boy's wish to perceive his mother as an unhappy victim of his father's domination; that is, she was forced to have sex with father. Many boys, in their competition with their fathers, like to feel that father is abusing mother sexually so that they can have reason to save her and possess her. This belief is often played out in the fantasy of many boys and men who imagine themselves rescuing a whore from other men who exploit her.

After the man rescues his woman, there is an initial feeling of mutual elation. The man feels victorious and the unhappy woman feels protected. However, as in all immature forms of love, the elated feeling diminishes and disillusionment sets in. Because the rescuer is unconsciously rescuing a mother figure, he begins to feel guilty about his conquest (i.e., he damaged father) and then "turns off" sexually and interpersonally. In addition, because the unhappy woman is hardly in a position to give her partner very much, he feels deprived. The unhappy woman begins to feel that she really wasn't rescued and instead of feeling grateful and happy for what she got, she begins to feel unloved all over again.

Ellen C., a woman in her thirties was in an unhappy marriage. Her husband neglected her, beat her physically, and rarely wanted to have sex with her. She began to have an affair with Fred, a single man, and spent a lot of time telling Fred about her horrible marriage. Fred felt enormous sympathy for Ellen and kept on telling her what an immature and sadistic man her husband was. He also told her that she should move out of her home and that he would take care of her in his apartment and marry her. Ellen accepted the offer gladly.

At first, as Ellen described it to her marriage counselor, life with Fred was "ecstatic." She "thrived on his kindness, sensitivity, and sexual attentiveness." However, the sexual relationship between Ellen and Fred, which was mutually enjoyable for several months, began to deteriorate. Fred became impotent and, of course, Ellen felt very deprived. The mutual elation turned into mutual anger and despair, and when Ellen and Fred sought marriage counseling, they were seriously considering a divorce.

Compulsive Love

Individuals who are compulsive lovers are usually plagued by self-doubt. Their compulsive love serves the purpose of warding off a variety of feelings and fantasies which induce anxiety. By having compulsive sex with a member of the opposite sex, they try to prove to themselves that they have no homosexual inclinations; by declaring their love constantly to their partners, they can deny their hatred; and by involving themselves in a love relationship in which they receive constant attention, they can buttress their shaky self-images and low self-esteem.

The compulsive lover usually attracts a very needy person. For a short period, both partners believe that they have found a means of overcoming distress. However, the compulsive lover rarely gets much pleasure from his love relationship because his real conflicts are not being resolved. Like an addict, he receives a temporary high but then has to return to living with his self-doubts. Consequently, he begins to resent his lover. His needy partner feels upset with his angry displays and withdrawal and usually withdraws and sinks into a depression.

Grace D., a woman in her thirties, was very attracted to Hank, a man in his late twenties. Grace found that Hank, in contrast to other men she had dated, "could tolerate and even enjoy" her insatiable sexual drive, her desire to be with her man constantly, and her open declarations of admiration. Hank, a man who had experienced a deprived childhood and who felt like "a second-class citizen" next to most people, was very stimulated by Grace's openness, sexuality, and wish for symbiotic togetherness. For many months, the couple enjoyed an idyllic relationship and, without any ambivalence, married.

While their mutually enjoyable relationship continued for a few months into the marriage, both partners soon began to suffer. Hank kept feeling that he had "no space" whatsoever and became infuriated with Grace's "demandingness" and "clingingness." In response to Hank's lack of receptivity, Grace handled her own rage by having an extramarital affair.

While Grace was having an affair without Hank's conscious knowledge, she felt more relaxed and less demanding of him. This shift in Grace allowed Hank to feel more relaxed himself. But, when he turned to Grace with affection, she felt so guilty about her affair that she couldn't relate to Hank comfortably. As is true with many spouses involved in extramarital sex, Grace unconsciously arranged for Hank to discover her affair (Strean, 1980). Outraged, Hank yelled, screamed, and physically abused Grace until she felt appropriately punished. Both of them needed several years of psychotherapy before they could overcome their immature expressions of love.

Unrequited Love

Many individuals seek for the perfect parent. The more unavailable and/or unattainable the love object, the more lovable the object seems to be. Because loving feelings, and particularly erotic fantasies, toward a parent usually induce profound guilt, an unavailable object is safer to love. If the unavailable and unattainable person responded, it would be like having sex with a much loved parent—something that is taboo and something that must be rejected. Teenagers, particularly, often love actors, actresses, or other heroes and heroines from a distance. They can feel their passion but do not have to act on it and therefore, can avoid feeling guilt and torment.

Clinicians frequently see in therapy men and women who ardently love the unavailable object, but become full of disdain if the unavailable object, or anybody else, responds warmly to them. While these clients are full of rationalizations about their likes and dislikes, what they need to confront and master is their search for a perfect parent. They need to come to grips with their wish for the perfect parent. They also need to see how guilty they feel about their incestuous wishes and realize why they reject the unavailable object or anybody else who responds affectionately toward them.

Ian E., age 35, was in therapy because he could not sustain an attachment to any woman. He sought out the most attractive women he could find, usually those for whom other men were competing, and earnestly tried to woo them. If a woman responded to him, he quickly rejected her, but if she didn't respond to him, he strove even more valiantly to woo her. When Ian failed to attract a woman, he became depressed for long periods of time.

In his treatment, Ian eventually learned that he was carrying on a futile battle to win mother from father. He also learned that as soon as he thought he had won over a mother figure he had to disparage her, to avoid feeling "so dirty." Ian also learned that as guilty as he felt about winning over a symbolic mother, if he didn't, he thought he was an incomplete man. This vicious cycle took Ian some time to untangle in therapy.

Celibate Love

Another immature form of love that derives from the pursuit of a parent is celibate love. Many individuals, if not most, unconsciously make their mates parental figures. They then have to cope with uncomfortable sexual feelings toward their partners who remind them of their mothers or fathers. When incestuous wishes are powerful, one way of dealing with a lover or marital partner is to have a relationship which is exclusively nonerotic— then there is nothing much to feel guilty about.

One of the reasons that couples can live together with relative ease but become very unhappy when they get married is that the marriage bond unconsciously symbolizes home and family. As long as the individual is having sex with a person who is not home and mother (or father), life is reasonably comfortable. It is many a potent man who becomes impotent with a woman when he makes her his bride; it is many an orgastic woman who becomes frigid with a man when she marries him and then sees him as a father figure.

Mature love involves a willingness to fuse tender and erotic feelings toward one object. Celibate people feel so uncomfortable about their erotic feelings toward those they love that they have to renounce them and try to rationalize away their neurotic inhibitions. The popular writer Erica Jong in *Fear of Flying* (1973) stated the conflict very well: "I cannot fuck the one I love, and I cannot love the one I fuck."

Jill F., a 27-year-old woman, told her therapist that she and her husband Ken "made mad passionate love" while they were living together but within weeks after they got married, "we both turned off to each other" and hardly had sex at all. While Jill and Ken had all kinds of rationalizations to explain their lack of interest in each other—hard work, different sleep patterns and so on—they both were really amazed and acutely upset when they noted that their blissful love affair had turned into an asexual, dull marriage.

It took many months of psychotherapy for both Jill and Ken to realize that the main reason neither of them could sustain their love for one another after they got married was because each had made the other a parental figure. As their therapists encouraged them to fantasize about the other, they were eventually able to see that their asexual marriage protected both of them from facing unacceptable incestuous wishes which created enormous anxiety for them both.

Homosexual Love

From a psychoanalytic point of view, most men and women who become homosexual have had very frustrating childhoods. Usually they have experienced parents who were cool and detached with one another, both physically and emotionally. Having experienced poor role models who failed to demonstrate that love between members of the opposite sex can be enjoyable and enriching, homosexual men and women are in an acute rage most of the time—even though much of their rage is unconscious. In almost every case they are very frightened of their sexual fantasies toward the opposite sex; consequently, they regress and have an imaginary mother-child relationship with their homosexual partners (Socarides, 1977).

Leo G., age 20, came for therapy after being jilted by his homosexual male partner. After his therapist helped him mourn his loss, Leo felt less depressed and more self-confident. In what he described as his "new psychological state," he told his male therapist that he had actually been in conflict about his homosexual love life and wanted to understand it better.

As Leo reviewed the story of his life, he recalled memories in which he felt "indignant toward my cold father but had to suppress it." He also remembered many sexual fantasies toward his mother which he also had to deny most of his life. Of particular importance in his therapy were dreams and fantasies which strongly pointed to the fact that Leo was "so frightened to compete with men for women" that he decided early in life it was less threatening to submit to men "like a woman" than "to be a man and get clobbered."

Critical Love

In determining the selection of a mate, the complementarity or "fit" of the two partners is of importance (Lutz, 1964). Psychoanalysts and other clinicians have for some time noted the complementarity of the sadist and the masochist, the dependent alcoholic and the indulgent spouse, and the deceiver married to the individual who unconsciously gets gratification from being deceived (Waelder, 1941). What marriage counselors of many different persuasions have also been able to demonstrate is that regardless of how much a spouse criticizes a partner's sadism, sloppiness, gambling, or alcoholism, unconsciously he admires it and receives vicarious gratification from the partner's temper tantrums, indifference to manners, and so on.

In critical love, the partner who criticizes seizes upon a quality in the mate which he cannot tolerate within himself. Instead of facing his own childish wishes, for example, sadistic or competitive thoughts, the critical lover attacks the partner, saying covertly "It's not me who has these negative qualities, it's you! What's wrong with you?" He overuses the defense mechanism of projection.

The critical partner usually finds a guilt-ridden mate who feels a strong need to be punished for real or imagined transgressions. As in the sadomasochistic relationship, the partners often exchange roles and take turns in criticizing and being criticized. Usually both partners have weak self-images and derive some temporary comfort when they demean the other.

Madeline H., a woman in her forties, was in therapy because of a very conflicted, sadomasochistic marriage that was in its fifteenth year. One issue that became prominent in her treatment was that she became very furious when her husband watched wrestling matches on television. Although she was extremely critical of the "viciousness" of the wrestlers, their "barbaric" habits, and their "uncivil attitudes," she came closer to understanding her unconscious identification with her husband's interest in wrestling: One day she found herself bellowing, "Anybody who watches such a brutal sport like wrestling ought to be shot."

Loving the Partner's Parents

While I have already alluded to the fact that many people fall in love because they believe their partner is a perfect parent, there is a related phenomenon in which the individual is unconsciously attracted to the fiance's father or mother, and usually much more to them than to the future spouse. The partner's family, in effect, is what is really loved and the individual looks forward to becoming a prized son or daughter— something very much wanted for many years prior to meeting the prospective mate.

Usually the partner of the man or woman feels deprived and unconsciously identifies with the prospective mate's wish to have a new, different, and better family.

Norman I., age 24, was engaged to Olive for about six months. Although he enjoyed being with Olive alone, more than half of their time was spent with Olive's family. Norman particularly liked talking with Olive's father about sports, business, and other mutual interests. When Norman found out that Olive's parents were going to move to a different country, and one where it was impossible for Norman and Olive to live, Norman broke the engagement and never saw Olive again.

It was very clear that Norman was much more attracted to Olive's father than he was to Olive, and when he saw he couldn't have Olive's father, he lost interest in her.

Revengeful Love

Many individuals have felt like scapegoats in their own families and yearn to get even with the parents and siblings they feel mistreated them. One way of trying to erase old pains that derive from real or imagined family mistreatment is to choose a marital partner who will induce discomfort in one's siblings or parents.

Peter J., age 25, had a very hostile relationship to an older sister. He felt inferior to her and was very jealous of her superior academic gifts and social skills. One of the reasons that Peter married Roberta, he told his therapist, was to make his sister jealous and have her feel as uncomfortable as he had felt while growing up.

While Peter felt great during his courtship showing off Roberta to his sister and to others, Roberta soon tired of "feeling used and being treated like an object" and her relationship with Peter deteriorated.

The immature forms of love reviewed in this chapter are not chosen consciously or deliberately by the individuals. Rather, those individuals who love immaturely have never been helped to grow up. They cling to childish fantasies, are influenced by internal punitive voices, and are compelled to utilize maladaptive defenses. Unfortunately, the fate of a marriage is decided long before the marriage occurs. The human psyche is formed early in childhood and the result is enshrined in the person, usually without his or her awareness. A love relationship does not create anything really new in the partners—their wishes, defenses, and habitual ways of coping existed long before the partners met. There are few if any innocent victims of marital discord; their misfortunes were unconsciously arranged (Bergler, 1963). This is why it is important for troubled husbands and wives to understand how their life stories strongly influence their immature love patterns. In Chapter 3, to which we now turn, we will discuss how psychosexual development strongly influences marital dysfunctioning and marital unhappiness.

CHAPTER 3

Psychosexual Development and its Relationship to Marital Conflict

The way in which individuals cope with the vicissitudes of marriage is shaped by the stories of their lives. Each person enters marriage with an inner script. The way he perceives and relates to his mate is very much governed by experiences in previous relationships with parents and significant others. If life during a child's formative years was gratifying, the chances are high that the individual will be propelled toward a gratifying relationship in marriage. On the other hand, if the child experienced a great deal of frustration or was dealt with ambivalently or inconsistently, in all probability he will have a marital relationship that is frustrating, ambivalent, and inconsistent. As already implied in earlier chapters, this is not a conscious, deliberate process; rather, each spouse unconsciously recapitulates in marriage what transpired between himself and his parents and what transpired between his parents as a couple. To ensure a healthy and happy marriage, the prospective spouse not only needs to have had healthy, happy parents who loved him consistently, but he also needs to have had parents who enjoyed and loved each other consistently. A rather tall order!

In this chapter we will review the stages of psychosexual development through which all children traverse and we will attempt to demonstrate how a child's journey through his early life experiences will markedly influence how he feels and functions in marriage.

NATURE AND NURTURE

Clinicians sometimes overlook a very important variable that affects the individual's self-image and his interpersonal relationships. That variable is his native endowment or his constitution. Although one's environment certainly influences how intelligent and how energetic one becomes, these aspects of the personality are largely inherited. No matter how benign their environment and no matter how appropriately stimulating their care-takers, some children can never become brilliant, beautiful, charming, or creative. If parents cannot accept a child's limitations, but reject and/or pressure him instead, the child will incorporate these parental responses into his psyche. He, in turn, will anticipate rejecting and pressuring re-sponses from others, including his spouse.

Harry Stack Sullivan (1972) pointed out that the image an individual has of himself is largely "an introjection" of how he thinks other people have viewed him. While the color of the eyes, the shape of the body, the drive endowment, and the intellectual capacities of a child are essentially inherited and by themselves shape his interaction with others, how sig-nificant others respond to these constitutional givens is extremely pertinent. Certainly if a child is handsome, bright, and energetic, he has a better chance in most families to love and be loved than if he were ugly, stupid, and lethargic. However, many parents find it difficult to tolerate a bright, energetic, good looking child, and their subtle or overt repudiation of him will strongly shape his self-image and his eventual marital interaction.

Jerry Z., age 24, was in marital counseling because he could not cope with his wife's "constant criticisms." Over and over again, his wife Rena would make disparaging remarks about Jerry, citing his poor intelligence, sloppy demeanor, and nonexistent sense of humor. While Jerry, in re-sponse to Rena, would vacillate between exhibiting angry temper tan-trums and depressive withdrawals, his therapy revealed that in many ways he unconsciously agreed with Rena's criticisms.

Inasmuch as Jerry was a successful professional who had already demonstrated his intellectual potential and social skills, his male therapist Dr. A. was able to point out to him the discrepancy between the objective facts about himself and his own self-appraisals. As Jerry brought in memories from his childhood it became clear that his parents, particularly his mother, had had difficulty in really appreciating an energetic, bright, good looking boy. His recollections from his childhood revealed that his spontaneous curiosity, his enthusiasm, and his wit induced a great deal of anxiety in his parents, and by criticizing Jerry they were unconsciously trying to wipe out his native strengths.

While Jerry was attracted to Rena because she was "bright" and "com-petent," his therapy unearthed the fact that he felt very uncomfortable about his strengths and married someone who would sustain and rein-force his negative self-image.

While many parents are threatened by their children's native strengths, we have already suggested that some parents cannot accept their son's or daughter's constitutional limitations. Many fathers and mothers need to believe that their children are superathletes, brilliant geniuses, or Hollywood stars, rather than recognize that their children are average or below average mortals. They make their children narcissistic extensions of themselves and constantly idealize them and fantasize that their children are close to omnipotent.

A child who has not been helped to face his realistic limitations expects the world to cater to his grandiosity; he can never tolerate criticism and is usually full of anger toward anybody who does not indulge him. Obviously this kind of individual becomes a narcissistic spouse who is very difficult to live with.

Mary Y., age 30, was in therapy because she "needed help in divorcing Jack," her husband. She described Jack as "stubborn, intolerant, and unromantic." As she perceived her marriage, her "needs were never met." In her treatment Mary eventually was able to see that she wanted Jack to treat her the same way her parents did, which was to praise her constantly and never criticize her.

Both of her parents wished to experience Mary, an above-average looking girl, as "a Marilyn Monroe." Though she was of average intelligence, Mary's parents continually told her she was brilliant and would be the first woman to be a Supreme Court Judge. When Mary received B's or C's in her school work, she was told by her mother and father that her teachers were either threatened by her or were too limited to appreciate her.

Mary had many romances but they all ended within a few months because her boyfriends were "not good enough." Although she felt Jack could appreciate her, he too "did not come up to par" and she grew to hate him.

Part of growing up is learning to face one's native endowment as it is. When children are not helped to view their intelligence and physical attributes realistically, they either become too self-effacing or too grandiose as spouses.

THE ORAL STAGE (TRUST VS. MISTRUST)

The first phase of maturational development has been referred to as the "oral period" (Freud, 1905) because the interests and wishes of the infant center around the mouth. To be fed and made comfortable through nursing are paramount desires at this time. The feeling of being loved, wanted, and played with is a crucial part of the infant's diet, and the intake of nourishment and acceptance of love should proceed simultaneously (English and Pearson, 1945). Direct investigation of children has shown beyond any doubt the tremendous importance of love for the well-being of the child (Spitz, 1965). Loss or withdrawal of an important person is the most devastating experience a child can have, and its effects are disastrous for a later feeling of well-being. The acronym TLC (for "tender loving care") has become current as a result of research on child development. In animals as well as in humans, tender loving care in childhood is essential for a happy adulthood (Fine, 1981).

Erik Erikson (1950) called the first year of life the "trust-mistrust phase" because he was able to demonstrate that if the child has a warm, consistent, empathetic relationship with the mother during the first year, the child develops an "inner certainty" and a trusting attitude which helps immeasurably in the enjoyment of interpersonal relationships.

For a marital relationship to be enjoyable, both partners must be able to depend on and trust each other. If both have experienced a warm feeling at their mothers' breasts, have enjoyed being caressed and hugged, and have learned that to depend on another person does not lead to envelopment or abandonment, then there is a strong likelihood that they can give and take with one another in a relatively conflict-free atmosphere. On the other hand, if they experienced their mothers as ambivalent, inconsistent, frustrating, or unloving, they will tend to view their partners the same way.

Many sexual and interpersonal problems in marriage evolve from the oral period. The fondling, caressing, and other movements in sex are very reminiscent of the early mother-infant interaction during the first year of life. If these experiences as an infant were upsetting, the adult spouse will inhibit these desires because he or she will worry about being frustrated, abandoned, or mishandled.

If a child never learned to trust his mother, he will not trust his spouse. Many husbands and wives who are extremely suspicious of their partners' motives and behavior and who see injustices occurring every day in their marital lives are individuals who could not trust their mothers. The psychoanalyst Melanie Klein pointed out that the child who is frustrated severely during the first year of life is full of fury and views the mother as having "bad breasts" (Klein, 1957). This view of the mother becomes displaced onto the marital partner, and whether the partner is husband or wife, he or she is regarded as ungiving, hostile, and sadistic.

Joan V., age 24, was in marital counseling because she was convinced that her husband hated her. She suspected him of having extramarital affairs, spending their money secretly, and planning to leave her. In her transference relationship with her male therapist, Dr. C., she experienced him the same way. Joan also reported that in her contacts with previous therapists, both male and female, she "could not trust any of them because they were all very selfish people."

In her treatment with Dr. C., Joan was able to understand how she was recapitulating her relationship with her mother with virtually everybody who was important to her. It turned out that Joan's mother was very ill during her first two years of life and eventually died. All of the fury and all of the mistrust that Joan felt toward her mother was transferred onto her husband and others.

During the first year of life the infant is dominated by the "pleasure principle" (Freud, 1905) and therefore wants instant gratification. However, he is inevitably going to be rebuffed and eventually has to accept the "reality principle"; that is, that he cannot always have what he wants when he wants it. For example, the infant may want continued suckling at the breast when his biological equipment makes weaning more appropriate. He may want to be carried when he has the capacity to crawl.

Weaning, frustration, and the ability to renounce gratification at times are prerequisites for healthy maturation. However, many parents have difficulty saying "no" to their children; consequently, their children never learn to relinquish some of their infantile narcissism and grow up thinking that a breast should be available at all times. Those children who have their narcissistic wishes constantly gratified, grow up to become adults who expect their spouses to gratify them constantly. They become furious if the spouse says "no" to them.

Judith T., age 40, had been through three marriages. When she was ready to leave her fourth husband, she thought it would be a good idea to consider marriage counseling. In her therapy with Dr. D., a woman therapist, she spent most of her sessions complaining about her tendency to choose "ungiving" men. However, when Dr. D. attempted to have Judith describe her husbands' inconsiderateness, it turned out that all of her men were far from ungiving; rather, Judith was dominated by the pleasure principle and was extremely narcissistic. As a child she had intimidated both of her parents and they indulged her excessively. In her treatment, it took her several years before she could learn to take "no" for an answer.

The psychiatrist and psychoanalyst Margaret Mahler (1968) described three phases of development which all infants traverse. The first phase is the "autistic," the second is the "symbiotic," and the third is "object constancy." The autistic phase refers to the first two or three months of life when the infant is exclusively preoccupied with his own interests and demands and cannot appreciate the fact that other people have their own needs. Hence, the infant at this time of life is extremely narcissistic and is dominated by the pleasure principle. As the infant matures and learns to appreciate the availability of a mother and enjoy her ministrations, he moves into the symbiotic phase and wants to be one with his mother. While the symbiosis is mutually pleasurable, a healthy mother-infant dyad advances toward what Mahler referred to as "separation-individuation." If the child feels loved while autonomous, he can begin to internalize this positive experience and feel a healthy self-esteem away from his mother.

We have already referred to the autistic spouse who is very narcissistic. The symbiotic marital partner is one who becomes a clinging vine and can never separate from the spouse. He or she must make every decision with the spouse and wants the partner to do the same. The symbiotic partner feels demolished and desperate when the mate shows any autonomy. This person was never helped to enjoy feeling separate and individuated as a child and insists on a symbiosis in marriage.

Mark S., age 40, came into treatment after his wife, to whom he had been married for 15 years, started to work. She had been at home throughout their entire marriage and Mark responded to her autonomous act as if he were "being killed." He was desperate, depressed, and dejected. He reported that he had nothing to live for.

In treatment it was discovered that Mark's mother was a very possessive woman who, when Mark was a child and a teenager, insisted on knowing about his every activity. Mark realized as an adult that he received tremendous gratification from his mother's constant attention and chose a wife who would treat him "like mommy did." It took Mark several years before he could learn to tolerate some degree of separation from his wife.

The symbiotic spouse usually invests his partner with a great deal of omnipotence. Consequently, physical or emotional distance from the partner tends to induce the same kinds of emotional responses that are observed in an infant when separation occurs. Psychiatrist John Bowlby (1969) described the sequence of protest-despair-detachment-vegetation and possible death when a child is threatened with loss of his mother. Many symbiotic spouses such as Mark S., mentioned above, demonstrate the same emotional reactions when confronted with the possible loss of their partners, even if the loss is a temporary one. It has often been observed that when adults think their love relationships are about to break up they react with loss of appetite, insomnia, depression, and desolation (Strean, 1980).

All love relationships for both sexes tend to recapitulate the early mother-infant reaction to some extent. While certainly not the sole determinant, the oral phase of development seems to establish a lasting association between affection and the need for others. If children have received consistent warmth from an empathetic mother, they will be more inclined to trust themselves and their partners in a loving marital relationship (Erikson, 1950). Some authors have contended that the child's intense attachment to the mother is one reason why monogamy has existed as an ideal for many people throughout the ages (Spotnitz and Freeman, 1964). As demonstrated through case examples, if the first year of life has been characterized by inconsistent mothering, the adult will be suspicious of the spouse, feel strong hostility toward him or her, and anticipate rejection.

THE ANAL STAGE (AUTONOMY VS. SELF-DOUBT)

If during his first year of life the infant has received appropriate physical and emotional gratification and has been weaned without trauma, during his second year he can begin to derive satisfaction from the mastery of impulses and increase his range of intra- and interpersonal experiences and his repertoire of social skills. However, regardless of how benign his first year of life was, it is not easy for the child to mature. The baby, who during the oral period of development has been "all id" (i.e., living a life of constant gratification), is not eager to change. On being asked to be a giver, he still wants to be a receiver. On being told to take some responsibility, he still wants others to be completely responsible for him. Consequently, a great deal of ambivalence is characteristic of children during the learning and training period of the second year of life. Out of love for their parents children want to please, but they also feel hatred toward their parents for imposing rules, regulations, and controls which seem arbitrary and unnecessary.

Many husbands and wives experience the act of giving to their spouses as "doing one's duty." They unconsciously make their marital partners controlling parents and feel humiliated and controlled when their partners want something of them or when they think something is expected of them.

Carole R., age 37, was in therapy because she could "not stand her husband's demands." When he initiated sex, Carole felt "like a child sitting on a pot having to do my duty." She told her therapist, "I have to hold back from him, otherwise he'll dominate me all of the time." Carole felt that her "space was always being invaded" and she found herself feeling either furious or depressed when with her husband.

In her treatment, Carole was able to understand that her resentment of her husband evolved from her relationship with her parents. She experienced their rules and regulations as arbitrary demands and felt helpless in coping with their controls. As she saw how she was unconsciously making herself a little child next to her adult husband, she was slowly able to diminish some of her hatred toward him.

If a child has been trained harshly or prematurely during the second year of life, he frequently becomes an intimidated adult with a harsh super-ego or conscience. He then feels that he must perform regardless of what his own individual preferences are. As a marital partner this individual feels an enormous obligation to please the spouse although he really resents it.

Erikson (1950) has described the conflict of the second year as one of autonomy versus shame and doubt. If a child does not feel too hostile toward his parents he can enjoy his independence and autonomy. However, if he feels he must rebel to gratify his own desires, he worries about how much he is destroying his parents and reacts with shame, doubt, and guilt. Many marital partners cannot feel free to enjoy themselves away from their spouses because they feel that they are destroying their partners while being independent. Feeling guilty each time they are autonomous, they anticipate punishment and rejection.

Bob O., age 45, was in a depression. Married for over 15 years, he told his therapist that he had felt "like a dog on a leash" throughout his marriage. When he wanted a night out with the boys, even the desire itself made him feel ashamed of himself. If he had an opinion contrary to his wife's, he invariably doubted himself. While he projected a great deal of his difficulty onto his wife, it was clear that in Bob's mind any act of autonomy on his part meant that he was hurting his wife.

When Bob's childhood experiences with his parents were explored in therapy, it became clear that the only time Bob had liked himself was in those situations where both his parents had unqualifiedly approved of him. Otherwise, he had doubted himself and felt ashamed. "Independence was dangerous," Bob told his therapist, "I always thought I was sending them to their graves when I told my parents I disagreed with them."

When husbands or wives have not resolved the problems of the second year of life, their conflicts frequently enter into their sexual lives. Not wanting to gratify their partners—who they feel are selfish and controlling like the parents of their past—they often have an unconscious wish to either frustrate their partners' desires or to use them and abuse them in sex. These husbands and wives are full of sadistic fantasies and unconsciously want to urinate or defecate on their partners when they are involved with them sexually. Consequently, they either inhibit their sexual desires because they are frightened of becoming too animal-like, or they become selfish, inconsiderate lovers and rebel against spouses who appear to them as controlling parents.

Sandra N., age 25, was in marital counseling because she could not enjoy sex with her husband. While she had many rationalizations to account for her lack of sexual desire, explorations of her fantasies eventually revealed that she wanted to be "a wolf" with her husband. As a wolf, Sandra would "make a meal of him, bite him, hurt him, and then shit all over him."

Inasmuch as bowel and urine training is one of the first strong demands that parents place on the child, conflicts are inevitable. How these conflicts are resolved will, in many ways, determine whether the individual will be a cooperative marital partner or one who wishes to be defiant, rebellious, and obstinate.

THE PHALLIC-OEDIPAL STAGE (INITIATIVE VS. GUILT)

At about the age of three, the youngster begins to give love as well as to receive it. Initially, children love both parents indiscriminately, but between the ages of three and six they turn their affection with greater intensity to the parent of the opposite sex and compete with the parent of the same sex (Freud, 1905). The anthropologist Malinowski (1922) studied familial patterns in several cultures and concluded that the oedipal conflict or family romance is a universal phenomenon.

The oedipal conflict is different for each of the sexes. First, let us look at the oedipal conflict in boys. From birth, a little boy is primarily dependent on his mother for security and comfort. He continues to value her as a source of sustenance, but by the time he is three years of age he begins to feel wishes of a romantic nature toward her. In much the same way that he notices his father loving his mother, the boy wants to be his mother's lover. He competes with his father, and in the boy's mind the father becomes a dangerous rival for his mother's affections. Because of the boy's competitive fantasies toward his father, the boy fears father's anger, disapproval, and retaliation. From dreams and fantasies of children and adults, it is clear that the boy unconsciously fears his father will castrate him for his oedipal desires. Inasmuch as the boy needs and loves his father, he often feels "bad" for wishing to displace him. Very often, out of fear of father's wrath, the boy submits to father and becomes very compliant toward him.

Many of the marital problems of men are caused by their unresolved oedipal conflicts. They can experience the "winning" of their wives as a hostile triumph over their fathers and then feel guilty for any pleasure they have with their wives. Because men can unconsciously arrange to make their wives mother figures, closeness to their wives, particularly sexual closeness, feels like a dangerous act of incest. They then can become impotent and/or defend themselves against intimacy. Some married men can only enjoy sex with women who are not their wives, because sex in the home is like sex with mother—a forbidden act. Finally, there are many men who feel they are guilty oedipal conquerors and have been disloyal to their fathers; these men need to spend as much time as they can "out with the boys" so as to placate their fathers toward whom they feel they have transgressed.

Jack M., age 30, came into treatment because he wanted to leave his wife but was worried about the effect it would have on his two children. He was very uncomfortable with his wife and felt very controlled by her. He explained that his sexual impotence with his wife was due to the fact that "her breath smells exactly like my mother's and I feel smothered by her." Jack could further rationalize his impotence because he was very potent with his girlfriend.

Jack's attitude toward his marriage shifted a great deal after he went away for a week with his girlfriend. As she assumed many of the traditional wifely responsibilities, such as cooking and sewing for him, Jack became impotent with her. He later told his therapist, "When I'm with a woman for too long, she becomes like a mother and then I feel like a mother-fucker. I get guilty and depressed and begin to feel that the only life that is O.K. is to be gay and be with men only."

The girl's oedipal conflict is usually more difficult for her than the boy's is for him. The girl, in contrast to the boy, becomes a rival of the parent who has been her main emotional provider. Consequently, she is caught in a powerful dilemma: whether to relinquish the dependency on mother which has been so gratifying and so necessary, or to try to maintain it while risking its disruption as she pursues father.

As is true with married men, unresolved oedipal conflicts in married women occur when they turn their husbands into father figures and then experience intimacy with them as forbidden incest and deserving of punishment. Other women can never feel content in marriage because they are looking for an idealized father figure. Also, some women, like oedipal men, experience fulfillment in marriage as an oedipal victory over their mothers and have to be punished. Their guilt in some cases is so severe that they give up men and regress to overt or latent homosexuality.

All children have omnipotent fantasies and want instant gratification. All boys want to give birth to babies and fantasize having breasts and vaginas. Similarly, when girls turn toward their fathers, they want to own his penis. It is a part of father, whom they treasure, and like all children, they want to own everything in sight. Penis envy is usually buried in the unconscious and becomes manifest only through its derivatives: low self-esteem, lack of assertiveness, or constant competition with men.

Beth K., age 23, was in marital counseling because she could "experience no joy with my husband." She was "turned off" sexually and experienced her husband most of the time as "a sad-sack." Exploration of Beth's past revealed that she was "Daddy's little girl." Beth had many memories of being alone with her father and feeling like his "little Princess." When she got married she cried a great deal at her wedding because she was going "to miss my Daddy."

Beth constantly demeaned her husband and told him how inferior he was to her father. After realizing in therapy that she was always looking for a fight with her husband, she tried to be warmer and more receptive. However, her dreams and fantasies showed that sex with her husband was experienced as "telling mother to go to hell and screwing Daddy" and she felt very guilty about her pleasure. Still later in her treatment, she had fantasies of biting off her husband's penis and her father's. She wanted "to merge with their power but they never let me."

As Beth explored her oedipal fantasies and penis envy in treatment, her marriage became much more satisfying.

The maturational dilemma to be resolved in the oedipal period for both girls and boys is that of taking initiative versus feeling guilty (Erikson, 1950). Children who feel guilty about their oedipal fantasies may become docile, passive, and unassertive. However, if the oedipal period has been relatively free from too much conflict, the maturing youngster will enrich his or her capacity to achieve and to love. Such a child will be able to form an enjoyable, trusting attachment as a carry-over from the oral stage, to be cooperative and yet feel autonomous because the anal stage was successful, and to admire the loved person of the opposite sex and take initiative with the partner.

THE LATENCY STAGE (INDUSTRY VS. INFERIORITY)

If the child has resolved most of his oedipal conflicts, he is able to move from his family to the social world of peers. While he still needs the comfort and security from his family, by the time a child is six or seven he should be increasingly able to forgo childish impulses and begin to empathize with the needs and wishes of others. The period from age six to ten has been called "the latency period" because the intensity of the child's instinctual impulses is temporarily subdued. During this time the child attempts to renounce his romantic attachment to the parent of the opposite sex and to reduce his competition with the parent of the same sex. The degree of renouncement of romantic preoccupation during the latency stage depends a great deal on the climate of the particular culture in which the child is being socialized. Consequently, the degree of sexual preoccupation in latency varies widely (Roheim, 1952).

Early in the latency period the child has his first love affair with a youngster of the opposite sex. This is observed in most children and recalled by most adults. What sparks the first love affair, which usually occurs around age six or seven, is that the child cannot give up the attachment to the parent of the opposite sex too easily; hence, he or she needs a substitute. A child who does not have a first love affair with a peer during early latency has not succeeded in liberating himself from his parents. This usually has serious consequences for later personality formation (Fine, 1975).

During the latter half of the latency period, many children confine themselves to same-sex groups and often express a great deal of contempt toward members of the opposite sex. Rather than acknowledge his sexual attraction, which would reactivate oedipal conflicts, the child defends himself by denying love and expressing hate. This defense is known as "reaction formation," that is, expressing the opposite of what one really feels.

When oedipal conflicts are not resolved, the latency child tends to avoid close one-to-one relationships and utilizes gangs or other groups for protection. If his anxiety is not resolved, as a marital partner he will frequently want to escape from intimacy by being active in groups, usually of his own sex. Frequently, married couples who are involved in switching and swinging are individuals who cannot tolerate the anxiety they feel in the one-to-one intimate relationship of marriage.

How a child copes with latency issues is an excellent way of determining how he will cope with marital conflicts inasmuch as the latency period requires the child to take on new responsibilities which involve another person. The child who enters school, like the adult who enters marriage, must share more than he did previously. He can no longer be exclusively concerned with his own interests and desires. Like marriage, relationships in school and elsewhere require empathy, mutuality, compromise, negotiation, problem solving, and frustration tolerance. Just as the latency child must expand his ego functions and postpone gratification in order to be successful in his dealings with others, a successful marital partner is one who can forgo certain narcissistic preoccupations, lessen omnipotent desires, curb infantile desires, and tolerate limitations in both himself and the other person.

Many adults handle their marital frustrations in the same manner that the latency child deals with his infantile wishes—by projecting immature desires onto someone else. Many husbands and wives criticize their partners for being immature, unkind, and unrealistic, not realizing that in so doing, *they* are being immature, unkind, and unrealistic. A favorite pastime of latency children is "squealing" on another child who does the very thing he wishes to do but finds forbidden. Similarly, many husbands and wives unconsciously enjoy collecting injustices and pointing out how and why their partners are "unfair" or "not playing the game."

Max J., age 37, had been married for 12 years and sought marriage counseling because he could not tolerate his wife's "enormous immaturity," "constant obsessiveness," and "ever-present helplessness." He told his male therapist, Dr. E., that he constantly pointed out to his wife how she was an immature woman, but his wife never seemed to respond to "constructive criticism."

When Dr. E. pointed out to Max that he found himself constantly criticizing and demeaning his wife, Max responded with enormous anger. On Dr. E.'s listening to Max's anger without comment, Max became helpless and obsessive, and talked about how he wanted a wife and a therapist to take care of him and let him be a child. As Max studied his own immaturities, he eventually became more tolerant of his wife's.

The task of the latency period is to resolve the conflict between "industry and inferiority" (Erikson, 1950). Marital partners who have resolved the tasks of this stage of development feel relatively sure of their internal resources. Feeling confident and not inferior, they are free to love and enjoy their spouses.

ADOLESCENCE (IDENTITY VS. IDENTITY DIFFUSION)

For many young people, anatomical, emotional, physiological, intellectual, and social factors combine to make adolescence a turbulent stage of development. As hormonal changes define the onset of puberty, the adolescent storm begins, and sexual and aggressive drives express themselves with greater intensity. Teenagers want to be treated like independent adults in many ways, yet with so many changes occurring they feel a strong yearning for parental direction. Ambivalence is characteristic of adolescents. They want independence, yet they are afraid of it and want to cling. They want to be given to, yet feel humiliated by their passive longings. They want sex but they often feel guilty and frightened about gratifying themselves. They are ambitious but they feel squeamish about surpassing their parents and other figures of authority.

Those clinicians who have worked with teenagers have all noted the adolescent's tendency to recapitulate his complete psychosexual development at this time and to reexperience old conflicts (Blos, 1967; Esman, 1979; A. Freud, 1958). Oral conflicts manifest themselves in adolescents' frequently peculiar food habits and their occasional flirtations with vegetarianism. They can be very symbiotic one day and the next appear autistic and narcissistic. Conflicts with anality are very apparent in their frequent desire to be obstinate and rebellious. They can appear filthy and, at times, love dirty clothes and dirty jokes. Adolescents can move from promiscuity to celibacy within a week as they struggle with their revived oedipal conflicts. They can frown on success and achievement for a day and then emerge the next day as intellectual giants philosophizing about life.

If the adolescent does not establish a cohesive identity and master the anxieties that interfere with intimacy, then he has a turbulent, chaotic, ambivalent marital relationship. He will feel half adult and half child with his spouse. He will feel guilty about sexuality, frightened of autonomy, and terrified of dependency.

Dorothy G. was a 22 year old married woman who sought marriage counseling because she and her husband "could agree on nothing." Dorothy liked to travel and her husband liked to stay at home. She liked sex frequently; he liked it occasionally. Dorothy hated to visit parents and in-laws; her husband enjoyed visiting.

As Dorothy progressed in her therapy, it became clear that she and her husband were both two ambivalent teenagers who did not have stable identities and were extremely unsure about their real feelings about most aspects of life. It took many years of therapy for Dorothy (and for her husband, who later entered individual therapy) to resolve her ambivalences. It was only after they could examine their childish wishes and childish attitudes that they were able to have a stable marriage.

As I have suggested several times, in every marriage the history of individual psychosexual development is recapitulated in condensed form.

Each person follows an inner script. That is why handbooks on marital techniques have only limited value. In order for an individual to resolve marital conflicts he must feel ready to trust and be trusted in a relationship where he is not frightened of mutual dependency, mutual admiration, mutual sexual pleasure, and mutual devotion. Unfortunately, few individuals are capable of this kind of interaction.

CHAPTER 4

The Dynamics of Marital Conflict

The philosopher Schopenhauer wrote a tale which has been a popular fable for many decades. In the fable Schopenhauer tells of some freezing porcupines who huddled together for warmth but were repelled by the sting of one another's quills. Each time the need for warmth brought them together their mutual anger began all over again. Consequently, the porcupines were continually attracted to each other to get warm, but they were also alienated by the pain they caused each other.

The dilemma of the porcupines seems to be the fate of many marital pairs. Husbands and wives are attracted to one another because they believe they can give and get warmth and security from one another. However, they can also cause one another pain by their joint neuroses and by their conflicting wishes. Like porcupines, when men and women get closer to one another and their emotional reactions are intensified, they can hurt one another (Eisenstein, 1956).

As indicated in earlier chapters, people can never marry themselves out of their neuroses. Whenever two unhappy people get married, each adds the problem of his or her own neurotic conflicts to those of the other. It has been noted that at the present point in the evolution of human culture the neurotic process is universal, that there are masked neurotic ingredients in every human personality, and that, except in rare cases, these masked neurotic ingredients play a distorting role in marital choices and interaction (Kubie, 1956).

STAGES OF MARRIAGE AND INEVITABLE CRISES

Although each marriage and the individuals who comprise it are unique, all married couples do go through several predictable stages. Inherent in these stages are inevitable conflicts. As early as 1931, the sociologist Sorokin and his colleagues presented a four-stage, family life cycle. Over

38

the years, Glick (1947, 1957), Rodgers (1964, 1973), Hill (1970), Duvall (1971, 1979), Freeman (1982), Barker (1984) and others have delineated six or more stages in the marital life cycle which are often accompanied by crises. Some of these stages occur when the partners leave their respective parents and establish their own home, when they decide to have a child, when their youngsters become teenagers, and when their own children leave home. Let us look at some of these stages of marital development in more detail.

Leaving Home

It is frequently overlooked that when a man and woman get married each goes through a personal transition. The psychologist Daniel Levinson and his colleagues (1978) called this phase of life "the early adult transition," and the psychologist and popular writer Gail Sheehy (1976) referred to it as the "pulling up roots" phase. Young people at this time are separating from their parents and establishing their own identities, their own modi vivendi, and their own priorities.

The reason leaving home and getting married reaches crisis proportions for many young people is that they unconsciously experience their separation and individuation (Mahler, 1968) as an attack on their parents. Breaking up the old family symbiosis can be experienced by young people as weakening their parents' powers and arranging for their parents' decline and possible destruction. Said one young bride, "As soon as we left the church after the wedding, my parents looked like they were fading away." And a young groom said, "After our honeymoon, we visited my parents' home and they looked quite desolate." While parents of newlyweds often do feel desolate and abandoned, young people feel guilty because they worry about whether they have caused their parents' distress. Most of the time they are unaware of their own unconscious wishes to hurt their parents by leaving them; instead they experience an inexplicable feeling of guilt and discomfort.

Leaving home often conjures up oedipal associations and the young person can unconsciously view the consummation of marriage as hostilely surpassing the parent of the same sex and becoming sexually involved with the parent of the opposite sex. Many marital arguments during the first several months of the union are caused by the guilt that young people feel about dissolving symbioses and/or gratifying oedipal fantasies. While the overt fracases do not usually involve these issues directly, the issues tend to appear when the arguments are subjected to clinical investigation in the client's therapy sessions.

Virginia A., age 20, sought counseling because she was "miserable" in her marriage of six months. Every time she sat down for a meal with her husband, Virginia found herself in an argument with him. They debated about "trivia"—the cost of the food, the number of calories in it, the necessity of desserts, and so on. Very often they left the dinner table not talking to each other and, in their mutual anger, slept in different rooms.

When Virginia was asked by her therapist what she was feeling and fantasying at the dinner table with her husband, she became quite teary-eyed. She talked about missing her own home and thought of the joyous times she had had with her parents and siblings. Virginia also pictured her parents looking sad while they ate meals without her and she began to realize how much she viewed her getting married as "an assault" on her parents.

As Virginia faced her guilt about assaulting her parents, her arguments with her husband tended to diminish. Their sexual life improved a great deal when Virginia realized that her mother and father still had each other and that she, Virginia, was "not exactly a crook."

A Child is Born

When any dyad becomes a triad there is inevitable conflict. If a husband and wife have a child, a crisis is almost inevitable (Barker, 1984; Litz, 1968). Roles have to be reassigned, status positions shifted, values re-oriented, and needs met through new channels (Parad, 1965). In a study of 46 essentially "normal" couples, LeMasters (1965) found that 38 of them reported "extensive" or "severe" crises in adjusting to their first child and that this crisis reaction was *not* the result of not wanting children. Furthermore, LeMasters' data supports the belief that the crisis pattern occurs whether the marriage is "good" or "poor." Considerable evidence exists in the study that the crisis pattern in the 38 cases "was *not* the result of maladaptive disabilities."

Just as the institution of marriage has been romanticized in our culture, the same can be said for parenthood. Although our society idealizes the role of "parent," there is little preparation for parental roles. As one of the subjects of the LeMasters' study exclaimed, "We knew where babies came from, but we didn't know what they were like."

Many sociologists have commented on the overidealization of parenthood in our society, and the little direction given to its attendant difficulties. Green (1958) suggested that many couples find their parental roles in conflict with such other interests as work, recreation, and socialization. Benedict (1958) pointed out that young people in our society are often victims of "discontinuity in cultural conditioning"; that is, they have to unlearn previous training before they can move on to the next set of roles.

Clinicians have observed that new parents tend to become unconsciously envious of their newborns because they, the parents, would like to be the recipients of what the infants receive emotionally and physically. Most husbands and wives unconsciously make their spouses parental figures and when the infant gets so much attention from the spouse, the husband or wife can feel displaced and angry.

Every time Harold B., age 26, saw his infant son at his wife's breast getting milk, he got an acute headache. Although Harold found all kinds of rationalizations to account for his headaches, his therapy revealed that he was extremely envious of his son, felt displaced by him as if he had a new sibling, and experienced all kinds of death wishes toward his son. As Harold was able to verbalize his resentments to his therapist, his headaches diminished a great deal.

Marriage and the Terrible Teens

In Chapter 3 we discussed how adolescence is a turbulent period. Inasmuch as all parents vicariously relive their childhood and adolescent years through their children (Strean, 1979), a parent is reminded of his teenage years when his son or daughter reaches this stage. Because teenagers are preoccupied with romance and sexuality, the parent who identifies with a son or daughter feels romantically inclined and wants to be a Romeo or a Juliet. When a parent in his or her forties or fifties fantasies having an exciting romantic partner, the spouse can appear quite mundane in comparison to the fantasy. Then the spouse can become the recipient of enormous hostility.

Sally C., age 45, found herself more furious toward her husband than she had ever been during their entire 20 years of marriage. What became clear in her therapy was that when her 15-year-old daughter started to date boys, Sally, without realizing it consciously, wanted to be a 15-year-old also and "have a ball with the boys." She felt acutely frustrated being a 45-year-old woman and was angry at her husband for not making her feel younger and for not being younger himself.

Many times a parent, in his or her strong desire to become a teenager again, makes his or her daughter or son a psychological lover. At the same time the parent distances him or herself from the spouse. This usually induces a great deal of anger and jealousy in the spouse and a powerful crisis can emerge.

Jon D., age 47, came to a family agency reluctantly at the urging of his wife. She was very upset because they had not had sexual relations for almost a year. Exploration of the family dynamics revealed that when the D.'s daughter became 14, Jon began to unconsciously view her as a girlfriend and turned his wife into a prospective mother-in-law. Jon, in effect, wanted to regress to his teenage years and begin a romance all over again.

The Empty Nest Syndrome

Often when children leave the home the parents do not feel needed. In those marriages where the major source of satisfaction for both spouses was in the role of parent, the marital relationship is in serious jeopardy. Sometimes parents work hard to hold on to their children in order to preserve the marriage. Others throw themselves into a career and try to forget about their marriage (Henton et al., 1983). Many begin having extramarital affairs (Strean, 1980) and a large number get divorced. Brody and Osborne (1980), in *The Twenty Year Phenomenon,* have described this period as one in which marital partners who were held together by their children feel a decline in their self-esteem and a blow to their self-image. When there have been many dissatisfactions in the marriage and the children are gone, divorce is a very real possibility.

Jean and Fred E., both in their fifties, had been married for over 25 years. Their three children had all left home and the E.'s found themselves in constant battles. Both realized that what they were arguing about was inconsequential but they also realized they were harboring a great deal of hatred toward one another.

In marriage counseling both recognized they had really grown apart years before, but did not want to break up until their children left home. When the children left, they finally decided to divorce.

NEUROTIC COMPLEMENTARITY

One aspect of marital conflict that has been noted by many clinicians but not discussed too much in the literature is how marital unhappiness gratifies and protects the marital partners. Most unhappy husbands and wives would like to believe that they are victims of circumstance and that if they had another partner, all would be well. On many occasions, therapists can be seduced into concurring with their clients that indeed their clients are victims of abuse, indifference, hostility, and criticism.

As the clinician looks beneath the surface of his client's marital complaints, he inevitably sees that the very issue the client moans and groans about is the one which he unwittingly and unconsciously sustains and reinforces. Married men and women who habitually complain about their spouses' sexual unresponsiveness are those who constantly disparage their spouses' attempts to respond sexually. Those husbands and wives who deride their spouses for their lack of cooperation are also those who frequently frustrate their partners' attempts to cooperate. And those marriage partners who chronically complain that their spouses are poor parents for their children are frequently sabotaging their spouses' efforts to relate to their children.

Every chronic marital complaint is therefore, an unconscious wish. The husband who insists that his wife is "a frigid bitch" needs and wants such a woman. If his wife responded to him with warmth he would be frightened; that is why he stays married to her and why he unconsciously sought her out in the first place. The wife who laments that her husband is too passive, too impotent, and too unassertive, needs and wants such a husband. She married him because his passivity attracted her and protected her. An assertive man would have frightened her too much.

Adele F., age 32, constantly complained that her husband, Jack, was "terribly unromantic." He never brought flowers home, hardly ever bought her perfume, and was extremely inept sexually. One day Jack, instead of complaining constantly that Adele was "a ball buster," made a determined effort to try to please her and brought home flowers and expensive perfume. At first Adele seemed pleased, but when Jack and Adele were having sex later in the evening, Adele turned to Jack and asked with impatience, "How come your penis is so small?" Jack reacted by becoming impotent and for weeks withdrew from Adele sexually and emotionally, and stopped trying to be attentive to her. Adele could now declare that Jack was an inattentive husband and lover with some justification.

Unconscious Collusion

As is quite clear from the above case illustration, there is frequent unconscious collusion between marital partners; that is, they "cooperate" to sustain and reinforce their individual neuroses. Adele F. needed and wanted an unassertive husband and Jack "cooperated" by fulfilling this role. Jack in turn needed and wanted a woman who would criticize and demean him and Adele "cooperated" with him in this venture. Also, when Jack departed from his habitual way of coping in the marriage and became more assertive and more sexual Adele felt threatened and attempted to demean Jack. And, once again, Jack colluded with Adele and became the passive man she wanted, while Adele resumed the role of the critical wife that Jack unconsciously desired.

When the notion of collusion (Bowen, 1966; Dickes, 1967; Eisenstein, 1956) is utilized by the marriage counselor in assessing clients and planning treatment, then there are no saints nor sinners, no innocent victims nor guilty abusers. Rather, both partners are seen unconsciously at work protecting themselves from anxiety and gratifying infantile wishes. In an implicit manner both partners form a contract to preserve one another's neuroses by perceiving the partner as the partner needs to perceive him or herself (Dickes, 1967; Paolino and McCrady, 1978; Sager, 1976).

Lloyd and Paulson pointed out that in a conflicted marriage each partner "maintains an internal world that the other supports. By confirming one another's projections, they help each other to maintain a closed internal system, protected from modification by reality" (1972, p. 410). It is usually when these intrapsychically agreed upon roles break down that the couple, or one member of the dyad, becomes very anxious. As Gurman stated, "Thus, even among couples who initially appear to want change, there is a tremendous internal pressure, generated by the desire to maintain one's own self-esteem and psychic boundaries, to continue to behave in modes that reinforce one's perception of one's spouse and, thereby, of one's self" (1978, p. 490).

Just as an individual who is terrified of intense sexual or aggressive feelings "needs" to be phobic lest he or she be in terror, and just as the acutely guilty person "needs" to be obsessive, the anxious, frightened spouse "needs" a collusive partner. If a man who is unconsciously frightened of his sexuality does not have a withholding wife, he will be terrified; if a self-effacing masochistic wife does not have an alcoholic or gambling husband to nurture, she will feel worthless.

Millie G., age 42, frequently complained about her husband's drinking. She hid the bottle from him, didn't speak to him when he was drunk, and tried to praise him when he was sober. When her husband, Sam, went into therapy and then went "on the wagon," Millie became depressed. In her own therapy she was eventually able to realize that criticizing Sam and trying to control his drinking gave her "a feeling of importance." When Sam stopped drinking, Millie confessed that she "missed his drinking."

It is important to recognize in marital conflicts that not only is the chronic marital complaint an unconscious wish, but very frequently the complaining spouse also receives vicarious pleasure as he or she observes the marital partner drinking or gambling excessively, having temper tantrums, or being involved in sexual escapades. Because the complaining spouse receives vicarious pleasure from the partner's maladaptive behavior, he or she subtly but persistently encourages it.

Jason H., age 40, was extremely critical of his wife Peggy's obesity. When Peggy went on a diet and lost more than 25 pounds, Jason decided to reward her by taking her out to dinner. At first, Jason subtly tried to encourage Peggy to eat foods which would have had the effect of increasing her weight. When Peggy resisted, Jason himself ate huge quantities of food and gained several pounds.

When clinicians hear spouses deriding their partners it is important for them to keep in mind that these spouses are unconsciously attracted to the very practices they condemn. Many an abused husband or wife secretly admires the spouse's sadism and many an abstainer secretly admires and even envies the spouse's overeating or overdrinking. The clinician can recognize this dynamic by observing the interactions of marital dyads. They usually find that the very issue being criticized and condemned was apparent even during the couple's courtship.

Anne I., age 33, was in treatment because her husband, George, had just started his third extramarital affair within three years. As the dynamics of Anne's collusion in George's affairs were reviewed in her therapy, it became quite apparent that Anne was deriving unconscious gratification from his affairs. She told her therapist that George always seemed warm and soft after he came home late from the office and this made her feel good. She even had a few fantasies of picturing George in bed with other women and was "turned on" by the fantasies. Furthermore, several times during their courtship Anne had learned that George was off with other women but she only mildly objected. As Anne concluded after several months of treatment, "I guess I accepted his affairs before and during our marriage. They must do something for me."

As we consider the notion of collusion in marriage and note that one member of the dyad is attracted to the very characteristic that he or she overtly condemns, we can infer that individuals who become married to one another are usually at the same level of maturity. Each spouse unconsciously is attracted to and reinforces those personality patterns which protect and gratify his or her individual neurotic patterns (Meissner, 1978). When one partner modifies his habitual patterns, the other partner fights the change, and when the partner who tries to change recognizes his spouse's objection, there is "a regression in the service of the spouse"

(Fine, 1982). By this we mean that both spouses have formed a contract to preserve a neurotic equilibrium. When one partner attempts to alter the neurotic equilibrium in any direction, the other partner works hard to restore the equilibrium (Bertalanffy, 1973).

As we have now seen, many, if not most, marital partners are burdened by unresolved or only partially resolved developmental tasks (Erikson, 1950). These developmental conflicts are carried over into their marital relationships, with their interaction being fraught with tensions, hostilities, and difficulties (Meissner, 1978).

It is helpful to review how a spouse unconsciously arranges for the partner to mirror or become part of his psychic apparatus so that his neurosis is supported and maintained. It will also be helpful to note the gains that each spouse derives from this arrangement.

The Spouse as Superego

Every marital clinician recognizes how common it is for married people to arrange, unconsciously, for their spouses to be parental figures. One aspect of making the spouse a parental figure is that the individual looks to the spouse for praise and criticism. Many married people, like children, can only approve of themselves if they think their "parent-spouses" applaud what they do. Likewise, many married people dislike themselves if they believe their spouses disagree with them or are critical of them.

Perhaps one of the most common complaints of married men and women in and out of treatment is that their partners do not validate them enough and undermine them too much. As we now know, behind every chronic complaint is an unconscious wish; therefore those married individuals who rant and rave about their partners' constant criticisms need and want their partners to criticize them. What purpose does this serve?

In the process of growing up most individuals, if not all, have found it very difficult to give up infantile wishes. When they reach adulthood, they still want omnipotent parents to make all their decisions, provide them with an eternal Garden of Eden, and never frustrate them. Furthermore, many adults cope with reality's frustrations by wanting to strike out and hurt, similar to the way children behave. Finally, many adults retain residues of their oedipal conflicts and want to gratify incestuous and murderous longings. All of these wishes, which are usually unconscious, create anxiety and guilt. Guilt is superego punishment.

It is much easier for most individuals to attach themselves to a superego figure in the form of spouses who criticize and punish them than it is to forever punish themselves for forbidden wishes. The reason this is easier is that these individuals can retaliate when the superego-spouse criticizes, and feel misunderstood rather than guilty, self-righteous rather than worthless. Finally, self-esteem is protected when a spouse can say, "I'm a good person. I just have a critical partner." It is much more difficult to say, "I have forbidden oral desires, unacceptable anal wishes, and complex oedipal conflicts and I feel I should be punished for my incestuous and sadistic fantasies."

When one member of the marital dyad unconsciously arranges for the other to be a punitive superego who will criticize and demean, the one who assumes the role of superego figure will inevitably be an individual who is unconsciously attracted to, but condemning of, a spouse who is more open with his id wishes. This arrangement provides for a neurotic complementarity that on one hand creates havoc but on the other hand supplies both partners with protection and gratification. The superego figure protects her partner from acting out forbidden id wishes and also gratifies his wish for punishment when he does so. For herself, the superego figure receives gratification from observing her partner exhibit id wishes (which are really her own forbidden hidden desires) but she can feel self-righteous as she punishes her partner by saying in effect, "You are the infant, not me!" This collusive relationship creates havoc because neither partner is able to get much pleasure from his or her instinctual drives and neither spouse can like the other. The partner who wants to gratify his id wishes feels controlled and criticized while the superego figure feels threatened and angry a good part of the time.

When one spouse makes the other his superego figure, the superego figure in turn usually makes her partner an id. However, this is not always a static arrangement. From time to time couples switch roles. They can alternate roles fairly easily because each partner is really psychologically quite similar to the other and both partners are usually at about the same level of maturity. Both have strong id wishes which they would like to gratify. Both feel strong anxiety when they feel like gratifying their id wishes and both feel very guilty and want to be punished for their infantile wishes.

Bruce J., age 36, told his therapist that living with his wife Eileen for the past 10 years had been "holy hell." He pointed out that whenever he performed a domestic chore, offered an opinion, or accomplished something positive in his business, he could "count on" her to deride him. Furthermore, Eileen was against almost anything that Bruce thought pleasureful. She resented his "strong sex drive," opposed his watching television, downplayed his sense of humor, and hated all of his friends.

It took Bruce a long time in his therapy to realize that he was unconsciously making Eileen the mother of his past whom he regarded as a very forbidding figure. Furthermore, while Bruce had many loving feelings toward his mother, as he did toward Eileen, he felt that showing these feelings to either of them was taboo. Actually, everything that gave Bruce pleasure aroused guilt in him. His sexual fantasies activated incestuous and oedipal guilt, his success in business made him worry that he was defeating people, and his desire to watch television and have other forms of recreation reminded him of forbidden childish sex play. Consequently, it was understandable that he would marry someone like Eileen who stimulated him on one hand, but prohibited him on the other.

During the course of Bruce's treatment he began to feel more accepting of his instinctual wishes and less guilty about them. Therefore, he did not react as strongly to Eileen's criticisms. As a result, Eileen, instead of being a superego figure, began to relax and become more fun-loving. Interestingly, this frightened Bruce and he began to find himself trying to limit Eileen and control her as she became more libidinal. She became his id and he had to use his own superego to punish her.

One of the reasons that marriage can be so confining for so many people, is that they unconsciously arrange to find a partner who will limit them and confine them. And one of the reasons that marriage can be so anxiety-provoking is that many individuals make their spouses "forbidden ids." Each time the "forbidden id" wants to gratify himself, his partner gets frightened because her own unacceptable and forbidden id wishes become activated, as was true in the case of Eileen.

The Spouse as a Devaluated Self-Image

In the process of growing up there are many people who do not form stable and positive self-images. Men and women can dislike their bodies, hate their instinctual drives, and be irritated with their maladaptive defenses. However, it punctures the individual's narcissism to acknowledge his limitations. It is much easier to project what is unacceptable about one's self on to somebody else, and a convenient "somebody else" can be one's marital partner (Paolino and McCrady, 1978; Willi, 1976).

When a husband projects all that he does not like about himself onto his wife, he receives much protection and gratification. He can feel that all his unhappiness is caused by something external to himself rather than by something internal. Instead of feeling small, he can feel a certain strength and power in belittling his spouse. He can also avoid facing his own neurotic problems by calling his wife stupid, boring, or asexual.

Usually when a spouse is scapegoated, she gets gratification and protection from being demeaned. Her guilt is assuaged, her own unacceptable sadism is controlled, and she does not have to face her own lack of self-esteem, because she can ascribe it to her unhappy marital fate.

As we have pointed out, individuals who marry have many similar psychological conflicts. In the dyad we are discussing, both individuals hate themselves and neither individual truly accepts his or her instinctual wishes. Their unhappiness, which existed long before they met, is ascribed to their marriage and both can take turns scapegoating the other.

Carol K., age 39, came for marriage counseling because she wanted help in divorcing her husband Irving. She pointed out that she had never loved her husband but had married at the age of 24 because she thought it was "getting late and it was time to settle down." She chose Irving because he would offer her "security," but he turned out to be "boring, stupid, unstimulating, asexual, and a patsy." Furthermore, Carol was very upset with Irving because he passively accepted all of her criticisms. "I wish he would fight back," she lamented.

When her therapist asked her what she was feeling when she wanted Irving to "fight back," Carol's response afforded insight into her marital difficulties. "I'd like him to prove that I'm wrong. If he really was not the jerk I made him out to be, he would protest." As Carol thought some more about her wish to get Irving to fight back, she was reminded of the many times that she was belittled in her own home by her parents and siblings and never argued back. She eventually realized that she was placing Irving in the same psychological position she was in when she was younger. As she focused more on her childhood, she got in touch with her own fears of asserting herself, her own anxieties about sexuality, and her own poor self-esteem.

As Carol became more introspective, she was less derogatory toward Irving. While Irving responded positively to Carol's change of attitude, this was short-lived. He began to provoke her and really asked to be put down. Occasionally, he tried to put her down. This, however, did not work well since Carol liked herself better and didn't respond to Irving's provocations. Eventually, Irving went into treatment.

As we review our case illustrations and consider the dynamic interplays between the marital partners, we see the validity of the statement made by the psychoanalyst Edmund Bergler (1978, p. 11) who said,

All stories about a normal woman who becomes the prey of a neurotic man, and vice versa, a normal man who falls in love with a highly neurotic woman, are literary fairy tales. Real life is less romantic; two neurotics look for each other with uncanny regularity. Nothing is left to chance, as far as emotional attachments are concerned.

The Spouse as Ego-Ideal

In Chapter 2 we pointed out that in choosing a mate there is a tendency on the part of many individuals to project their own lost narcissism onto the prospective partner. All of the strengths that these people wished they could have, but never owned, are projected on to the object (Freud, 1914). If an individual has dreamed of being brilliant, powerful, very sexual, and omniscient, these are the qualities that are "observed" in the other person. In the beginning of a romance all is idealized, "I looked across a crowded room and there she was, and when I saw her, I knew from that moment." In such a romance, the mate is considered able to fulfill all of one's fantasies (Mason, 1977).

In previous chapters we concluded that the realities of life inevitably puncture one's unrealistic hopes. Yet many marital partners persist in trying to make their mates "better halves," idealized penises, and super-heroes (Stein, 1956). However, the attempt to make the spouse an ego ideal is bound to fail for several reasons. First, nobody can be an omnipotent giant for too long. No man or woman can possibly live up to such an unrealistic, distorted image. Second, when a spouse does not live up to his partner's childish demands, the partner will react with strong rage. In the rage, she will rant and rave about how she was fooled and point out that in reality, her mate is quite average or below average. On being labeled average or below average, the mate who has been idealized feels and acts furiously as his narcissism is frustrated; consequently he begins to attack his partner, thus providing her with more fuel for her argument that she has been duped and is deprived. Finally, because the wish for the partner to be omnipotent is a fantasy that is created to compensate for internal wounds, the fantasy—even if it is partially gratified—is not much of a compensation because no fantasy ever healed internal psychological wounds. Nonetheless, wounded people do not like to examine their internal wounds; they persist in looking for artificial crutches which eventually break down.

Laura L., age 35, married Mel who was a physician. She told her therapist that "it was love at first sight." According to Laura, Mel was brilliant, bold, sexy, and open. Laura's intense admiration bolstered Mel's self-image and the couple had an idyllic courtship. Soon after they were married Laura felt very jealous of Mel's long hours in his medical practice, experienced herself as neglected, and began to have temper tantrums. Laura's reactions infuriated Mel and he began to demean her more and more. As a result, both partners became very unhappy and their romance deteriorated into a war.

When Laura went into therapy she soon learned that her wish for an omnipotent man was her attempt to compensate for her ugly self-image. In growing up she felt very inferior to her two brothers and thought that being a girl made her "second-rate." She hoped that Mel would fill "an inner emptiness." Because Laura felt that only by owning a penis would she be "first-rate," she had to possess Mel all of the time. That is why his absences made her feel so worthless and empty.

When Laura made some gains in her therapy and liked herself more, she was not as possessive of Mel. At first Mel felt relieved by her change in attitude, but after a while he missed her old ways and he began to attack her. Fortunately, he was able to sense that he had his own neurotic attitudes and did go into treatment.

It is important for the marriage counselor to constantly keep in mind that couples are usually attracted by shared developmental failures (Skynner, 1976). Thus, "overt stylistic differences and apparently needs in ongoing marital interaction often reflect conflict over the same more fundamental dynamic theme" (Gurman, 1978, p. 451). Because marital partners have similar developmental conflicts, many of the dyads cited in the literature create the erroneous impression that marital dyads are static. It is usually not correct to assume, for example, that A needs nurturance and is attracted to B who needs to be nurturing. Usually both A and B secretly yearn for nurturance and constantly shift positions with one another. Inasmuch as both members of the dyad have similar wants and similar internal prohibitions they take turns in being parent and child, desirer and prohibitor.

Let us look at some of the dyads often cited in the literature and try to see how the partners are quite similar (Mittelmann, 1956) although described as different.

The Dominant-Submissive Dyad

In this type of a relationship, one member is described as being aggressive, sadistic, and out to humiliate and hurt his partner, while the other member is chiefly dependent and submissive. While this picture can describe the couple's interaction in many ways, it is somewhat short-sighted. We have to keep in mind that a sadistic person is one who has many passive, dependent, masochistic desires which he cannot tolerate. His sadistic behavior defends against the anxiety that his passive-dependent wishes create. He chooses someone to dominate him and by so doing can dominate or control his own unacceptable wishes.

The dependent spouse is usually one who is very frightened of her sadistic and dominating desires and defends against them by being passive and dependent. She chooses a partner who will reinforce her defenses so that she can say, "It is you who is sadistic, not I," just as her partner can say, "It is not I who is passive and weak, it is you."

When one partner is dominant and the other is submissive, neither of them maintains this equilibrium for too long. The dominant partner begins to feel guilty about his sadism and submits while the submissive partner begins to feel resentful about being placed so frequently in a submissive position. Consequently, when we talk about a dominant-submissive dyad, we are referring to two people who have a great deal of sadism in them and who feel guilty about their wishes from time to time. At different times each partner needs to submit and be passive and, therefore, they alternate roles with one another. We have seen several examples of this dynamic constellation in the case illustrations in this chapter and in earlier ones.

The Detached-Demanding Dyad

In this dyad one partner attempts to appear self-sufficient and emotionally detached while the other partner appears very intense and openly demanding of love. If one partner, let us say the husband, violently demands love, the wife becomes fearful and the husband feels humiliated. Because he feels so humiliated after showing his craving for love, he defends himself by becoming detached. When the husband becomes detached, he arouses his wife's interest in him and she becomes openly demanding of love. Hence, the couple repeats the same cycle over and over again.

In trying to understand the interactions and transactions of this dyad, it is important to keep in mind that both husband and wife are very frightened of their strong dependency longings. The detached member defends himself with a pseudo-independence and a deriding of his partner's wishes for contact. The demanding spouse has unconsciously selected someone who will deny what she craves but fears. As a result, both partners work together to express unacceptable dependency wishes and to fight them.

Rod M., age 27, complained to his marriage counselor that his wife, Faye, was "a sheet of ice." She pushed him away when he was affectionate and didn't want to listen to him when he desired to converse. In his treatment Rod learned that he was actually very critical of his own wishes for attention and used Faye as a superego. As he felt less critical of himself for his longings, he did not become as defensive when Faye put him down. When Faye saw that Rod was less defensive, she became more respectful of him and started to allow herself to be more dependent on him. At first Rod became frightened of Faye's changes and withdrew. Further therapy helped him understand that Faye's expression of dependency reminded him of his own longings: As he became more respectful of himself he could respect Faye more.

As we pointed out earlier in this chapter, when one member of a dyad makes changes, the neurotic equilibrium of the marital interaction is disturbed. Most couples seek to restore it. However, when one member of the dyad is in therapy, as was true in the case of Rod M., if the therapy is working well, "regression in the service of the spouse" (Fine, 1981) can be minimized, and, instead, progression in the service of both spouses can be enhanced. We will discuss this issue in more detail in Chapter 5.

The Helpless-Considerate Dyad

When one member of a dyad is extremely helpless and feels like a weak, vulnerable child, he wants instant gratification from an omnipotent parent. If his spouse does not relieve him of every pain instantly, he becomes furious and resents his partner's inability to be a perfect parent. His considerate spouse, who usually lacks self-confidence and has low self-esteem, often responds to her partner's anger with depression and eventually becomes helpless herself. Again, we have a vicious cycle in which both partners exchange roles and neither is satisfied. At any given time, one partner feels imposed upon while the other feels deprived. In reality, both members of the dyad feel like weak children and both yearn for an omnipotent parent.

Arthur N., age 45, was an acutely depressed man who frequently felt "guilty," "hopeless," "desperate," and "always unhappy." His wife Sara tried her best to take care of him and for days at a time would smile patiently and support him consistently. Inevitably Arthur would find something that Sara had not done just right and would physically beat her. Sara often responded to the beatings by apologizing to Arthur and vowing to be a better wife. However, after a series of beatings, she would become violent and place Arthur in the same position he had placed her. Arthur then would become a self-effacing, considerate husband for several days and try to nurture Sara. His considerate demeanor, however, soon turned to one of helplessness, weakness, and hopelessness and the vicious cycle between Arthur and Sara repeated itself again and again.

In our examination of various types of marital conflicts, it is important to keep in mind that the dyads we have described are not mutually exclusive. By this we mean that it is quite possible for a helpless-considerate dyad to also show features of detachment and dependency and switch dominant and submissive roles as well. At times each member of the dyad can ascribe superego and ego ideal qualities to the other partner and utilize each other in many different ways. No individual marital partner and no married couple can be neatly categorized. Each husband and wife is unique and the complexities and idiosyncracies of each is important to consider in the diagnostic assessment and treatment of marital conflict, to which we turn in Chapter 5.

Therapeutic Principles in Treating Marital Conflicts

When helping professionals have sensitized themselves to some of the historical and sociological features of the marital institution, have given some thought to why people fall in love and marry, have reviewed salient aspects of psychosexual development, and have examined some of the pertinent dynamics of marital conflict, they are ready to consider their role-sets in treating individuals who are in marital conflict.

In this chapter we will discuss the important ingredients in the therapeutic process of marriage counseling. Although some of the clients who seek help from social agencies, mental health clinics, and private practitioners do not present their marital problems as the immediate issue for which they want help (their marital conflicts arise later in the treatment), this chapter will examine the dysfunctional marriages whether or not this was the presenting problem. Even though some of these individuals come for help as marital dyads while others come alone, many of the therapeutic principles involved in helping married couples conjointly are the same as treating husbands and wives individually. While we will comment on some of the differences, it is important to note that helping people in marital difficulty—regardless of the treatment modality—does involve a distinct process: gathering data, making a psychosexual assessment, choosing an appropriate therapeutic modality, and, finally, helping the individual or couple resolve their marital conflicts.

GATHERING DATA

In order to help someone who is in marital difficulty, the professional must know the individual very well. The same overt symptom—for example, sexual abstinence—has a meaning for Mrs. Smith which is quite different from the meaning of Mrs. Jones' abstinence. The etiology of Mr. Adams' difficulties that provoke him to abuse his wife is probably very different from what prompts Mr. King to beat his spouse. Each client's conflicts, history, personality, and cultural background is unique. Consequently, each client's psychosexual assessment must be individualized and each treatment plan should relate to the particular client's modus vivendi and idiosyncrasies.

The clinician gathers data and makes an assessment through interviewing. Let us consider some of the important features of the initial interviews.

The Initial Interviews

One of the major reasons that close to half the people who apply for therapeutic help leave treatment prematurely is because they have not felt empathy from the therapist in the initial interviews (Perlman, 1968; Strean, 1978). All too often clients are bombarded with numerous questions, given premature solutions, or presented with too many interpretations.

It takes practitioners a long time to become genuinely convinced of the fact that a good interviewer is a good listener. They have to see over and over again that the individual who stays in counseling is one who has been given an opportunity to have a concerned listener attend to his feelings, thoughts, ideas, and memories on a consistent basis. Experienced clinicians know that what helps people the most is pouring their hearts out and telling what is on their minds to somebody who spends most of his time empathically listening. Throughout the whole treatment process and particularly in the initial interviews if most of the time is spent with the clients talking while therapists listen, in most cases the clients' tensions are reduced, their thoughts become clarified, and energy previously utilized to repress disturbing thoughts and feelings becomes available for more productive and enjoyable psychological and interpersonal functioning.

An old axiom of casework and psychotherapy is "begin where the client is" (Garrett, 1951; Kadushin, 1972; Strean, 1978). If clients are to feel free to be themselves and expose their angers, vulnerabilities, guilts, and embarrassments to the therapist, they have to feel that what is of concern to them at the moment is what the therapist most wants to hear. All too often therapists bring their own agendas to initial interviews and, as a result, cannot be sensitive to what is on the client's mind. If a therapist is too eager to get a history while the client is disturbed by the practitioner's office arrangements or waiting room decor, the client will feel alienated and annoyed. If the therapist is too interested in talking about fees, absences, and number of sessions while the client is experiencing doubts about entering counseling in the first place, the client will feel irritated and misunderstood. And, if the therapist has a particular modality which he believes helps most clients and tells the client that he should be in conjoint therapy, family therapy, group therapy, or long term therapy while the client has other notions, the chances that the client will drop out of treatment become strengthened (Strean, 1985).

All clients who come to the marriage counselor for the first time have doubts and feel ambivalence about being there. They worry about being accused and blamed, they fear revealing their sexual and aggressive thoughts and their sexual and aggressive behavior, they anticipate being told that their situation is hopeless, and they are apprehensive about the therapist's not thinking well of them. All of these issues must be borne in mind by helping professionals when they gather data on the client's marriage and other pertinent aspects of his life.

In applying the notion of "beginning where the client is" to initial interviews, therapists can be assured that all they have to do at the first meeting with most clients is to greet them cordially, ask them to sit down in a chair that is for them, and wait for them to start telling what is on their minds. Beginning therapists are often surprised to learn that most prospective clients are quite ready to talk to them if they see a receptive expression on a receptive face. For those clients who do not feel ready to begin talking and are silent, the interviewer can ask—after around ten seconds of silence—"Where would *you* like to begin?" This is frequently all these people need in order to tell their story.

Where reluctant clients often like to begin is by telling the interviewer that they do not want to be in the therapist's office and do not want to be in counseling. It is important for these clients to feel that they can voice their resentments about treatment to an empathic person who gives them permission to feel antagonistic. Often when a prospective client who resents being referred for treatment is helped to voice his resentments, anger subsides, and his cooperativeness increases.

Michael Z., age 26, was referred to a marriage counselor by his physician. Michael was sexually impotent, had psychosomatic problems ever since he married the year before, and was furious that his wife did not realize that "all of the marital difficulties are her fault." He told Dr. A., the therapist, that he felt manipulated by his wife and his physician to come to see him "but there's no reason to see you because I haven't got anything wrong with me—it's all my wife's problem."

Tempted to argue with him, but realizing that he would become one more of Michael's enemies if he did so, Dr. A. said, "They've ganged up on you and made you feel like the culprit, and it feels as if I'm joining them; I don't blame you for feeling angry and upset about being here!" Because Dr. A. met Michael where he was, Michael felt understood and after voicing some more resentments toward his physician and his wife admitted that he knows he's "always been suspicious of people and I do get into a lot of arguments." When Dr. A. merely nodded, after a moment or two Michael said, "You seem to be an all-right guy, I'll try you out for a while."

In their zeal to help people and buttress their doubts about their professional competency, beginning therapists often find it difficult to help a client discuss *his* doubts about being a client. Too often they try to argue with the client and convince him that he needs therapy. Some clinicians become so disappointed about the client's lack of motivation that they react with passivity and give up trying. If therapists want to help their clients grow, they have to accept the fact that all clients resist treatment from the first session to the last and that some individuals are so suspicious of another person they cannot afford to risk being in treatment (Fine, 1982; Strean, 1985). However, if the client genuinely feels that the therapist will not impose treatment on him and that he does have the right to reject the therapist's services, the chances are much greater that he will become a client.

When Marilyn Y., age 24, met her therapist for the first time, she told Dr. B. that she was seeing him "under orders" from her husband. Her husband had told Marilyn that if she did not begin psychotherapy immediately, he would divorce her. On Dr. B.'s asking Marilyn how she felt about beginning therapy "under orders," she brought out a lot of anger toward her husband, but also recognized that she was frightened of his leaving her. Consequently, she had to be in treatment.

Dr. B. told Marilyn that he realized how frightened she was to be alone without her husband; he also told her that he never saw therapy work when the person was "under orders." Feeling understood and accepted by Dr. B., Marilyn said, referring to her husband, "If he doesn't accept me with my neurosis, he can't love me all that much and I should question what I'm doing with him."

Marilyn decided that she could not be in treatment "under orders" and if her husband insisted that her being in treatment be part of the marriage, she was willing to risk not being married. Three weeks after her husband was willing to accept her without her being in treatment Marilyn called Dr. B. and began treatment "under my own steam" and not "under orders."

Many times prospective clients need several interviews to discuss their doubts about being in treatment. Psychodynamically oriented therapists recognize that the ambivalent spouse will be ambivalent about being in treatment and that part of this client's treatment is being offered the opportunity to discuss his ambivalence about therapy and the therapist as long as he needs to do so. When this is done in a safe atmosphere, the client may be able to move toward trying to understand his own ambivalence in his own marriage.

Promises of Help

When clients discuss their marital problems in their initial interviews and appear helpless, hopeless, and despondent about their marital woes, it is often very tempting for the therapist to reassure them and say that he can help. If we keep in mind that all clients resist change and find it difficult to view themselves or their spouses differently from their current perception, the idea of things being different can be threatening. In addition to creating anxiety in clients if they are promised help in their initial interviews, clients are very wary of one who promises something so soon. They wonder if the therapist is too eager to build his practice, too zealous to use his expertise, or just too narcissistic and egocentric.

Sometimes the depressed, overwhelmed client does ask in the first or second interview if the therapist can help. Usually this question reflects doubts about the therapist and the therapy, and it is much better if the therapist does not say "yes" or "no," but tries to find out what the client is feeling when he asks. If the therapist can do this, the client's doubts come to the surface and can be explored further by therapist and client.

Mitchell W., age 36, had discussed his marital problems with Dr. C., a female therapist. Toward the end of their first interview, in which Mitchell had been quite articulate, he asked Dr. C., "So, what do you think of all this? Do you think you can help me?" Dr. C., sensing that behind Mitchell's questions were thoughts and feelings that he had not expressed, asked Mitchell, "Could you tell me what you are thinking and feeling right now that prompts your question?" Mitchell responded with irritation, "You seem to be a classical shrink! You answer questions with questions! To tell you the truth, I have my doubts about whether you understand me or can help me!" When Dr. C. asked Mitchell what his doubts were about her competency, Mitchell said that Dr. C. was "too young" and "a woman."

Dr. C. and Mitchell then spent the next several interviews discussing Mitchell's resentments toward young women and therapy. Because Dr. C. was not defensive or argumentative, but helped Mitchell discharge what was on his mind, he slowly began to experience her as an ally and stayed in marital counseling with her.

When the therapist does not promise but tries to understand, does not reassure but listens, does not advise but tries to empathize and identify with the client, there is more possibility for the client to stay in treatment and work out his problems. It should be remembered that most people who become clients do so because there is no one in their social network to hear them out. Most nonprofessionals, on hearing someone else describe his marital conflicts, feel an obligation to advise, take sides in the disputes, blast the individual's partner for not being appreciative, offer notions and behaviors that worked for them, or change the subject. They have not been sensitized to the notion that one of the most effective means of being helpful is to permit the client plenty of latitude to voice what is on his mind (Barbara, 1958). Psychologist Carl Rogers (1951) described effective, nonjudgmental listening as offering the client "unconditional positive regard."

More On Answering Clients' Questions

Part of nonjudgmental listening involves empathically dealing with a client's questions as was demonstrated by Dr. C. in the foregoing illustration. Many clients, especially in their initial interviews, ask questions about the therapists' qualifications, his own marital status, how marriage counseling works, what the therapist thinks of the client's spouse, who is right and who is wrong, and so on. Some beginning marriage counselors— and some experienced ones as well—take the position that the client "has the right" to know about the therapist's professional qualifications, his marital status, and his success and failure rate with previous clients in marital conflict. Otherwise it can be asked, "How does the client know who he is really dealing with?" And it can be said, "In an atmosphere which is designed to be one of equals, the therapist has a responsibility to the client to reveal himself, particularly his professional qualifications, his marital status, and his views on marriage."

If therapy is for the client and not for the therapist, then the therapist's job is to help the client discover himself. A therapeutic relationship, unlike any other one, has as its exclusive focus the unfolding of the client's feelings, thoughts, fantasies, memories, and so on. When the client has questions about the therapist or the therapy, what can be more helpful to him than anything else is to discover just what motives prompt his questions. Often his questions, when their meanings are examined more carefully, can help him discover unknown psychological facts about his marriage.

June V., age 40, was seeing a marriage counselor for the first time. She asked the counselor, Ms. D., "Are you married?" Ms. D. responded, "I don't mind telling you, but more important, what are you feeling and thinking about me that makes you ask?" June, a bit irritated on having been frustrated, said, "Frankly, anybody who is married, in my opinion, is a slave. I committed myself to slavery when I got married and if you are a slave, I don't want to have anything to do with you!"

Further exploration of June's notion that "marriage equals slavery" brought out a long history in which she was involved in many sado-masochistic relationships. She really felt that to be in an intimate relationship one had to be a slave. While June spent several years in treatment focusing on her unconscious wishes to be masochistic and on her need to defend herself with sadism, and though she improved a great deal in therapy and her marriage became more enjoyable and more fulfilling, it was never necessary for Ms. D. to reveal her own marital status.

A client is reassured of the professional's qualifications and is helped to feel that treatment can work when he sees that the therapist is exclusively focused on empathically relating to the client's concerns, feelings, and motives. Sometimes, in order to help a client grow, it may be necessary to frustrate him. Questions from the client, if explored fully, will usually tell us something more about the client and his marriage. Whatever information the counselor reveals about himself usually has limited positive effect on the outcome of treatment. Therefore, questions that the client asks should be answered only under very rare circumstances. Whether the client's questions are about the therapist's married life or about something else, the same principle holds: *Find out* why the client is concerned with the issue at hand. This is "beginning where the client is" (Strean, 1978).

On Asking Clients Some Questions

While the clinician involved in marriage counseling is primarily a good listener, he does need data about the client's present and past in order to make an assessment and plan treatment; consequently, he has to ask questions about the client's life, particularly about his married life.

Earlier in this chapter we pointed out that the competent clinician does not bombard the client with questions when the client wishes to discuss other concerns. Usually the best way to ask questions of a client is to pose them when the client is discussing something close to the data that is necessary to procure. For example, as we shall discuss a little later in this chapter, to understand a client's marital conflicts it is necessary to know a great deal about his past and present relationships with his parents. When the client has discussed one or two incidents that involve his mother, or incidents involving mother figures, it may be quite appropriate and well-timed to ask the client, "What was it like with your mother while growing up?"

A question that truly engages the client will be one that clarifies ambiguities, completes a picture of the client's marital situation, draws out more detail on the client's thinking, and elicits emotional responses (Kadushin, 1972). In order for a question to be considered helpful by the interviewee, he has to experience it as one that, if answered in full, will enhance him in some way. Questions that can be answered with "Yes" or "No" do not really help the client explore his marital situation more fully or increase his understanding of it. For example, asking a client "Are you unhappily married?" gives him little opportunity to reflect on his marriage, discharge his complaints, or examine his role in it. However, if the clinician asks, "Could you tell me what's going on in your marriage since the two of you have been experiencing difficulties?" more data will be elicited and a fuller exploration of the client's marriage may ensue (Strean, 1978).

Not only must the clinician time his questions according to the client's pace, but questions should also be brief and clear (Fine, 1982). Furthermore, the professional's use of language should take into consideration the client's social, economic, intellectual, and cultural circumstances. The sensitive interviewer recognizes language differences among different ethnic, socioeconomic, and age groups. We will comment further in this chapter about how the client's cultural and ethnic backgrounds should be part of a good psychosexual assessment.

The Presenting Problem

One of the first pieces of data that the clinician involved in marital counseling has to procure for the psychosexual assessment is the client's presenting problem and his view of it.

It is certainly the rare client who comes to a marriage counselor and states, "I have a conflicted marriage and I realize I am handling the relationship neurotically. I would like to understand my own role in the difficulty—particularly how my unconscious wishes and history make me blind to what is going on." Rather, clients usually talk about not being able to handle an unresponsive spouse; they invariably point to their own strengths and castigate their partners. Frequently, they want help with separation or divorce but are afraid of the impact that disrupting the family will have on their significant others. Sometimes an individual or couple will not even refer to their conflicted marriage in the first few interviews, but seek out a therapist for child therapy or family therapy to deflect from examining their marital problems.

Although therapists realize that clients have to defend themselves against recognizing the real truth about their marital conflicts, therapists nonetheless have to respect their clients' manner of presenting their problems and what they, the clients, deem paramount. When a husband presents as his problem his wife making him impotent, or when a wife presents as her problem being a victim of abuse, it is imperative for the clinician to enter the client's world and to respect the way the client views his marital problems. This is what Carl Rogers means by "unconditional positive regard" (1951).

Telling a spouse that he has his problems too and that he's not just a victim of circumstances, or pointing out that the marriage should be saved, compounds clients' resistances and alienates them from the therapeutic process. Beginning therapists make two common errors in relating to the presenting problems of individuals experiencing marital conflict. They are often inclined to take the clients' requests too literally and begin proceedings for things like separation, divorce mediation, or child therapy. When they do this they fail to help the client look beyond manifest purposes to more basic latent ones that may be present (Hamilton, 1951). There is another error that inexperienced therapists tend to make: telling the client too soon that what he presents is only superficial and that the real problem is something else.

When a client asks the counselor for advice on how to divorce, reconcile, or interact better, it is important for the therapist to differentiate between the client's requests and the client's therapeutic needs. In order to move beyond the client's superficial presentation of his problems, the therapist has to subject the client's requests for the kind of help he wants and the way he perceives his problems to careful examination. Every client's request for help with his marriage, no matter how farfetched, needs to be heard in all its details and explored further. At all times what the client presents and how he presents it has to be respected by the clinician.

Saul U., age 50, applied for help to a family agency because he needed "a divorce mediator." He had decided on the day he called the agency that "25 years of marriage is enough." He told the social worker at the agency that he needed divorce mediation because his wife would not accept his decision to leave her. Saul had not yet told his wife about his decision to leave her but he "had concluded that divorce mediation was the treatment of choice."

When the social worker Mr. E. showed a great deal of respect for Saul by asking Saul to tell him how he felt divorce mediation would help him, Saul pointed out that without divorce mediation he would "have a fight on my hands." He was convinced that his wife would be "furious" about his leaving her and he would "end up a loser." With careful exploration of Saul's conviction that he'd end up a loser, Saul was able to discuss his marital conflicts in more detail. He brought out that he had always been under his "wife's thumb" and had always had to submit to her and placate her. As Mr. E. stayed with Saul's own ideas and his own fantasies, and continued to show a great deal of respect for Saul's definition of his marital problems and how he wanted them solved, Saul was eventually able to move the discussion to an examination of his repressed anger, his need to submit, and his unresolved dependency problems.

When the therapist stays with the client and empathizes with his definition of the problem without agreeing or disagreeing, the client is usually able to explore his conflicts in more detail and to expose many problems of which he was not previously aware. When therapists hear their clients' prescriptions about how they want or expect their problems to be solved, it is at times tempting to show them other ways and means. In the initial interviews especially, this dashes the clients' hopes and punctures their fantasies too abruptly. Meeting the client where he is usually helps him to talk about himself in more detail.

The Client's Social Context

In order to make a comprehensive psychosexual assessment of the client and his marital conflicts, it is important to know the circumstances in which he lives. This is essential for at least two reasons. First, if a couple is living with in-laws and/or with children, their interactions and transactions with these significant others will affect their marital adjustment. Sometimes the presence of in-laws creates a great deal of tension for a married couple and it will be crucial for the couple to understand how they are using the in-laws to aid and abet their own conflicts. Certainly, the same can be said about the presence of children or stepchildren. Second, it is important for the therapist to get in tune with the social context of the client's life; in many ways a client's social context defines what is and what is not a marital problem. Different socioeconomic, ethnic, and cultural groups proscribe and prescribe different roles for married people.

Among certain religious groups, for example Orthodox Jews, it is not infrequent for women to take a subservient role to their husbands. Within certain ethnic groups, such as Italians and Poles, physical means of expressing aggression are occasionally prescribed. Given the poor socioeconomic conditions for many Blacks, unmarried motherhood is not rare. These role injunctions are internalized by clients and deviating from them can create anxiety (Stein and Cloward, 1958). As we suggested in Chapter 1 when individuals stray from what their parents and extended family deem appropriate, they often become ambivalent and guilty and cannot relax with their spouses.

In this day and age of alternate life-styles it is important for the clinician involved in marriage counseling to relate to the excitement, ambivalence, and anxiety that some of their clients have as they think of experimenting with new styles which have been proscribed by their parents and significant others.

Marjorie R., age 40, was in marriage counseling because she had many difficulties with her husband. Among the problems was that she wanted to do some "switching and swinging" but her husband was opposed to it. Although Marjorie spent several sessions advocating swinging and switching and condemning her husband for disagreeing with her, it became clear from the way she was trying to enlist her therapist, Ms. F., as an ally, that she really had a great deal of ambivalence herself about swinging and switching. In effect, she was projecting her internalized voices of her parents and others, that is her own superego, onto her husband. In this way she could externalize an internal battle and keep herself unaware of her own conflict.

When the client deviates or wants to deviate from the values that his social context has prescribed, it is almost inevitable that he will have mixed feelings about it. Sometimes it is difficult for the helping professional to recognize the ambivalence because the client projects one side of his ambivalence onto the spouse and it appears on the surface that he just has an oppositional partner. While the spouse is frequently made the embodiment of parental injunctions, the spouse can also be made into a tempting id who wishes to violate internalized standards. In the case above, Marjorie R. was experienced by her husband as the tempting id who wanted to overthrow social standards.

The Client's History

As pointed out in Chapter 3, each individual's past participates in and shapes his present functioning. In order to help husbands and wives resolve their marital conflicts, much of their therapy should consist in the counselor showing them how they recapitulate their pasts with their marital partners. Inasmuch as marital partners tend to turn their spouses into parental figures, it is essential for the marriage counselor to know how the client experienced his parents. What is crucial in understanding a client's attitudes and behavior is not only what actually transpired between the client and his parents, but of equal if not more importance is the meaning the client has given to these events.

Shirley P., age 24, was in marital counseling because she constantly feared that her husband would leave her permanently and without notice. She seemed convinced of her husband's imminent departure because she felt "very unlovable." In examining her history, it turned out that Shirley's father, a physician, was suddenly drafted into the army without much advance notice when Shirley was a young girl. Shirley *interpreted* her father's going into the army as an act of rejection aimed at her; therefore, she reasoned that her husband, who she had made into a father figure, would do the same.

One of the important dimensions of a client's history is his impression of how his parents related to one another. If a child is reared in an atmosphere where parents love, respect, and communicate well with one another, the child will tend to replicate this behavior in his own marriage. Not only do children tend to identify with the parent of the same gender and behave in their own marriages the way that parent did, but they expect their spouses to have similar attitudes and values to their own parent of the opposite sex. Very often the way a child saw his parents cope with problems is the way he believes problems should be coped with in his own marriage.

Tom O., age 24, found himself sulking frequently in his marriage. This occurred even when he was feeling warmly toward his wife. When his history was explored, he brought out that the image he constantly had of his father during his childhood was one of "a sulky, depressed weakling." Tom identified with his father and on becoming a husband he unconsciously behaved with his wife the way he had observed his father behaving, particularly when with his mother.

In addition to understanding the client's past family life and the atmosphere in his home, it is important to review the client's psychosexual development as he experienced it. While clients vary in their ability to recall childhood memories, again what is important is the interpretation the client gives to childhood events. For example, in discussing his first year of life, about which he will probably have no conscious recollection, what is pertinent are the client's *beliefs* about whether he was a wanted child, what life at the breast or bottle was like, how loved he felt, how much he was able to trust, and so on. Similarly, his own thoughts about toilet training are very important for a comprehensive psychosexual assessment even if he has no memories of the "autonomy versus shame and doubt" (Erikson, 1950) stage of life. The same can be said about getting sexual information, starting school, and so on.

Central to assessing a client's history are two concepts, *regression* and *fixation.* When an individual experiences a great deal of anxiety in coping with a particular psychosexual task, he may attempt to diminish the anxiety by returning to less mature modes of functioning. For example, a five-year-old child who has difficulty accepting certain sexual wishes or has difficulty accepting the birth of a sibling may cope with these problems by returning to wetting the bed or to thumb sucking (even though he had been successfully toilet trained and had already given up thumb sucking two or three years before). Similarly a married man who feels guilty about his sexual wishes toward his wife may regress by getting drunk frequently. Regression implies that the individual has successfully mastered certain psychosexual tasks but he returns to previous, less mature gratifications when certain demands induce anxiety.

The term fixation is used to describe individuals who have never matured beyond a certain point of psychosexual development and are unable, in many ways, to mature further. Individuals may be fixated at any level of development: oral, anal, phallic-oedipal, and so on. As part of the assessment, the therapist has to determine where the client is fixated. Has he ever learned to trust? Has he ever established sufficient autonomy? Has he ever learned to relate intimately to another human being?

It is not always easy to determine whether a particular marital conflict is a manifestation of regression or fixation. In order to be sure the therapist has to take into consideration the many dimensions of the client's current functioning, his ways of relating to other people throughout his life, and the way he relates to the therapist.

After seeing Ted N., age 32, for about 10 interviews, his therapist, Mr. G., was able to determine that Ted's alcoholism was an oral fixation. Ted had a long history of social isolation, was extremely mistrustful of his wife, of Mr. G., and of most people. Ted's mistrust bordered at times on paranoia. For example, he was convinced that his wife and Mr. G. were collaborating to get him to admit he was "crazy."

Ted's mother had died when he was only six months old, and his father had sent him from one foster home to another. Feeling angry and abandoned, Ted relied on alcohol rather than people for gratification.

Sid M., also age 32, also suffered from alcoholism but was not fixated at the oral stage. He regressed to alcoholism because conflicts at a higher stage of development were too overwhelming for him.

After Sid's wife, Sue, became pregnant, he became impotent. The idea of his wife becoming a mother was threatening to Sid because he was unconsciously making her his own mother. Therefore, sex with her activated incestuous fantasies in him for which he felt very guilty. To cope with his guilt he not only made himself impotent but he withdrew from Sue and turned to men for interpersonal gratification. Homosexual fantasies toward men disturbed him a great deal so he regressed further and "drank to drown out unpleasant thoughts."

In focusing on the contribution of the client's history to current functioning, the clinician should consider not only the history of the client's adverse experiences and their meaning to him, but also, as social worker Helen Perlman (1957, p. 176) advised,

> The history of his successful or unsuccessful adaptation to them—his "solution" of his difficulties . . . by retreat, by entrenchment, by blind fighting, or by compromise, detour, and constructive substitutions—this history of his development as a problem encountering, problem-solving human being may provide . . . an understanding of what the client suffers from and what the extent of his coping ability is likely to be.

The Client's Psychic Structure

According to Freud (1938, 1939) the human psyche is comprised of *id, ego,* and *superego.* The id, the most primitive part of the mind and totally unconscious, is the repository of the drives and is concerned with their gratification. The ego, which develops out of experience and reason (although its potential is, to some extent, inherited), is the executive of the personality and mediates between the inner world of id drives and of superego commands and the demands of the external world. Some of the functions of the ego are judgment, reality testing, frustration tolerance, and interpersonal relations; the ego also erects defenses against anxiety. By assessing a client's ego strengths and weaknesses the therapist can determine how well he is adapting because the more severe the client's disturbances, the less operative are the ego functions and vice versa.

The superego, to which we referred in previous chapters, is the judge or censor of the mind and is essentially the product of interpersonal experiences. It is divided into two parts: the conscience and the ego ideal. The conscience is that part of the superego which forbids and admonishes while the ego ideal is the storehouse of values, ethical imperatives, and morals. Therapists sometimes overlook the fact that a client with a punitive and exacting superego usually has strong id wishes, often of a murderous nature, that cause anxiety. Rather than constantly live with unbearable anxiety the individual arranges for the superego to admonish him not to enjoy pleasure.

In assessing an individual's marital conflicts it is extremely important to understand how the individual's id, ego, and superego function and interact. Many clients cannot derive pleasure from their marital relationships because their superegos are so punitive. These clients are forever repressing id wishes to depend, to aggress, and to have sex. Often these clients cannot tolerate the infantile nature of their id wishes and their egos cope with anxiety through the utilization of the defense mechanism of projection. They constantly castigate their spouses for being infantile instead of looking at themselves.

Many spouses experience marital difficulties because their ego functions are so weak. They cannot delay gratification, they cannot absorb frustration, and they cannot empathize or identify with their spouse's wishes and fears. Clients with weak ego functions persist in trying to get their partners to indulge them unrealistically, or they feel so weak and overwhelmed in their marriages that they withdraw.

In sum, an assessment of the client's psychic structure—id, ego, and superego—and the way they interact, will go a long way in helping the clinician understand what hinders the client in enjoyable participation in marriage.

The Assessment

After clarifying the client's presenting problems and helping him through the initial interviews to move toward participating in a helping process, and after gathering the pertinent data that we have been discussing, the therapist is ready to formulate a psychosexual assessment. It should be stressed that the gathering of data is never a static process; new information, such as the client's history, current problems, and cultural background is always forthcoming. Consequently, the assessment is always being enriched, enlarged, and occasionally modified.

The process of assessment is an attempt to ascertain what troubles the client, why it troubles him, and how it seems to contribute to his marital problems. As we have implied, such professional judgments should be supported by evidence and should be checked and rechecked to assure their validity and reliability (Siporin, 1975). The assessment takes into consideration how the client's history is recapitulated in his marriage, how his psychic structure of id, ego, and superego is utilized to create and sustain his marital conflicts, what his modes of relating to the clinician in the interviews reveal about the way he copes with intimate relationships, and how his social context supports, aids, and abets his marital conflicts.

In the assessment the professional seeks to explain the client's marital conflicts. Is Mr. X's sexual impotence a function of his oedipal conflict in which he is making his wife the mother of his past? Or is he unable to trust—an oral problem? How strong or weak are his ego functions as he tries to cope with his marital conflicts? Is his superego punitive or full of lacunae? How much of his dysfunctional behavior is a regression or fixation? What about his social context? What fantasies did he have when he fell in love? What motivated him, consciously and unconsciously, to choose his mate? How does he relate to his marital partner and what parts of his history and his psychic structure are played out with her? Is she his superego? Is she his id? How are their cultural backgrounds similar or different? These are some of the questions that the helping professional must answer in order to make a comprehensive psychosexual assessment that will help him choose the appropriate therapeutic modality for the client and engage the client in an individualized treatment process of marriage counseling.

CHOOSING THE MODALITY

There is ongoing debate among practitioners as to which treatment modality is the treatment of choice in helping resolve marital conflicts. Sometimes proponents of individual long-term therapy and advocates of conjoint therapy (treating the couple together) appear to be political rivals rather than colleagues who are trying to determine the most appropriate treatment for their clients. If practitioners carefully make comprehensive psychosexual assessments of their clients and do not impose their own theoretical predilections and therapeutic biases on them, they will find that different modalities suit different clients at different times.

In most instances, but far from all, the psychodynamically oriented therapist has favored individual long-term therapy for the treatment of marital conflict. The rationale for this is as follows: First, inasmuch as chronic marital complaints are unconscious wishes, and inasmuch as the unconscious can be best helped to become conscious in a one-to-one therapeutic relationship, individual therapy seems to be the treatment of choice. Second, inasmuch as an unhappy spouse is an unhappy, neurotic individual, his marital difficulties can be resolved when he overcomes his neurotic conflicts. Neurotic conflicts, the psychodynamically oriented therapist alleges, can best be worked through in a therapeutic relationship where the focus is exclusively on the individual. Here, the client will recapitulate his neurotic problems in the transference relationship with the therapist and emotionally experience how he writes his neurotic marital script. As Meissner (1978) pointed out, individual therapy requires that the client assume responsibility for his own personal growth and change. Particularly when partners have different conscious aims and goals for the marriage does individual treatment allow for independent work.

While advocates of conjoint therapy have pointed out that there are really no secrets between marital pairs (Ackerman, 1958; Sager, 1976), proponents of individual therapy have averred that the resolution of marital conflicts is best conducted in an atmosphere of confidentiality. They have noted that many spouses would find it extremely difficult, if not impossible, to discuss extramarital affairs, homosexuality, certain childhood experiences, and feelings and fantasies toward the therapist and others in front of their partner.

Individual therapy for marital conflicts has been criticized because it can, in some cases, result in serious psychological disturbances in the mate (Sager, 1968), lead to divorce, and become long and expensive. Furthermore, the therapist doing individual treatment is often unaware of the nature of the real marital interactions and the actual distortions his client makes about the spouse. The therapist may also be unable to recognize that his client's partner has gross deficiencies in being able to communicate and solve problems (Meissner, 1978).

Conjoint treatment attempts to treat the neurotic interaction between two individuals rather than treat the individuals themselves. Advocates of this approach point out that dysfunctional marriages are not so much the result of a neurotic collusion but of a lack of role complementarity and dysfunctional role expectations. In contrast to their psychodynamically oriented colleagues, they contend that neurotic people can and do make good marriages, while many healthy individuals maintain unhappy marriages. They believe that the psychological status of a marriage is determined less by the personality difficulties of each partner than by the way the two personalities interact (Ackerman, 1958).

Therapists involved in conjoint therapy also believe that in the conjoint format, both the underlying interpersonal dynamics and the unconscious aspects of "the marital contract" become clear quite soon. Spouses have the opportunity to understand each other in greater depth and to develop empathy for each other. In front of a neutral observer, marital partners have the potential for perceiving each other more realistically. The therapist also has the opportunity to see how partners distort each other's communications. According to Martin (1976) the therapist in conjoint therapy is better able to limit destructive behavior and to facilitate the development of the observing ego of each partner, enabling them to test reality more effectively.

Some of the disadvantages of conjoint therapy are that most of the time the unconscious motives of the individuals cannot appear spontaneously, and that confidentiality is not assured; therefore, many individual secrets are not forthcoming. Because of the nature of the format the couple can use it to discharge complaints without getting to their wishes and defenses which keep these complaints alive. A possibility in conjoint therapy is that the partners may unite with each other and project onto the therapist their negative feelings about authoritarian or omnipotent parents, and therefore they can defeat the therapist's efforts to effect change (Meissner, 1978). With its emphasis on the here-and-now conjoint therapy can ignore crucial dimensions of individual history which are important etiological factors in the conflicts.

Frequently, advocates of conjoint therapy overlook the fact that to participate in this treatment requires reasonably strong egos in both partners. Husband and wife have to be able to identify with one another, empathize, tolerate frustration and anxiety, control hostility to some extent, and share the therapist. Many clients who have marital problems do not possess these abilities and it would appear that conjoint therapy is contraindicated for them.

Conjoint therapy seems to be the treatment of choice for those couples who have many ego functions intact, communicate well with each other, and want to share the therapist without experiencing too much sibling rivalry. These clients should be able to share secrets with their partners in a way that is neither too disruptive to their marriage nor to their treatment. In sum, mature, well-integrated individuals can probably use conjoint therapy quite well.

There are also couples who are so symbiotic that to see them in individual therapy is to hurt them. Usually they protest about being separated and their opposition to individual therapy has to be respected—often for some time.

As noted, the emphasis in conjoint therapy is on the here-and-now and the history of the individuals is often overlooked. For those couples who have a strong resistance to examining their pasts and who wish to concentrate exclusively on current issues, conjoint therapy is usually welcome.

Both individual therapy and conjoint therapy may be long or short. In long-term treatment, the husband or wife has the opportunity to see how his or her history, marital complaints, and neurotic complaints are recapitulated in the transference relationship with the therapist. This can provide fundamental and sustained change which short-term treatment cannot offer. However, there are many clients who fear a sustained long-term treatment approach and their resistances to it must be respected. Often, when the client who fears intimacy and is suspicious is offered short-term treatment, he relaxes and may move on to something more extensive when he feels more secure. Even if clients cannot move on to more extensive treatment, short-term work is better than nothing.

Some clients cannot tolerate either individual or conjoint therapy but feel more secure in a group where they can hide if need be, and where they can feel better when they learn their problems are not unique. Group therapy has been recommended for marital problems that are chronic and ego syntonic; for example, the problems appear to be a way of life (Grunebaum, Christ, and Neiberg, 1969). In the group setting, a couples' marital interaction is described and enacted with another group member with immediate feedback. A group composed of individuals with similar developmental problems and capacities for object–relatedness facilitates the process (Neiberg, 1976).

Among the disadvantages of couples' groups is the mutual communication of hopelessness, or the potential for members who are very destructive or disturbed to disrupt group interaction and prevent group cohesion. When there are family secrets or the fear of self-revelation by one marital partner this modality is contraindicated. It may also be seen as threatening to an individual who is restrained or insecure in groups.

THE TREATMENT PROCESS

While there are several differences between individual treatment and conjoint therapy, there are certain aspects of any treatment process which all clinicians who treat marital conflicts should master.

While conjoint therapy concentrates more on the here-and-now, individual treatment tends to concentrate on how the past is recapitulated in the present. While conjoint therapy focuses on marital interaction, individual treatment tends to focus more on the individual's fantasies, memories, and dreams. And while conjoint therapy deals mainly with conscious thoughts, individual treatment tries to make the unconscious conscious. Even with these differences both therapies must take into account notions such as transference, countertransference, resistance, confrontation, clarification, interpretation, and working through.

Transference

Transference is a universal phenomenon of the human mind and dominates the whole of each person's relations to his environment. Transference exists in all relationships: in marriage, in the classroom, in business relations, and in friendships (Freud, 1926). Because of our unique histories, ego functioning, superego mandates, values, and social circumstances, each of us brings with us to every new relationship wishes, fears, anxieties, hopes, pressures, defenses, and many more subjective factors. These have evolved from previous relationships and may or may not be appropriate in the new situation. Inasmuch as these universal phenomena are largely unconscious, we cannot will them away or consciously modify them. They influence our perceptions of the people we meet; very often, therefore, the reasons we give for responding to people with love, hatred, or ambivalence are rationalizations.

The intimate relationship of client and therapist recapitulates the feelings and fantasies as well as the emotionally charged experiences that the client had with parents, siblings, and significant others. If therapists do not understand how they are experienced by their clients, they cannot be too helpful to them. All clients respond to their therapists' interpretations, clarifications, and other remarks in terms of their transferences to their therapists. If the client loves the therapist, he will be inclined to accept most of his therapeutic interventions; if he hates the therapist, even the most neutral statement or question will be suspect. If the client has mixed feelings toward the therapist, all of his interventions will be responded to ambivalently.

Much of psychodynamically oriented therapy is an attempt to help the client understand why he responds to the therapist the way he does. Assisting the client in feeling and understanding his transference reactions will be one of the major means of helping the client resolve his marital problems.

As we have pointed out several times, chronic marital complaints are unconscious wishes. If clients want what they complain about in marriage, then they will unconsciously arrange to transfer onto the therapist the very complaints they have of their spouses. It is when clients observe that they experience their therapists the same way they experience their partners, that they gain some conviction of their own roles in their marital conflicts. Of course, this will occur only if the clinician sides neither with the client against the spouse nor with the spouse against the client. The clinician, if he is to help the marital transference develop in the therapy, must remain a quiet listener who exposes conflicts without imposing his own values or biases on the client's productions.

Jack L., age 40, was in marital counseling with Ms. H. because of his sexual impotence. He described his wife as a "cold, frigid, bitch who always wants to castrate me." During his sixth month of twice-a-week therapy, Jack came into a session with Ms. H. and told her that he was going to divorce his wife, Grace. "She is continually unreceptive, has no sexual appeal. I've tried everything and I'm leaving!" he bellowed. After a silence, Jack asked Ms. H., "What do you think of all this?" When Ms. H. did not present her own opinion but asked Jack, "What are you feeling right now that prompts your question?" Jack responded with enormous rage and told Ms. H. that she was "a cold, hostile bitch" who frustrated him. On starting to threaten to leave treatment, Jack paused, and with some insight said, "I guess I need to fight it out with all you dames!"

Repeated occurrences of the type of interaction that occurred in the above session gradually gave Jack the conviction that he "was attracted to cold women with whom I can fight."

When a clinician recognizes that transference always exists, he can look at his therapeutic results more objectively. If the client wants his spouse to be an omnipotent parent, he will probably transfer this wish on to the therapist and will try to achieve a similar relationship with the therapist where he is the indulged child. Then any time the client feels the therapist is not gratifying this desire, he will become hostile and feel the same rage that he feels toward his spouse when his wishes for the omnipotent parent are not gratified. If the client unconsciously turns his spouse into a superego, he will look for the same kind of punishment in therapy that he does in his marriage. Regardless of the client's transference to the spouse it will be recapitulated in the therapy provided the therapist remains neutral.

Inasmuch as the client views all the therapist's interventions through the lens of his transference, one of the therapist's major tasks is to help the client see why he wants to distort the therapist the way he does, and what gratification and protection this provides for him.

As noted in Chapter 4, many clients turn their marital partners into their unacceptable ids. They criticize their partners for their intense dependency, insatiable hunger, and perverse sexuality. In the treatment situation, they inevitably experience the therapist the same way: he becomes their attractive but frightening id.

Elinor K., age 34, was in marital counseling because she found her husband "disgusting, demanding, and sexually overstimulating." She resented his "constant orders" and was thinking of leaving him. For several months in her treatment with Dr. I., a male therapist, Elinor was detached, polite, and essentially uninvolved. When this pattern became quite clear to both therapist and client, Dr. I. suggested that it might be further explored in the treatment. Elinor then began referring to her therapist as "a dirty old man," "an oversexed Freudian," and "a hungry bastard."

Much of her treatment was an attempt to show her how she renounced her own id impulses and transferred them onto both her husband and her therapist.

While transference reactions are almost always traceable to childhood, there is not always a simple correspondence between the past and present.

Although there is sometimes a direct repetition—such as when the client is quite convinced that the therapist is almost identical to a father, mother, spouse, or sibling—there is frequently a "compensatory fantasy" (Fine, 1982) to make up for what was lacking in childhood; that is, the client fantasies that the therapist is somebody he would have liked his parents or siblings to have been. It can be inferred from such fantasies and dreams that overt positive and loving feelings expressed toward the therapist may be covering up negative and hateful feelings. Similarly, hostile statements toward the therapist can defend against warm feelings toward the therapist.

It should be reemphasized that transference exists in all relationships. There is no such phenomenon as a client who has "no transference." As client and clinician accept transference as a fact of therapeutic life, they gain an appreciation of the client's conflicts and aspects of his history that are contributing to his dysfunctional marriage.

In working with clients to help them understand their transference reactions and to help them see that their reactions to their therapists are identical to their reactions toward their spouses, the therapist needs patience. He cannot immediately point out the similarities when they occur. The client must feel these similarities over and over again before he is able to acknowledge them and see how he creates them.

It should be pointed out that in conjoint therapy there are multiple transferences. Each marital partner has transference reactions to the therapist and to the other partner. In addition, the couple forms "a conjoint transference" to the therapist. All of these transferences have to be understood and mastered.

Countertransference

Countertransference is really the same phenomenon as transference, except that it refers to those wishes, fantasies, anxieties, and defenses of the therapist that interfere with his objective perception and mature treatment of the client. Therapists can make their clients their mothers, fathers, siblings, and so on. They can turn them into their ids, egos, and superegos. Most frequently, the client represents for the therapist an object of the past onto whom past feelings and wishes are projected.

In marriage counseling, countertransference reactions are easy to develop, yet they can interfere with helping clients resolve their marital conflicts. One of the most common countertransference problems is joining the client in his attacks on the spouse and forming a love-and-be-loved relationship with the client. The spouse becomes the enemy and the client does not have to explore his hatred toward her: the therapist legitimizes it. Usually when this occurs, the therapist is overidentified with the client and the client's partner is experienced as a hated object of the therapist's past.

Sam I., age 26, was in treatment with Mr. J., a male social worker of approximately the same age. When Sam described his marital difficulties to Mr. J. and referred to his wife as "asexual, undemonstrative, and inhibited," Mr. J. advised Sam to consider having an extramarital affair or to divorce his wife. While Sam initially welcomed Mr. J.'s advice because it made him feel "more independent," and "like a man," after a while he began to oppose his therapist and left treatment prematurely.

When Mr. J. reflected on his countertransference reactions in his work with Sam, he realized that he had failed to see how much Sam utilized his hatred toward his wife to ward off the anxiety that the intimate relationship of marriage aroused. Furthermore, Mr. J. also realized that some of his own repressed hostility toward his own wife was being vicariously discharged by encouraging Sam to do what he, Mr. J., wanted to do but was frightened to face in himself.

If the therapist forms a love-and-be-loved relationship with the client and supports him against the spouse, the client can never feel his hostility in the transference relationship with the therapist. Consequently, the chaotic marriage continues while therapist and client indulge one another. A positive countertransference, while a desirable attitude, must be studied as carefully as a positive transference (Fine, 1982). When the therapist is overidentified with the client he begins to overlook the client's contributions to his own problems. This can strengthen the client's self-pity and intensify his wishes to be an indulged, omnipotent child.

Therapists are human and consequently can feel hostility toward some of their clients. Just as a negative transference has to be understood, a therapist's negative countertransference has to be understood. Frequently when the marriage counselor does not like a client it is because the latter reminds the therapist of a disliked parent or sibling. Most often a negative countertransference is activated because the client demonstrates attitudes and/or behavior that the helping professional cannot tolerate in himself.

Marsha F., age 30, was in marital counseling because her husband told her that he would leave her unless she straightened herself out. As Marsha discussed her marriage with her therapist, Ms. K., it became obvious to both client and therapist that Marsha was very subservient to her husband, behaved quite masochistically with him, and frequently was self-demeaning, blaming herself completely for the marital problems.

As Ms. K. listened to Marsha's accounts of her marital struggles, she found herself irritated with Marsha's self-demeaning attitude. She began to lecture Marsha about how she was "taking a lot of crap" from her husband and that she should tell him off. Marsha tried to carry out Ms. K.'s directions but felt too frightened to do so. In response to Marsha's opposition, Ms. K. pressed her harder and Marsha became even more inhibited. The sadomasochistic relationship that Marsha formed in her marriage was recapitulated in her treatment; it was then compounded because her therapist behaved sadistically with her. After several months of treatment with Ms. K., Marsha quit, saying she was helped by Ms. K. to have a better marriage. However, a review of the material showed that Marsha was merely placating Ms. K. and really wanted to escape from her.

When Ms. K. reflected on her behavior with Marsha, she eventually realized that Marsha's passivity and masochism reminded her of some of her own passivity and self-hatred which she tried to repress and deny. When Ms. K. saw parts of herself in Marsha, she wanted Marsha to get rid of these characteristics quickly, much the same way she tried to get rid of these characteristics in herself, instead of facing them and understanding them.

Countertransference, like transference, appears in all therapeutic modalities. In conjoint therapy the therapist can join one partner against the other, indulge both of them, hate both of them, or react untherapeutically in a variety of other ways. Just as there is no such thing as a client who has "no transference," there is also no such thing as a therapist who has "no countertransference." A practitioner who is able to face countertransference reactions is in an excellent position to help clients resolve their marital problems without being too influenced by his own irrational loves, hates, and ambivalences.

Resistance

Although unhappily married people come to a helping professional to resolve their marital conflicts, anybody who has tried to help them therapeutically has observed a universal paradox in their treatment—they all want to preserve the status quo and, therefore, fight change. Regardless of the setting in which they are seen and regardless of the modality in which they are treated, all clients present obstacles to their feeling better and to their functioning better (Strean, 1985). Therapists who accept resistance as a fact of therapeutic life are accustomed to hear the impotent husband extol the virtues of celibacy, the masochistic wife resignedly say that misery is inevitable in marriage, and the battling couple insist that a fist fight often clears the air.

As suggested earlier in this chapter, most clients welcome the idea of saying what comes to their minds to a quiet, attentive listener. However, sooner or later therapy becomes painful and creates anxiety for most clients. As the client discovers parts of himself that have been repressed, such as sexual and aggressive fantasies, he may feel guilt, shame, or embarrassment. Then he may become silent and evasive or want to quit therapy altogether.

When the client stops talking about himself and ceases to examine himself, it is called resistance. Resistance is any action or attitude that impedes the course of therapeutic work. Because every client, to some extent, wants to preserve the status quo, all treatment must be carried on in the face of some resistance.

One way to understand the nature of a client's resistance is to think of his dysfunctional marital interactions. For example, if a client refuses to take responsibility for his marital battles in daily life and projects them onto the spouse, he will probably spend a lot of time in the treatment situation making disparaging remarks about the spouse; in addition, he will probably make disparaging remarks about the therapist and other people. If a client in his daily married life is frightened of intimacy, he will resist discussions that border on this issue in treatment and will try to turn the therapeutic situation into an intellectual dialogue or something else that is more comfortable for him. And, if a client must defend against homosexual fantasies in his married life, then he will resist discussing anything that may have a homosexual connotation in treatment.

What are referred to as defenses in the client's daily life (operations by the ego to avoid anxiety, for example, denial, repression, projection) become resistances in treatment. It is extremely important for the marital counselor to recognize that the presence of a resistance always means that the client feels in danger and is trying to ward off potential pain. Resistance is not something good or bad; it is an unconscious operation that the client feels forced to use to protect himself.

Resistance is not created by the therapy. The therapeutic situation activates similar types of anxiety that are aroused in married life and the client then uses habitual mechanisms to oppose both therapy and the therapist (Greenson, 1967). The practitioner will find that resistance can take many forms: The client can arrive late for sessions, cancel appointments, refuse to talk or pay his fees. Also, resistance can take a subtle form: The client can become overcompliant, somaticize his conflicts, or be unduly deferential with the therapist.

As client and therapist study the dangers that are being warded off by the form the client's resistance takes, they can both become more sensitized to the dangers that exist in the client's marriage.

Sanford and Rhoda D., a couple in their early thirties, were in conjoint therapy because they both felt that "the chemistry was missing" in their interpersonal and sexual lives. At home and in their sessions with their therapist Mr. L. they battled each other constantly and seemed to be deeply involved in one-upmanship power struggles. Occasionally, their fracases involved hitting one another physically.

Although they came to their sessions on time and seemed to be cooperating with Mr. L., the therapist noted that from time to time Sanford and Rhoda would come 15 or more minutes late to their interviews. When Mr. L. noticed this pattern and shared it with them, clients and therapist were able to figure out that the D.'s came late to sessions after they did not fight in the previous session. Feeling warmly toward one another and toward Mr. L. frightened them. They had to spend much time in their conjoint therapy trying to understand what felt dangerous to both of them when they experienced warm feelings.

While lateness for the D.'s was their way of resisting intimacy, lateness for another couple or individual could express a fear of expressing aggression, an anxiety about sexual fantasies, or some other danger. The meaning of a client's resistance is unique to the client and it may take several sessions for the meaning of the client's resistance to be determined.

While the term "counterresistance" is not foreign to most therapists, there have been few systematic attempts in the literature to discuss the therapist's contribution to the evolution, maintenance, and intractability of client resistances. From the moment the client calls on the phone for a consultation to the termination of the contact, the therapist has fantasies and feelings toward the client which can influence the client's activity and inactivity in the treatment (Strean, 1985). Often the therapist has a responsibility in the client's absenting himself from the interviews, in the client's tardiness, in the client's non-payment of fees, and in other forms of client resistance (Langs, 1981).

Interventive Procedures

We have pointed out several times that one of the best things a marriage counselor can do is be a good listener. As the client has an opportunity to pour out his heart and spontaneously discuss his thoughts, he feels valued by the therapist and his self-esteem rises. Then he is able to examine resistances, transference reactions, history, and conflicted and frequently embarrassing aspects of his marriage.

The therapist has to be more than a listener and questioner during the treatment process. At times he has to confront the client with behavior and attitudes which are aiding and abetting his marital difficulties. As we saw with Sanford and Rhoda D. in the above case illustration, the therapist had to confront his clients with their tardiness. Confrontation is most helpful when the client has some inner conviction about what the therapist is presenting. Latenesses, absences, and nonpayment of fees are obvious facts; frequently, however, when clients are confronted with their resistive behavior, they feel that they have to protect themselves. Often a confrontation is experienced as an accusation.

Although Sanford and Rhoda D. were able to talk about their tardiness, later in treatment when Mr. L. confronted them with their occasional absences, they became very defensive and argumentative, and told Mr. L. he "was making too much of nothing." Both of them experienced Mr. L. as a punitive teacher who was criticizing them. When Mr. L. listened to their complaints with empathy and did not retaliate when the D.'s voiced their anger at him, the D.'s were eventually able to acknowledge that, indeed, they both found him to be authoritarian at times and resented him for this.

The decisive question with regard to the therapist's activities (questions, confrontations, etc.) is not whether the statement is correct but how the client reacts to it, and in turn what the therapist does with the client's reactions (Fine, 1968). Perhaps in the majority of cases the clinician offers the "correct" question, confrontation, or interpretation; but if the client needs to oppose him, that is what he must attend to (as Mr. L. did when the D.'s did not accept his statement that their occasional absences from interviews were something to examine).

Confrontation leads to the next step, clarification. Clarification refers to those activities of the therapist's that aim at placing the client's behavior in sharp focus and examining the issues that motivate it (Greenson, 1967). For example, in the above illustration Mr. L. suggested that Sanford and Rhoda D. think some more about their absences from interviews; therapist and clients then learned that the D.'s had many hidden resentments about therapy and the therapist. They learned that they experienced Mr. L. as authoritarian, arbitrary, and a bit pompous.

The next step after clarification is interpretation. To interpret means to make an unconscious phenomenon, such as a defense or a wish, conscious. More specifically, it means to make conscious the unconscious meaning of a given psychological event. The therapist goes beyond what is readily observable and by his interpretations assigns meaning and causality to a psychological event. In the example of the D.'s, Mr. L. interpreted as follows: "You are absent from interviews because you each experience me as the father of your childhood who you felt was authoritarian and made you always submit to him. You handle your anger at me in the same way you handled it toward your fathers—by running away from it."

The procedures of clarification and interpretation are intimately connected. Very frequently clarification leads to an interpretation which leads back to a further clarification.

Working through refers to the repetitive, progressive, and elaborate explorations of the client's attitudes and behavior which eventually lead to behavioral change. A variety of processes are set in motion by working through in which insight, memory, and behavioral change influence each other. As the D.'s examined their hostility toward Mr. L. and toward their parents, they were able to see how they were fighting old childhood battles with one another and were distorting one another in many ways.

Whether the clinician engaged in marriage counseling helps his clients in one-to-one treatment, conjoint therapy, or group therapy, clients will not enjoy the benefits of his help unless they begin to experience themselves differently. Correction of dysfunctional marital behavior and of immature attitudes toward marriage can take place only when the client is convinced that who he is, what he wants, what he fears, and what gives him pleasure are genuinely understood and accepted by the therapist. The husband and wife who fear sex cannot truly enjoy it until they are convinced that their sexual fantasies, fears, and practices are not rejected by the practitioner. The husband who has temper tantrums and physically abuses his wife will not be able to modify his behavior until he feels that his therapist empathizes with his intense anger and with the desperation that gives rise to it.

Only if the client feels genuinely accepted as he is can growth take place and the client usually senses how the clinician truly feels toward him. This is why the most brilliant interpretations of hostile therapists have little impact and why the occasional lapses of an empathetic and sensitive therapist are usually overlooked by the client.

CHAPTER 6

Treating the Symbiotic Spouse

Having familiarized ourselves with some of the salient features of the treatment process in marriage counseling, we are now in a position to relate some of the therapeutic principles we discussed in Chapter 5 to specific client groups. In this chapter we will discuss the treatment of husbands and wives whose marital problems are caused primarily by unresolved conflicts emerging from the first year of life.

As will be recalled, for an individual to participate with some freedom and enjoyment in a marital relationship he has to be able to trust the partner and feel that he can be trusted as well. In order to achieve this kind of interaction the individual should have received sufficient and consistent doses of tender love and care from a need-gratifying mother. If the child was the recipient of sufficient and consistent psychological and physical warmth, and if he enjoyed it, he is prepared in many ways to give and receive love in a marriage.

As we suggested in Chapter 3, many of the movements, caresses, and language between lovers are reminiscent of the caresses and "baby talk" that the infant received while being held by his mother. If the mother was experienced as genuinely loving, the child will transfer his or her positive feelings toward her onto the spouse. If, however, the mother was experienced as ambivalent, harsh, hostile, or depressed, the child—on becoming a marital partner—will feel furious with the spouse much of the time, distrust the spouse most of the time, and want to withdraw from the spouse almost all of the time. Psychiatrist John Bowlby (1969) has described the sequence of protest-despair-detachment when a young infant feels threatened with loss of his mother. Many married people who have conflicts on the oral level demonstrate the same emotional reactions in their marital relationships.

In addition to receiving tender loving care, another important experience that the child should have during the first year of life (around the age of 11 or 12 months) is weaning. Weaning helps the child accept the reality principle with some equanimity. It also aids the child in recognizing that he cannot be omnipotent nor can he expect there to be an omnipotent parent available for him all of the time. Weaning helps build ego strengths; it aids in the development of frustration tolerance and reduces infantile narcissism. If a child has been weaned in a sensitive, loving, and understanding manner, he will be prepared in many ways to accept frustration in marriage and to acknowledge that the partner has wishes and needs separate from his own. Furthermore, he will not be as likely to expect marriage to be a Garden of Eden. However, if the child was not appropriately weaned but indulged, he will be inclined to expect the marital partner to always be at his beck and call. He will not accept "no" for an answer; instead, he will insist that he must have what he wants when he wants it.

When a child has been weaned abruptly and harshly he retains large quantities of murderous rage within himself. He can either become a constant collector of "injustices" in marriage or he may turn his violent feelings inward and be constantly depressed.

Many clients who appear for marriage counseling have problems emanating from the first year of life. They pose various therapeutic problems.

THE WITHDRAWN SPOUSE

During the first couple of months of life the baby is autistic (Mahler, 1968) and preoccupied almost exclusively with his own sensations and wishes. He is extremely narcissistic and is unable to appreciate that other people have needs of their own. Only as he receives constant ministrations from a need-gratifying mother can he move from autism to object relatedness.

If a baby spends the first few months with a depressed mother, or with one who is ill, absent, or unavailable, he becomes fixated at the autistic level and has limited interest in other people. While many of these individuals never marry, some do. Although those who marry have retained the hope that, perhaps, a mother is available, they are not really convinced of this. They enter a marriage half-heartedly and are usually unable to relate very meaningfully to the partner. When they are in a marriage counselor's office, they are most suspicious of him and have come there because a physician or someone else has strongly advised them to do so; they rarely seek help on their own. Similar to their approach to marriage, they enter the therapist's office half-heartedly.

The therapist, in order to involve the withdrawn spouse in treatment, must respect the client's resistances to interpersonal relationships. He cannot be too active because emotional intimacy frightens this client. The client believes that emotional security is best achieved away from people.

Susan A., age 22, was referred to Dr. Z., a male therapist, by her physician. She had complained to her physician that after getting married about a year previous to her consultation with him, she was constantly nauseated, had hives all over her body, suffered from insomnia, and found it very difficult to concentrate on her job as a bookkeeper. When her physician could find no organic basis to account for her bodily ailments, he referred her for psychotherapy.

While Susan complied with her physician's suggestion she felt agitated, depressed, and frightened. When she met Dr. Z. she immediately told him that she did not see any need for psychotherapy. On Dr. Z.'s recognizing with her that it must have been irritating to be referred to a place where she felt she didn't need to be, Susan said, "Maybe the doctor knows something that I don't know." Dr. Z. then asked her, "What could this be?" After a long silence Susan said that she was "a lousy wife." She pointed out that although she had been married for over a year, she could not "stomach" sex with her husband, and found just being with him "hard to take." She also brought out material which suggested that during her whole life she found that being with people was repugnant to her. Toward the end of her first interview Susan said that she was a "hopeless case" and she doubted whether anybody could help her. On Dr. Z.'s suggestion that perhaps she might want to discuss her doubts about being helped by him in another interview, Susan said she'd come back but she "doubted if it would help."

Susan cancelled her next appointment and told Dr. Z. that she decided that she would prefer "to go it alone." Dr. Z. over the phone told her that he certainly did not want to pressure her to come to a place where she did not want to be, but he did feel it might be a good idea to discuss her skepticism about help a little more because a lot was bothering her. Susan did come for another appointment and pointed out to Dr. Z. that she realized he wanted to help her but she had "never trusted a soul." When asked by Dr. Z. what she felt was untrustworthy about him, Susan did not answer the question directly. However, she did spend several interviews discussing her parents.

Shortly after her birth, Susan's mother had become bedridden with cancer and therefore had had little to do with her. Occasionally Susan's maternal grandmother was available but Susan did not have any warm memories of her. Susan experienced her father as "overhungry," "demanding," and "slovenly." Like her mother, he had removed himself emotionally from the client when it came to meeting her maturational needs. Father had alternated between violent-tempered alcoholic bouts and periods of withdrawal.

Susan had a sister who was three years older than she. In describing her relationship with her sister Susan said, "Although she was my big sister, I had to take care of her." As she told Dr. Z. about taking care of her parents as well, her hives became visible and she became very nauseated. Dr. Z. pointed out here that taking care of others was obviously something that was hard "to stomach" and very upsetting. To this Susan remarked, "I know you'd like to help me but I don't trust you. I feel that you want me to tell you more and more, and what good will that do?" Dr. Z. suggested that she felt she had to work hard for him the same way she had to work hard for others. Once more, Susan did not respond to Dr. Z.'s transference interpretation but did go on to talk some more about her own history.

Evidently Susan had responded to teachers and students while at school the same way she had dealt with her family. She felt she had to "put out" for everybody and resented it. Consequently, she was withdrawn at school where she did only average work, made few friends, and daydreamed a great deal.

When Susan graduated from high school, she took a job as a bookkeeper and met her husband Frank, an accountant, at the job. She liked him because he was "quiet, sincere, and could provide stability." There was limited communication between Frank and Susan during their six-month courtship but there was no overt tension, either. They married and had not yet consummated their marriage when Susan entered treatment.

As Susan continued in her treatment she became more and more withdrawn and more and more verbally inhibited. Verbal activity on the part of Dr. Z. tended to exacerbate her hives and nausea. When Dr. Z. told her again that she felt she had "to put out" for him and that she resented it, Susan nodded but did not produce more material.

Although Dr. Z. began to feel impatient with Susan, he also realized that to pressure her to talk would only intensify her conviction that she had to produce for him and that would also aggravate her symptoms. Therefore, he told Susan what seemed quite clear to him, "I get the feeling that being close to somebody puts you under a lot of pressure. I think you feel pressured in your marriage, on your job, and with me. You seem to feel that the only way to get along with me is to put out a lot of thoughts, feelings, memories, etcetera." Susan did not say much at this time but by her facial expression and bodily posture she appeared to feel understood. To test Dr. Z., for the next several sessions she was extremely quiet while with him. Dr. Z. in turn was also quiet, feeling that the most helpful thing he could do for Susan was to refrain from putting pressure on her to produce.

As Susan, for the first time in her life, was having a relationship with another human being where she did not have to do all the giving, her mood and attitude changed a great deal and her hives and nausea disappeared. She was able to begin having sex with her husband and resented him much less in many areas of life.

While Susan started to feel better in her marriage and on the job, much of the repressed rage that she had been carrying around with her most of her life had not come out in therapy. While Dr. Z. was silently trying to figure out how to help Susan release this rage so that she would feel even more comfortable in her marriage and elsewhere, Susan, herself, provided some direction. She began to react to Dr. Z.'s rather consistent silence and told him that he reminded her of her "stupid, alcoholic father who sat around and did nothing." She began to feel that Dr. Z., instead of helping her, was having a good deal for himself. He "got paid to do nothing."

Dr. Z. recognized that Susan was recapitulating her relationship with her father and that in order to make her therapy a corrective experience he would have to provide something for Susan now. He said, "I'm pleased that you can tell me of your dissatisfactions with me. This helps our work. What would you like from me now that would make it worthwhile to be with me?" Susan, somewhat surprised at Dr. Z.'s benign attitude toward her, became tearful and talked about how much she craved understanding and affection while growing up. "It was never there," she lamented. "I never had a father and mother to discuss school, boys, sex, or anything. I had to figure it out all by myself."

Susan, on her own, was able to direct her interviews with Dr. Z. into such areas as sex, work, and relationships with people—areas that she had never discussed with her parents. She talked with Dr. Z. about her embarrassment in being naked while having sex, her feeling that a penis was something to rip off rather than enjoy, and her conviction that if she let people know about her emotional needs they would be "disgusted" with her.

As Susan became more emotionally intimate with Dr. Z. she began to have sexual fantasies toward him which she shared with him. As she had wanted to do with her father and her husband, she had fantasies of ripping off Dr. Z.'s penis because he was not with her enough of the time. "If I had my druthers," said Susan, "I'd have you and your penis in me all of the time."

Inasmuch as Susan could feel more self-confident and relaxed with Dr. Z., she was eventually able to feel more relaxed in her marriage. Initially Frank was overjoyed with her progress; however, he became frightened when Susan became more emotionally and sexually intimate and eventually went into therapy himself.

The treatment of Susan seems to provide some guidelines for the marital counseling of the withdrawn spouse. First of all, it would appear that the therapeutic modality of choice for this client is one-to-one long term treatment. Inasmuch as this client was never gratified in a one-to-one relationship, he or she needs the corrective emotional experience that only a one-to-one therapeutic relationship can offer. As the client feels his distrust and anger toward the therapist—who is initially experienced as an ungratifying mother—and as the therapist responds to the client's distrust and anger without retaliating and without becoming defensive, the client slowly feels more positive toward the therapy and toward the therapist. He begins to examine his marriage and himself. It should also be recognized that the withdrawn spouse has a great deal of difficulty relating to even one person. Consequently, if this client is presented with a conjoint-therapy format, it will feel much too overwhelming and create too much anxiety.

In working with the withdrawn spouse, the therapist has to feel reasonably comfortable, as he is constantly being tested and is frequently being rejected. When Susan A. began work with Dr. Z., she told him several times that he would not be able to help her. Initially, Dr. Z. had to accept Susan's perception of him as incompetent and, without contradicting her or pressuring her, had to "hang in" and invite her to discuss her doubts about him. When the client, in effect, is given permission to distrust, to question, and to voice irritation with the therapist—as happened in the case of Susan—the client usually progresses in the treatment.

The withdrawn spouse frequently experiences both marriage and therapy as "a pressuring business." We saw this clearly in the work with Susan. One of the most helpful things that Dr. Z. did for her was respect her silences and tolerate her wish to give him next to nothing. It is difficult for most marriage counselors to accept the fact that nothing much is going to be said or done during treatment for some time. If the therapist can weather this treatment crisis, the client eventually feels strengthened and becomes more cooperative.

In working with any client, but particularly with the withdrawn spouse, the therapist should not feel completely satisfied with some initial improvement. Initial improvement reflects that the client feels accepted by the therapist while he, the client, can behave the way he chooses to behave. It does not imply that there has been a working through of the client's problems. As we saw in the case of Susan, despite feeling more sexually relaxed in her marriage and more accepting of her husband and therapist, she needed time to pour out her hatred and mistrust before she could fully enjoy herself in her marriage.

It would appear that some proponents of short-term marital counseling (Balint, 1961; Eysenck, 1952; Freeman, 1981; Hepworth, 1979; Reid and Shyne, 1969) have failed to recognize that the changes that take place in the early phases of counseling are primarily due to "the honeymoon reaction" (Fine, 1982) in which the client experiences the positive effects of the unique relationship that therapy provides. It does the client a disservice and makes counseling appear like a gift from the gods when therapists and clients take the point of view that long-term problems with trust, anger, sex, and dependency can be resolved in six or less interviews.

In the therapeutic work with Susan, it was clearly demonstrated that the client recapitulates his marital transference with the therapist and perceives him much the same way he perceives his spouse. When the therapist does not take sides in the marital conflict but instead helps the client relive in the transference his habitual ways of coping with crucial individuals in his life, clarification and interpretation by the therapist of these habitual patterns in interpersonal relationships helps the client grow in the marriage.

As we reiterated in Chapter 4, a marital relationship is a system in which the two actors strive to maintain a homeostatic balance (Bertalanffy, 1973; Paolino and McGrady, 1978). When one member makes changes, the other member's psychic equilibrium is shaken. Frank, Susan A.'s husband, needed therapeutic help to cope with her positive changes and his neurotic reaction to them.

The withdrawn spouse often presents many disabling symptoms. He can be suffering from addictions such as chronic gambling or acute alcoholism. It is often tempting for the marriage counselor to try to help the client give up his symptom promptly with the hope that if this is done his marriage will become more rewarding to him and to his spouse. This approach is shortsighted. It fails to take into consideration the unconscious collusion in all dysfunctional marriages and it overlooks the fact that any neurotic symptom reflects a chronic disability to cope with one or more life tasks (Erikson, 1950). The complete person has to be addressed and respected when a serious neurotic symptom is part and parcel of the marital conflict. One cannot tell an alcoholic spouse to cease drinking or a gambling spouse to stop gambling. These problems need many interviews of therapeutic attention.

Lloyd B., age 36, was referred to a family agency for marriage counseling by hospital personnel who had treated him medically for his chronic alcoholism. Lloyd had a 15-year history of "being on and off the wagon,"

The Withdrawn Spouse 89

as he put it, and now that he was married to Madeline for over two years, he could see that his alcoholism was seriously interfering with their relationship. When he was drunk, Lloyd was physically abusive to Madeline and could not have sex with her because he was either very tired and/or depressed. In his intake interview at the social agency he told the social worker, Ms. Y., that he was resolved not to drink any more so that he could save his marriage.

Impressed with Lloyd's determination to give up drinking, Ms. Y. praised him for his "mature attitude" and told him that he would be in a much better position to reap the benefits of marriage counseling if he could refrain from drinking. Lloyd was very pleased with Ms. Y.'s remarks and was determined to become "a cooperative husband and a cooperative client."

For about three weeks Lloyd was euphoric. He had stopped drinking and was able to work well, eat well, enjoy sex, and be a devoted husband. However, during the fifth week of his once-a-week treatment, he came to the interview somewhat sheepishly and confessed that he had been drinking. Not willing to explore with Lloyd what he was feeling in treatment and/or in his life, Ms. Y. told Lloyd that he was not sticking with their contract and that his drinking would sabotage his therapy and interfere with his marriage. Lloyd agreed with Ms. Y. that she was "absolutely right" and vowed not to drink anymore. However, immediately following the session Lloyd—although not drunk—provoked Madeline into an argument and physically beat her. Not recognizing that Lloyd's abusive behavior with his wife might have been related to his anger toward his therapist, Ms. Y. told Lloyd that he was not talking enough about his marital conflicts but was acting them out instead. However, she praised him for being able to abstain from alcohol. Lloyd appreciated the praise and told Ms. Y. that he was going to stay "on the wagon" and was also going to refrain from beating Madeline. Ms. Y. told Lloyd that he was developing a very positive and affirmative attitude toward his marriage and toward life.

Lloyd tried his best to avoid marital conflicts and to avoid drinking. However, he was unable to do so. After having two more drinking bouts and two more physical bouts with Madeline, he was too embarrassed to face Ms. Y. and he quit treatment. Despite many efforts Ms. Y. was unable to convince Lloyd to return for more treatment.

The case of Lloyd B. demonstrates the futility, and perhaps the danger, of trying to convince a client in marriage counseling to give up maladaptive and destructive behavior without helping the client to understand why he needs the dysfunctional behavior in the first place. Lloyd B. was an alcoholic for 15 years. Consequently, his need for alcohol was strong. It was his means of coping with intense anxiety in and out of his marriage. He needed help to understand what had created the anxiety that precipitated his alcoholism.

Virtually every client who is told to cease and desist from enacting any form of behavior resents being put into this position. No matter how well intentioned the therapist is, he is going to be experienced by the client as a patronizing and authoritarian parent who is too frustrating. While the client may behave quite deferentially when the therapist tells him to behave, he will, in all probability, displace the inevitable rage he feels toward the therapist onto his spouse or onto someone else in his environment. This is what seemed to have taken place with Lloyd B.

When the marriage counselor imposes his own values onto the client, the client always feels guilty when he defies the counselor. As we saw in the case of Lloyd B., the client began to feel so guilty about not living up to his therapist's standards, he could not face her and had to dissolve their relationship.

One value that has permeated the practices of helping professionals is client self-determination: the right of each person to live his life in a unique way. Thus, practitioners usually do not impose their own goals or standards of behavior on their clients but concede their right to make and pursue their own decisions and plans. When withdrawn spouses are extended the freedom by their therapists to determine by themselves what is best for them, they usually involve themselves in treatment with less protest.

Norman and Ellen C., a couple in their early thirties, were referred to Dr. W., a male therapist, for marital counseling by their minister, Rev. V. Rev. V., while doing short-term pastoral counseling with the C.'s, learned that Norman and Ellen had not had sexual relations for over a year in their two-year marriage, and spent a lot of time drinking with each other. He recommended marital counseling to them "in order to give up your drinking and to learn to have a more intimate relationship with each other."

On meeting Dr. W., Norman and Ellen told him that they were in his office in order to stop drinking and to learn to have sex. Realizing that they were merely echoing Rev. V.'s admonitions, Dr. W. asked the C.'s if this was something they really *wanted* to do, or if it was something they felt *ordered* to do by their minister. Norman immediately responded and said, "Well, you know you're not supposed to go against your minister but frankly we like to drink and we don't go for the other stuff." Ellen agreed with Norman and said, "We don't drink that much, anyway. One of the members of the church reported us. That wasn't nice." Dr. W. told the C.'s that a lot of people were telling them how to live and this could be annoying. Delighted with Dr. W.'s approach, both Norman and Ellen felt very relieved when Dr. W. nodded to their question, "You mean we don't have to come here if we don't want to?" Dr. W. said, "If you don't want to have sex, nobody can make you." Again, Norman and Ellen seemed pleased with Dr. W. and also seemed to want to continue their talk with him.

Inasmuch as Dr. W. knew that Norman and Ellen were enjoying their interview with him but did not want treatment, he decided to engage them further by asking, "Did you people feel pushed around in growing up?" Both of the C.'s talked at length about their traumatic pasts. They revealed that they had alcoholic parents who were frequently psychotic. Neglected and abandoned, Norman and Ellen did not trust anyone and could get pleasure only from alcohol.

Dr. W. invited the C.'s to return and discuss their histories with him. He told them they might find talking about their histories interesting. They enthusiastically complied and spent several interviews taking turns discharging anger at those people in their pasts who neglected them or abused them. During their fifteenth interview, Dr. W. asked the C.'s if, in the process of growing up, anyone had ever hugged or kissed them. To this both of the C.'s tearfully discussed how deprived they were and were never caressed or kissed. As they discussed this with Dr. W., they began to touch and hold one another. With some help from Dr. W., Norman and Ellen began to discuss their inhibitions and anxieties in sex. Eventually each of them moved into one-to-one long-term therapy. Although they both gave up drinking after about two years of individual treatment and although they were able to have sex after about a year of treatment, Dr. W. never found it necessary at any point to tell Norman and Ellen to stop drinking or start having sex.

From a psychodynamic point of view, the withdrawn spouse is a depressed, angry, suspicious child who trusts no one. This client needs a sensitive therapist who is available but does not apply pressure and who is benign without being too stimulating.

THE PARANOID SPOUSE

During the first year of life when a baby is not sensitively held, hugged, fed, and diapered, he protests violently (Bowlby, 1969). If his anger is not discharged in an accepting atmosphere, he develops a paranoid view of the world (Klein, 1957). He believes that the world is a dangerous place and that people are out to get him. His murderous wishes are projected onto others and he is always ready to be attacked. Sometimes he believes people are silently talking behind his back and plotting against him. Occasionally his paranoia can reach delusional proportions as was true with one paranoid client who said, "When I go to a football game and watch the players get into a huddle, I think they are all talking about me."

The paranoid spouse frequently makes his partner the victim of his distortions. Without foundation he can be absolutely certain that his mate has been unfaithful to him and he will badger her day and night and point out how she is trying to destroy him. This client frequently pursues his arguments logically and forcefully and is convinced that he must right wrongs that have been perpetrated against him. Because he is so forceful and convincing, he can manipulate others into believing that he is very justified in his accusations. Some paranoid spouses have been able to bring their mates into court and convince judges and juries that they are the horrible victims of abuse. Occasionally some paranoid spouses can get their partners to join them to fight against an enemy; however, most of the time the partner is the victim of their paranoia.

Because the paranoid spouse makes injustice collecting a way of life, he is very threatened by anyone loving him: being loved disturbs a modus vivendi which protects and gratifies him. This client feels like a child who is constantly misunderstood and abused and he must retaliate. When someone is kind to him he responds by saying, "I hate people and if you are nice to me it frustrates me. I feel so much less vulnerable if I am hating. Don't be kind to me!" Consequently, paranoid spouses are extremely frustrating to their marital partners when the latter try to appease them or love them.

One of the best ways to determine what makes the paranoid spouse suffer so much is to listen to his accusations very carefully. The accusations that are levelled against his marital partner (and others) are usually projections. He angrily attributes to his mate what he secretly feels or what he would like to do but cannot tolerate in himself. Consequently, when he accuses his mate of trying to hurt, maim, or poison him, this is what he would like to do to his mate. When he is convinced of his partner's infidelity, in all probability he would like to have an extramarital affair. Very often the paranoid spouse projects his infantile narcissism onto his mate and tells her she is a very self-centered, egocentric baby who neglects him. But what is ever-present with this client is that he constantly projects his own intense hostility onto his partner and then feels that he is a potential victim of her attacks. He finds it extremely difficult to face the fact that he would like to attack his mate whom he experiences as his frustrating, cruel, and sadistic mother.

It comes as no surprise to the experienced clinician when he observes that the paranoid spouse is extremely suspicious of treatment and that he very often tries to make the therapist his enemy. On being made an enemy the therapist can feel quite vulnerable and can have countertransference reactions. It is often tempting to "point out reality" to the paranoid spouse and tell him that neither his mate nor his therapist is trying to persecute him. Because he is so suspicious, when he hears this he is inclined to refute it and distrust the therapist's sincerity all the more. Occasionally, the paranoid spouse can manipulate the therapist into stating that, indeed, the therapist has been unfair, unkind, or hostile. This maneuver, which has often been "successful" with his mate, gratifies the client for a while, but never for very long. Inasmuch as the paranoid spouse is psychologically a vulnerable, angry baby with little inner certainty and with very low self-esteem, he cannot genuinely believe that anyone really wants to get along with him. Everybody is his enemy and he trusts no one. Only when he hates and distrusts can he feel somewhat secure.

Another countertransference reaction that the paranoid spouse is often able to induce in the therapist is to manipulate the latter into believing that he, the client, is a constant victim of the partner's attacks. Therapists, to avoid being the recipient of the client's rage, can overidentify with the client and point out that the client's partner is indeed a vengeful, hurtful, or infantile person. While this offers the client some temporary gratification, inasmuch as he really trusts neither the therapist nor himself, reassurance does not provide sustained relief.

It is a trying task to steer clear of arguing or overidentifying with the paranoid spouse. It is equally difficult to avoid placating him. Yet, none of these countertransference responses helps the client; sometimes they even strengthen his suspiciousness. In order to help the paranoid spouse, the clinician must listen to the client's complaints without challenging the client's distorted perceptions of his partner and without concurring with him either. If the marriage counselor listens empathically and occasionally asks the client to enlarge on his story, in due course the client will grow suspicious of the counselor. As we have constantly reiterated, the client always recapitulates his marital transference in his treatment. Therefore, it is inevitable that a paranoid spouse will become paranoid with the therapist, providing, of course, that the therapist neither joins the client against his partner nor becomes too conciliatory or deferential with the client. When the client starts to project his own hostile or sexual wishes onto the therapist, it is crucial for the therapist to listen to what is "wrong" with him without agreeing or disagreeing, much like he does with the client's marital complaints. However, inasmuch as the client is really talking about himself as he projects onto the therapist, as the therapist encourages the client to examine the whys and wherefores of the therapist's "pathological behavior" and accepts the client's critiques, the client is eventually able to examine himself. When the client sees that the kind of examination of himself that the therapist permits does not damage the therapist, the client begins to identify with the therapist's ease at introspection and begins to introspect himself and see how he distorts his marital interactions.

Marvin D., age 36, a successful mathematics professor, was referred to Dr. V., a female therapist, by his lawyer. Marvin had informed his lawyer that his wife was driving him "crazy," "making" him impotent, doing things to "make" him furious, and trying to "make" him think he was a homosexual. His lawyer felt that the idea of divorce proceedings was premature because a psychologist had to get the facts first. Marvin got the impression from the lawyer, and with some justification, that if he could show Dr. V. that his wife Mindy was psychologically sick, Dr. V. would help him succeed in a law suit against her.

On meeting Dr. V. Marvin appeared charming, bright, and logical. He had reams of notes "to prove" his case against Mindy. Mindy was out to make him impotent, he was sure, because from time to time she would initiate sex in the mornings when she knew he was eager to get to work and therefore he could not feel stimulated at this time. Marvin also told Dr. V. that when he came home from work Mindy always smiled at him, but he was convinced that "behind her smiles she is harboring a great deal of rage and she really wants to overpower me." The reason that Marvin was convinced that Mindy was a "malicious" wife was because during his entire life no one else had ever tried to trap him and he had never before felt victimized by anyone. Things were getting worse according to Marvin because lately he overheard Mindy whispering to their two daughters, aged 8 and 10, that he was a homosexual and he was worried that she would get the whole family to plot against him.

Realizing that Marvin had developed a rigid paranoid system, albeit an encapsulated one whereby only Mindy was his oppressor while the rest of the world did not appear to be against him, Dr. V. asked Marvin to elaborate on his "facts" and to hypothesize about Mindy's psychodynamics. Inasmuch as this stance of Dr. V.'s did not threaten Marvin's psychological equilibrium nor intensify his deep feeling of vulnerablity, Marvin welcomed Dr. V.'s approach. Marvin continued to say that Mindy was a very angry person because she had very controlling parents and she was trying to make him feel weak because she felt weak herself. She craved love, Marvin pointed out, but she was afraid of it; he knew that if he ever responded to her smiles she would trap him and hurt him. Furthermore, it was Marvin's "strong opinion" that Mindy was unsure of her femininity and that was why she had to think that Marvin was a homosexual. Marvin smiled when he said this and quipped, "That's what you psychologists would call projection."

Marvin spent several interviews discussing "Mindy's psychodynamics" and particularly focused on Mindy's "contemptible family background." He stated with anger, "Her mother was schizophrenic and her father was paranoid." "What else can come out of a family background like that but a sick woman?"

After Marvin had been coming to his interviews on a twice-weekly basis for about three months, he told Dr. V. that the sessions were helpful because he was gaining further understanding of Mindy and he could "empathize" with her because he realized that she had a very unstable background. Because of his "increased empathy," he noticed that Mindy was whispering about him less and her attempts to victimize him were diminishing somewhat. Dr. V. realized what Marvin was implying but what he could not say directly: he was feeling better because he was being listened to attentively and not challenged. Therefore his self-esteem was increasing and his anxiety was diminishing. However, it was clear to Dr. V. that Marvin's paranoid system was still operational and that his terror had not disappeared.

Marvin went on in his interviews with Dr. V. to contrast Mindy's family background with his own. His parents were bright, competent people "who were not pathological like Mindy's." Dr. V. showed interest in Marvin's relationships with his parents and younger sister; initially Marvin welcomed this and gave some information to her about his childhood and teenage years. However, it was clear that Marvin was slowly becoming evasive and looked uncomfortable.

When Dr. V. asked Marvin if there was something about discussing his own background that was bothersome, Marvin denied it. However, when Dr. V. remained quiet in the face of Marvin's massive denials, his paranoia began to emerge in the treatment relationship. He told Dr. V. that she was trying to trap him. He had come to see her to bring Mindy to court but now he knew that Dr. V. was her ally and that by getting his history she was trying to make him the culprit. Recognizing that Marvin was projecting his own hostility onto her, Dr. V. felt that if Marvin could examine—in an accepting atmosphere—*her* motives in being so vengeful, maybe he would eventually consider subjecting his own motives to examination. Therefore Dr. V. asked Marvin, "Do you have any thoughts about why I want to be so cruel to you?" Marvin smiled and said, "Oh, you want me to be your psychologist!" and then went on to say, "You probably were exposed to an angry environment and want to get back at people." Similar to what he did with his wife, Marvin spent several sessions discussing Dr. V.'s "pathetic background," how frustrated she probably was as a child, and how she grew to question her own identity, particularly her own sexual identity.

As Marvin saw that Dr. V. was not defensive nor threatened by his "analysis" of her, he became less vitriolic. After a couple of months of "grilling" her, he slowly began to identify with her nondefensive approach to self-examination. Marvin started to tell Dr. V. about times he had felt his own mother was "cold, arbitrary, and sadistic." While Marvin tended to describe his own mother as "another psychiatric case," he was able to verbalize some anger toward her. Although he was very tentative in bringing out his own feelings of desperation and rejection, he started to examine himself a bit. This was, however, frequently interrupted by Marvin telling Dr. V. that she was "trapping" him again and trying to make him a patient. Whenever Marvin felt vulnerable in the therapy, he turned Dr. V. into a patient and tried to analyze her dynamics. Inasmuch as Dr. V. never stopped Marvin from analyzing her, Marvin was able to drop this defense more and more and talk about himself instead.

After two years of treatment on a twice-weekly basis, Marvin eventually started talking about his own wishes to be loved, about his own anger when love was not forthcoming, about his own homosexual fantasies, and about his own fears of intimacy. As has been true in many other cases that we have reviewed, Mindy, while at first elated with Marvin's changes, began to feel uncomfortable with his more loving attitude. She requested help from Dr. V. (which Marvin permitted), and after about six months of once-a-week help could accept herself and Marvin without too much anxiety. They began to enjoy a mutually satisfactory sex life and felt warmly toward one another much of the time.

What is particularly crucial in counseling the paranoid spouse is to permit him to ventilate rage and to project his own difficulties onto the mate and therapist. If we keep in mind that the paranoid spouse is psychologically a child who has never externalized his deep rage in an accepting atmosphere, the therapeutic task becomes clear. After the therapist becomes the recipient of the slings and arrows that emerge from this client's outrageous fortune, the client can begin to face his primitive yearnings for love. Usually this first takes the form of projecting these wishes onto the mate and then onto the therapist. When the therapist does not oppose the client when he calls the therapist "a baby" or "a homosexual," the client eventually can face his own infantile yearnings. As he doesn't fight his own yearnings as much, he loves more and hates less and therefore can enjoy his marriage with less conflict.

THE DEMANDING SPOUSE

Earlier in this chapter and in Chapter 3 we discussed how crucial weaning is for the child's successful maturation. By weaning we are not only referring to the cessation of breast or bottle feeding, but we are talking about the necessary process of helping the child learn to take "no" for an answer. Every child needs help to cope with an imperfect world, to accept that he cannot have all his wishes gratified promptly, and to recognize that he must be able to respect and to gratify other people's wishes. If this dimension of child rearing is neglected, the youngster grows up to be a demanding spouse who will neglect his mate.

The demanding spouse is an extremely narcissistic person. Not able to take "no" for an answer, this spouse constantly expects the partner to cater to him. He wants to be what Freud called "His Majesty the Prince (or Princess)" (Freud, 1914). He believes his home is his castle and his dining room chair is his throne. Not willing to share domestic chores and always fighting the notion that he is a person who has responsibilities, his frustration tolerance is extremely limited. Doted upon by his parents, he grows up to expect this form of indulgence from his partner. When his desires are not met immediately he has violent temper tantrums. Frequently, he becomes involved in extramarital affairs (Strean, 1980) and is always threatening divorce. Because this spouse insists that his home must be his castle and that his life must be a Garden of Eden, he often does divorce to continue the search for his Paradise, hoping to find an omnipotent parent in marriage.

Very often the demanding spouse presents himself to the marriage counselor as depressed. He says his mate is unresponsive, unloving, and ungratifying. However, when the counselor examines the client's marriage and reflects on the client's history, he learns that this client is like the depressed child who is crying because he did not get a third ice cream cone that day or was not taken to the circus three times in one week. When the client's depression is assessed dynamically, it turns out that the client is moaning and groaning because his desired throne is shaky and his yearned-for castle is merely a home.

The demanding spouse is hypersensitive to the mildest of slights. If his spouse does not greet him effusively when he returns home from work, he can have a violent episode, cry tearfully, or sulk for hours. If gifts are not given in abundance he feels neglected. If the spouse has interests away from him he feels betrayed. This client is dominated by the pleasure principle, reality does not count, and he spends a lot of energy either demanding the attention he feels is rightfully his, or being depressed about why it is not forthcoming.

On becoming a client the demanding spouse inevitably makes many demands on the therapist. He beseeches the therapist to give him techniques to make his partner more attentive and/or tries to get the practitioner to join him in damning the marital partner. When these maneuvers do not work, he attempts to get the therapist to love him more, and if that is not successful he threatens to quit treatment, much the same way he threatens to divorce his mate. Very frequently the demanding spouse goes from one practitioner to another trying to capture the blissful life which he thinks is so eminently attainable.

Working with this client can arouse intense countertransference reactions in the therapist. Many clinicians feel that they are being eaten alive by the client. His demands seem so insatiable and his rage so strong when he is frustrated that the clinician does not only feel under attack most of the time, but can also feel weakened by the client. It is not infrequent for a marriage counselor to respond with anger to this client who seems so uncontrollable and so insatiable. It is also not infrequent for a therapist to feel like giving up trying to help such a client. Because this client appears so agitated and so depressed, it is easy for the practitioner to feel guilty about not giving enough and to want to gratify the client's requests and demands.

For a client who needs to be weaned so that he can eventually learn how to empathize with his partner, gratifying his requests only makes him more and more demanding. It is probably the best way to turn the marriage counseling into a disillusioning process for the client and into a treatment failure for the therapist.

Rena E., age 40, was in treatment with Dr. U., a male therapist, because she had not learned how to get her husband, Sam, to be more attentive and more affectionate with her. Taking her requests literally, Dr. U. offered Rena several suggestions in order to help her get what she wanted from Sam. He advised her to bring Sam his slippers when he came home from work, to make his favorite dishes several times a week, and to dress in sexy clothes. While Sam did respond to some of Rena's overtures, his response was not satisfactory to Rena. "I have to initiate too much and it makes me angry," she complained to Dr. U. "I want to get him to the point where he can take some initiative himself!" Rena protested. To this Dr. U. suggested that she face this issue directly with Sam and tell him that she would like him to take more initiative. Again Sam did take more initiative and again Rena felt it was not enough. She started calling Dr. U. over the phone in between sessions asking for more and more advice. Each time Dr. U. offered another suggestion Rena tried it, and each time she used it with Sam, she never got enough. Eventually she quit treatment.

Dr. U. failed to appreciate many dynamic issues as he counselled Rena. He did not understand that Rena was an insatiable child and that whatever she got from Sam would never be enough. He also overlooked the neurotic collusion between Rena and Sam; Rena was probably very frightened of her voracious appetite and needed a husband who would frustrate her. Of perhaps more importance, Dr. U. did not recognize that Rena was recapitulating in her transference with him the same dynamic interplay that transpired in her relationship with Sam. Just as Sam was never able to satisfy her, neither was Dr. U. Whenever she wanted something from either of these men she was left frustrated and angry. The similarity between her reactions to Dr. U. and to her husband needed to be explored in treatment. It was not explored and Rena left treatment a very unhappy client and a very unhappy wife.

As we have already suggested it is often tempting for the practitioner, under the guise of offering firm limits to the demanding spouse who needs to be weaned, to "point out reality" and tell him that what he wants is unrealistic and that he is much too greedy. Whether or not the therapist recognizes his anger when he takes this approach, the demanding client feels criticized and reacts with more anger and depression.

When Doug F., age 30, told his marriage counselor, Ms. T., that his wife, JoAnn, was ungiving and neglectful, Ms. T. explored his complaints. Doug talked about JoAnn not complimenting him enough, not caressing him enough, and not telling him enough times that he was "greater than any man she ever met." As Doug's dissatisfactions were further elucidated it became very clear to Ms. T. that Doug did get some attention and affection from his wife, but his demands of her appeared quite excessive. She decided to tell Doug that what he wanted from JoAnn was similar to what a little boy wanted from a mother and that he was being unrealistic. Doug took Ms. T.'s comments seriously and said he had "never looked at it that way before." However, Doug began to arrive late to his sessions with Mr. T. and "kept forgetting" to pay her. Ms. T. asked Doug about his latenesses and his forgetfulness; Doug eventually was able to tell Ms. T. that he was very angry about her "accusations and criticisms." Again Ms. T., instead of studying carefully with Doug the whys and wherefores of his feeling accused and criticized, told Doug that he was acting like a child and distorting her attempts to help him. And again Doug felt "put down," and told Ms. T. that she did not understand him. He then quit treatment.

In the above vignette, Ms. T.'s statements about Doug's wish to be a little boy were accurate. However, Doug was far from ready to hear them. It seemed apparent that Ms. T. was irritated with Doug's demanding stance and his immaturity. Instead of tempering her irritation and moving more slowly with him, she used her interpretations to "hit him."

The demanding spouse needs to be weaned. But, if it is going to work to the client's advantage, weaning should not be an abrupt and hostile process. Just as a benign mother who weans her child listens to her child's cries and protests when he is frustrated, the benign therapist has to listen to the demanding spouse's marital complaints, study them carefully, and administer frustration in small and infrequent doses. Just as one cannot tell a chronic alcoholic spouse to abruptly stop his drinking in order to save his marriage, one cannot tell a demanding spouse to immediately control his demands. Weaning takes time and patience is something the marriage counselor needs to offer the demanding spouse.

Hilda G., age 30, was in marriage counseling with Dr. S., a male therapist. She came into counseling because she was "sick and tired" of her husband George's "inattentiveness, neglect, and lack of sexual interest." Married for five years, Hilda pointed out that she came from a very loving family and that her parents were always good to her. She had the "finest" clothes, went to the "finest" schools and colleges, and always had the "finest" dates. She married George because he came from an "elite" family and she was reasonably certain that he would treat her in the way she was accustomed to being treated.

In treatment Hilda soon became quite demanding of Dr. S. She wanted to know his opinion on many aspects of her married life. Should she get a divorce or stay with George? Should she get angrier at George and insist on getting more? Should she have an extramarital affair? Dr. S., rather than offering his opinion on these questions, told Hilda that she had a lot of mixed feelings about these issues. Perhaps it would be helpful to see what accounted for her ambivalence. Hilda reacted to Dr. S.'s neutral response with feelings of helplessness, hopelessness, despondency, and depression. She told Dr. S. that she could never make up her own mind and that he would have to take over. If he did not take over she would either go to another therapist or might even commit suicide. Dr. S. commented here that it was awfully tough for her when she couldn't get someone to direct her life. Hilda agreed and told Dr. S. that he was very callous and that she was quitting therapy. She abruptly got up from her chair before the session was over and left the session slamming the door.

When Hilda did not return for her next session, Dr. S. called her on the phone and told her he thought it would be a good idea for her to come in and see him. He realized that she was very angry at him and he suggested that her anger toward him might be discussed profitably in his office. Although Hilda said over the phone that she would probably never return again to see Dr. S., she did keep her next appointment.

When Hilda came to see Dr. S. she was full of complaints. She told him that he was a narcissistic, cruel man who lacked empathy, and that he was only interested in himself and in his own peculiar orientation to therapy. She needed advice and he'd better give it to her.

Recognizing that Hilda was projecting her own narcissism onto him and realizing that she was finding it very difficult to tolerate any frustration, Dr. S. told her that he knew how painful it was for her not to get immediate advice. Since she had such mixed feelings about so many issues, he thought it would be best for her if he could help her make her own decisions rather than tell her what he would do. Hilda, a little more subdued now, told Dr. S. that she liked his "giving attitude" and went on to talk some more about her history. She talked about the fact that when she was a child, she could always "turn to Mommy or Daddy for an answer." She realized that she was furious at Dr. S. for not doing this and furious at George for not being more decisive. Dr. S. again acknowledged how painful it was for Hilda to be on her own.

Hilda did try to explore more of her feelings about what to do with her marriage, but again she felt stymied. She reacted with despondency and depression and had suicidal thoughts. "If I killed myself, you and George would be happy, wouldn't you?" Dr. S. replied, "Apparently the only way you feel comfortable in showing your anger to George and to me is to think of suicide." Hilda then released enormous rage. She told Dr. S. that she really hoped that he and George could be attentive, responsive, men who would give to her, but all they seemed to care about was themselves. She had fantasies of maiming, castrating, and torturing George and Dr. S. and pointed out that she resented them so much because they always appeared "so damn self-sufficient."

After spending many sessions crying and yelling about not having an omnipotent parent and after seeing that Dr. S. did not censure her for her rage, Hilda slowly became more reflective. She began to realize that she had never given up her deep wish to be "a little princess" and that she was trying her "darnedest" to get George and Dr. S. to treat her in this fashion. She felt that if she weren't a princess she'd be a slave. As Dr. S. and Hilda worked on this conviction she was able to realize that in trying to get others to treat her like a princess, she wanted them to be her slaves.

It took three years of twice-a-week treatment to help Hilda resolve her wish for the ever-present breast and to face being weaned. On being psychologically weaned she could more readily appreciate George's assets and accept him as a human being with his limitations.

All children at some point in their development believe their parents are omnipotent gods and that their parents can give them anything they desire. As we observed in the case of Hilda G., many adults still harbor the belief that there is an omnipotent parent available. When an individual is emotionally convinced that a parent is or can be omnipotent, he expects the marital partner to be omnipotent too.

This expectation is always disappointed. No one is capable of anticipating his spouse's every wish and being a fount of wisdom all of the time. Just as the maturing child must sooner or later accept the reality that his parents are neither perfect nor all-powerful, husbands and wives—if they are going to enjoy what can be enjoyed in marriage—must be helped to accept with equanimity that their partners are human beings with vulnerabilities and limitations.

Although the yearning for an omnipotent parent is something that most individuals never completely abandon, particularly when they live in a society that whets the appetite for such a parent, persevering in this belief not only leads to deep disappointment in a marriage but also results in feelings of weakness in those who continue to nurture the fantasy. If one believes that the marital partner is omnipotent and omniscient then one must feel very small next to such a paragon. After a while the individual who ascribes superhuman qualities to a marital partner becomes full of rage because he feels overpowered by these very superiorities.

One factor that accounts for the fairly frequent phenomenon of a married couple alternating between periods of extreme passion and intense hatred is that they share a common, usually unconscious, fantasy. If the husband, for example, attributes grandiose powers to his wife, he will deeply love his perfect goddess for a while. Sooner or later, however, he will hate her for not being that goddess. Intensifying his disappointment and anger will be the feeling of powerlessness that evolves when he contrasts himself to his fantasized perfect partner. A common means of coping with disappointment and weakness is to aggress. This temporarily heightens his self-esteem but soon frightens him because he needs his "omnipotent mother." Therefore, he returns to loving her again only to feel disappointed and weak all over. Invariably a husband who seeks an omnipotent wife selects a woman with similar fantasies. Consequently, both mates are eternally on an emotional see-saw, loving a god and then hating the partner later for inducing disappointment and feelings of powerlessness (Strean, 1980).

Usually it is only through intensive therapy that this unrealistic wish can be tempered. As in the case of Hilda G., only when the client is able to bring out fantasies in an atmosphere of safety and is helped to deal with frustration and anger (when the therapist does not provide an ever-present breast) is the client able to grow both in and out of marriage.

THE PARASITIC SPOUSE

During the oral period the infant moves from a position of autism to one of symbiosis (Mahler, 1968). As the youngster receives the tenderness, warmth, and love, of a consistently gratifying mother he feels "one" with the mother and the mother usually feels the same way with him. Many mothers, during the symbiotic phase of their infants' development, point out that they intuitively know in the middle of the night when their youngsters are awake and when they need to be fed, diapered, held, or hugged. Their infants' pain is their pain, their infants' joy is their joy, and their emotional and physical hunger is their own hunger.

As we have already indicated in the previous section of this chapter, a child must be weaned in order that further psychological growth takes place. He must learn that individuation and separation can heighten self-esteem and that their mastery leads to real gratifications in life (Mahler, 1968). If the child is not able to achieve some autonomy, as an adult he will emerge as one who is plagued by doubt and tortured by the shame he feels for being so helpless (Erikson, 1950). He becomes a clinging vine, an emotional parasite.

Many mothers feel threatened when their children start to walk on their own instead of wanting to be carried. They resent weaning the child and in their desperation unwittingly engulf the child more and more (A. Freud, 1965). Because the child who is a year-and-a-half or so is very much a victim of his mother's preoccupations and wishes, he cannot exercise much independence if mother does not encourage independence. Instead, he remains very dependent on his mother and she remains very dependent on him.

If mother and child are not helped to individuate, separate, and temper their wishes to engulf each other, the child grows up to be an adult who can never stand on his own two feet (Fenichel, 1945). When he marries he wants to know every detail of his partner's life and cannot permit his mate any privacy. He becomes furious if the partner has loving feelings for others, interests apart from him, and secrets that are not shared. To him it is the height of indignity to be excluded from any part of the partner's life—whether it be activities or thoughts and feelings. The parasitic spouse has been described as an "oral character" because like an oral baby of less than one year he wants to devour anybody or anything that appears valuable to him (Fenichel, 1945).

The parasitic spouse cannot tolerate separation. He may call his partner four or five times a day from work, and if, for some reason, the partner is not available, he has an acute temper tantrum and/or becomes quite depressed. While the parasitic spouse with his insatiable appetite is very much interested in sex and may have intercourse three or four times a day (with bodily contact in between), he is also prone to acute sexual problems. Often he projects his own wishes to devour and incorporate onto the partner and then fears he will be gobbled up in sex and have no separate existence. Fearing the very thing he unconsciously wishes—that is, merging—the parasitic spouse often avoids sex altogether.

Another common sexual problem of the parasitic spouse is that he cannot tolerate the ending of a sexual encounter. To him, separation and ending are equivalent to the death of the partner; he would therefore rather avoid sex than confront the agitation and desperation he feels when sex ends. As has already been suggested, the parasitic spouse projects his hunger onto the partner. Consequently, he begins to feel like a small child who is smothered by a parental figure. One means of ridding oneself of the smothered feeling and the anxiety that strong dependency feelings generate is to have an extramarital lover (Strean, 1980). The individual who is having an affair does not have to feel too attached to either his marital partner or to his lover. As he moves from one to the other, he can convince himself that he is an independent human being who does not have to attach himself to any one person. However, he becomes quite desperate should either the mate or the lover threaten a breakup of the relationship; he is, in reality, a very needy person.

The parasitic spouse invariably marries another parasitic person. These couples, while very attracted to each other by their mutual dependency, also harbor a great deal of hatred toward each other. Their hatred is overdetermined. On one hand, they each feel smothered by the other and are constantly castigating each other for being too dependent and not allowing the other "enough space." On the other hand, each feels very vulnerable and constantly wants reassurance. However, all the reassurance in the world does not satisfy the parasitic spouse because each time he is not fully merged with the partner he feels he has been dethroned, despoiled, and victimized (Freud, 1932).

Because parasitic spouses feel misunderstood and deprived most of the time, they are well known to marriage counselors. They frequently consult counselors in order to try to rid themselves of their acute unhappiness and overwhelming rage. Parasitic spouses invariably come to the marriage counselor together and want to be seen together. Like Ruth and Naomi in the Bible, they powerfully contend: "Whither thou goest will I go and there shall I be buried." As clients they also insist, "Thy therapist shall be my therapist and he will never see thee alone."

When the clinician meets the parasitic dyad he is immediately impressed with how childish these two people are. If one of them sits nearer to the therapist, the other feels acutely hurt and betrayed. The partner sitting nearer to the therapist will, after a short while, feel very uncomfortable for experiencing himself as too grasping and too greedy. These people feel an enormous obligation to think alike, feel alike, and look alike. If one gets something the other does not have, he feels very guilty about what he thinks he has taken away; in collusion with him, the other partner feels very deprived. Consequently, both mates reinforce each other's parasitic modus vivendi and both unconsciously unite in a firm pact to be one. They never want to separate.

The treatment of choice for the parasitic couple appears to be conjoint therapy, at least at the beginning of the contact. The reason this form of treatment seems advisable is because the couple feels desperate if they are separated. If they are seen individually by one or different counselors each feels abandoned. When the therapist agrees to see them together they appear much less threatened and feel better understood. However, the therapist should concentrate on helping them understand the many reasons for their intense and mutual clingingness. One of the goals of counseling should be to help the couple individuate somewhat: This can be realized in part by helping each member of the dyad through a period of individual counseling before therapy is formally terminated.

Lillian and Abe I., a couple in their middle forties, were referred to Dr. R., a female therapist, by their clergyman. In his referral, the clergyman told Dr. R. that a day did not pass without the I.'s battling. They argued about which movie they would attend, at which restaurant they would dine, and which friends they would visit. Evidently these arguments began with the onset of their marriage and had continued for 20 years.

At their first visit with Dr. R., Lillian and Abe were already arguing in the waiting room. Each felt the other should begin presenting his complaints and neither listened to the other's reasons for his preference to go second. Dr. R. hardly had an opportunity to introduce herself because the I.'s continued their argument in her consultation room. After about 15 minutes of sustained quarreling, Dr. R. interrupted the I.'s and somewhat jocularly stated, "You people are quite helpful to me!" Lillian and Abe abruptly stopped arguing and both looked at her quizzically. Lillian asked, "What do you mean?" Abe repeated her question by saying, "Yes, what do you mean?" Dr. R. responded, "You're helping me by showing me one of your difficulties in your marriage. Neither of you wants to stand alone. You are arguing about who should talk first and both of you are frightened of the possibility." After a minute's silence, Abe said, "We never thought about that before! You mean, we are afraid of independence?" Lillian chimed in and repeated what Abe had said. She stated, "I never thought we both had that in common." After a few such interchanges in which Abe and Lillian repeated one another, Dr. R. showed them what they were doing in the session (i.e. repeating each other, never individuating). In characteristic fashion each took turns agreeing with Dr. R. At the end of the first interview, Dr. R. invited the I.'s to return and suggested that this propensity for each of them to mirror the other might be worth understanding better.

In their next several interviews both Lillian and Abe took turns agreeing with the other that they felt paralyzed whenever separation and independence from one another became a possibility. Dr. R., in order to help the I.'s experience this enormous problem in the sessions with her, suggested that this problem might have something to do with their histories. She further proposed that Lillian and Abe share their own histories with Dr. R. and with one another in the interviews. Again, the I.'s were stymied. They could not decide who would go first. Here, Abe told a joke about a woman who took some special pills so that she could give birth to a polite child. It turned out that this woman conceived twins but they were inside her for over 11 months. The doctor went into her womb and heard each twin say to the other, "You go first." "No, you go first!" As a result neither child could enter the world. When Lillian and Dr. R. both laughed at the joke, Abe suggested to Lillian that she tell a joke. Here, Dr. R. pointed out that Abe could not feel comfortable unless Lillian did the same thing he did, and that Lillian felt pressured to do exactly what Abe did.

The I.'s began to slowly recognize the seriousness of their marital problem and were eventually able to discuss their histories. When they both saw how obligated they felt to keep pace with the other and reflected on how their individual histories influenced this pattern, each talked about the close, intense, and controlling ties in their respective families. Both Lillian and Abe realized that each of them experienced independence and separation as akin to murderous acts.

Both Abe and Lillian felt uncomfortable in the interviews as they discussed the fact that separation and independence seemed so terrible. After six months of treatment, Lillian started to vent anger toward Dr. R. for putting them in an uncomfortable position, and, for the first time, Abe's reaction was not identical to Lillian's. Although frightened, he seemed to feel Dr. R. was trying to help them with something. Lillian was not sure that Dr. R. was being helpful and she was very angry at Dr. R.

The fact that for the first time in treatment Lillian and Abe disagreed with one another was utilized by Dr. R. as much as possible in the therapy. She felt that if the I.'s could disagree and see that it wasn't the end of the world they would be greatly helped. Consequently, she told them, "For the first time since I've met you, you are disagreeing and you are both uncomfortable. Let's see what makes you feel so upset." Spontaneously, Lillian and Abe talked about how, during most of their lives and during their whole marriage, they viewed disagreement as a hostile affront. They both felt that if they disagreed they were being provocative, and that if someone disagreed with them they were being provoked. Abe was able to admit that he could not feel hostile toward Dr. R. because he thought it would be the end of his relationship with her. Lillian confessed that when she was feeling angry toward Dr. R., she was worried that "it would be the end" (of their relationship).

As the I.'s tolerated differences between themselves and differences with Dr. R. with less anxiety, their marital arguments diminished, their sex life improved, and their loving feelings toward each other emerged both in the therapy and in their relationship at home. When it was clear that both Lillian and Abe had matured and were both capable of some independence, Dr. R. suggested some individual counseling for each. While Dr. R. eventually saw each of them for individual counseling, it took six more sessions of conjoint therapy before they were willing to consider the change of format. With the possibility of separation, they both lost confidence in themselves, started to argue more, and became somewhat infantile again. However, because they had had over a year-and-a-half of conjoint treatment in which their mutual dependency was thoroughly discussed, they had sufficient internal resources to make the move.

In their individual sessions Lillian and Abe saw individual treatment as a betrayal to one another. They needed time before they recognized that they could each have individual and unique experiences without worrying that they were being destructive or being destroyed.

As we suggested in Chapter 5, when the practitioner engages a couple in conjoint therapy, the emphasis must be on their interactions with each other and on their interactions with the therapist. There is a tendency on the part of some marriage counselors to conduct individual therapy in a conjoint format. With a parasitic couple this becomes unbearable because husband and wife feel too separate from one another. However, the major advantage of conjoint therapy is that the couple can examine just how they interact in the here and now. Consequently, it behooves the conjoint therapist to show them what they are doing to one another and with one another rather than focus exclusively on their individual psychodynamics.

When the clinician meets a parasitic couple it is very tempting to try to get them to become separate immediately. Their clinging dependency and infantile narcissism become apparent so readily that the countertransference reaction they are apt to induce in the therapist is a strong desire to help them get off one another's backs. One common way that this countertransference reaction is expressed is by prescribing that each member of the dyad be seen individually by separate therapists. However, nothing alienates the parasitic dyad more than this prescription. The couple, as we know, perceives separation as equivalent to death and they become extremely apprehensive about killing and/or being killed and abandoning and/or being abandoned. What usually happens when the conjoint format is not utilized for this dyad is that the couple joins forces with even more tenacity and tries to defeat the therapist.

Richard and Leona J., a couple in their early thirties, sought marriage counseling because they were constantly involved in power struggles. For hours at a time almost daily each labelled the other as "intrusive," "clinging," and "demanding."

On meeting their marriage counselor at a social agency, they quickly demonstrated their intense parasitic interaction. Ms. P., their social worker, immediately shared her impression with the J.'s that neither of them felt able or willing "to give each other enough space." While Richard and Leona tended to agree with Ms. P.'s formulation and provided further data to substantiate it, when Ms. P. recommended individual treatment for them, they balked. Leona and Richard pointed out that they were both contributing to their marital problems and both of them were needed to work together to resolve them. Instead of respecting their resistances to her idea, Ms. P. tried to persuade them that they needed separate therapists. The more Ms. P. tried to convince the J.'s about the validity of her ideas, the more the J.'s fought her. The power struggle that was so much a feature of the J.'s marital interaction became recapitulated in the counseling situation. Unaware of this, Ms. P. did not relate to their transference reactions but continued to harp away at her conviction. The J.'s, in response to Ms. P.'s lack of sensitivity, left the interview, never to be heard from again.

As we suggested in Chapter 5, it is imperative for the clinician to always respect the client's resistances. Even if what clients prescribe for themselves seems self-destructive, it is important to give clients opportunities to express their preferences. In the case of the parasitic couple it is not only necessary to let the clients discuss fully their wishes for togetherness, but it also seems necessary—especially at the beginning of treatment—to gratify their wishes for conjoint therapy.

Sometimes the powerful mutual dependency that exists in the parasitic dyad's interaction extends to their children. When this exists there is a strong desire on the part of the couple to also have their children participate in the treatment sessions. Again, the couple's resistance to separate interviews for themselves and their children should be respected. Consequently, family therapy seems to be the modality of choice when there is a strong parasitic network existing in a family. As the family is initially accepted by the therapist in the way they wish to be treated, a therapeutic alliance takes place. This alliance can be utilized by the therapist to promote some individuation for the family members.

Sol and Karen K., a couple in their late thirties, were referred for marriage counseling by their physician for help with their sexual problems. Although they had been married for close to 10 years, they had not had sexual relations for the past four.

When Karen spoke to the social worker, Mr. O., over the phone, it seemed quite clear that just Sol and Karen would appear at the initial consultation. However, when Mr. O. went into the waiting room to greet the K.'s, he was surprised to see that they had brought their son David with them. All three were standing up, ready to come into his office. Mr. O., though a little flustered, invited the whole family in.

While Karen and Sol were talking animatedly to Mr. O., David covered his eyes. Since this familial interaction recurred several times during the interview, Mr. O. asked the family about it. After some resistive remarks on the part of all the family members, it came out that they all slept in the same bedroom and that David frequently was in bed with them. Furthermore, while Sol and Karen were talking about how this was a good arrangement, David covered his eyes and closed his ears, obviously showing his enormous discomfort.

It took several months of family therapy for the K.'s to face the fact that no member of the family felt comfortable doing anything alone, and that Karen and Sol felt they were depriving David if they did not have him sleep in their bedroom. Both Sol and Karen also reported that when they were children, they had slept in the same bedroom as their parents.

As the K.'s discussed how thoughtless and unkind they felt when they were independent and how frightened they all were to do anything alone, they began to experiment with some independence in the family interviews. Eventually they were able to disagree with one another on occasion.

It took over a year before the K.'s were able to have separate interviews and over a year-and-a-half before Leona and Sol could feel comfortable enough to have their separate bedroom and enjoy a sexual life away from David's eyes and ears.

As our case illustrations suggest, the parasitic couple presents a tremendous challenge to the marriage counselor. However, if the practitioner respects their resistances to separate and individuate and does not impose his own goals on them, this couple does have the capacity to use treatment in a way in which they can eventually have a more rewarding marriage.

THE PSYCHOTIC SPOUSE

A frequent visitor to the marriage counselor's office is the spouse who is psychotic. This client may be suffering from hallucinations or delusions, have a powerful paranoid system operating, be acutely manic, or so intensely depressed that he is actively planning to commit suicide. His judgment is poor, his frustration tolerance is weak, his grasp on reality is tenuous, and his attitude is narcissistic and infantile. Usually the psychotic spouse has a psychotic marriage partner and the dyad appear like little children to most observers. In warm moments, they seem like toddlers at play; in angry moments, which are many, they appear like murderous siblings who are out to torture and possibly kill each other.

There is continuing controversy among clinicians about the etiology of psychoses. Some contend that the dysfunction is strictly a constitutional and biological phenomenon that should be treated by pharmaceutical agents, while others view it as evolving from faulty interpersonal experiences. The psychodynamically oriented practitioner never denies constitutional and biological vulnerabilities, but he views the psychoses as primarily maturational problems that derive from negative interpersonal experiences early in life.

The two major psychoses are schizophrenia and manic-depressive psychoses. In schizophrenia the client has breaks with reality, hallucinates, has delusions, and frequently withdraws from people and talks to himself. In manic-depressive psychoses there is rapid alternation of moods. Within an hour or less the individual suffering from manic-depressive psychosis can shift from acute depression to intense joy—as if an extremely helpless, agitated, and depressed infant who had lost his mother (and therefore his whole world) were suddenly transformed into an extremely happy child who had been reunited with the mother.

There is now abundant literature affirming the notion that the schizophrenic client was deprived of normal physical handling and stimulation by a maternal figure during the first year of life (Brenner, 1955). Consequently, many of his ego functions have failed to develop properly, and his capacity to relate to and deal with his external environment is severely impaired—so much so that he may appear feeble-minded (Spitz, 1965). He is convinced that most people are his enemies and therefore withdraws from reality and remains quite seclusive, sometimes talking *only* to himself. Because he has not had appropriate responses from a trustworthy person, he is always angry and cautious, feeling that his environment is full of sinister forces. Rage pervades his entire psyche and prevents him from maturing, just as powerful infectious toxins retard physical development (Josselyn, 1948).

Because the schizophrenic client has withdrawn his libido (energy) from other people and directed it toward himself he feels estranged, depersonalized, and preoccupied with bodily sensations. The regression to, or fixation at, the infantile narcissistic state accounts for his megalomania; he fantasies that he is somebody very special, such as an emperor or queen.

Erikson (1950) has described the schizophrenic client as one who has either lost or never gained a basic sense of trust and therefore has to resort to a narcissistic, paranoid orientation to the world. His thinking falls back from the logical to the prelogical level, and he is consumed by archaic wishes that give rise to hallucinatory and delusional thinking.

As we have already suggested, the schizophrenic spouse is usually married to another schizophrenic individual. Often they victimize each other by their delusions: Each contends that the other is an evil persecutor. They rage and withdraw at the slightest frustration and are unduly sensitive to the mildest of criticisms. Although schizophrenic spouses hate one another with a passion, they are also very dependent and clinging. While only a minority of them divorce (Eisenstein, 1956), those that do divorce stay in contact with one another, fighting it out for years (Bychowski, 1956).

The manic-depressive's mood swings seem to mirror a situation in which the baby is alternately abandoned and loved intensely, only to be abandoned again. Differing from the schizophrenic client who seems to have suffered from a great deal of estrangement, the manic-depressive appears to be the product of a very tempestuous, unpredictable environment that offered pain mixed with sporadic pleasure. However, as Glover (1949) pointed out, the exaggerated self-love of the manic-depressive client during the manic phase is also indicative of pathology because it is often accompanied by a flight of ideas and actions. It is as if the client is desperately holding on to a joyful state but wondering when his mother's comfort will be withdrawn and his joy destroyed. In the depressive phase of the manic-depressive psychosis, one can usually see that the client has suffered decisive narcissistic injuries. He has severe and agitated crying spells and appears like a child who is very disappointed in his parents for not loving him and not strengthening his self-esteem (Fenichel, 1945). The manic-depressive client seems to be continually moving between hunger and satiety. Pleasure is expected after every pain, and pain after every pleasure. In his mind is the primitive idea that any suffering bestows the privilege of some later compensating joy, and vice versa (Fenichel, 1945; Strean, 1979).

The manic depressive client usually marries a manic-depressive spouse. Often while one is manic, the other is depressed; they take turns mothering each other. Both have very critical superegos. One of them is busily punishing the other at any given time. Each feels very deprived and each tries to extract love from the other. Both are always disappointed (Jacobson, 1956).

Marriage counselors, like many other clinicians, tend to reject psychotic spouses and often declare that they are untreatable. In doing so, they overlook certain theoretical issues pertinent to psychoses and do not examine certain countertransference reactions that the psychotic spouse induces. The major theoretical issue that is often overlooked in the assessment and treatment of the psychotic spouse is that the difference between a psychotic individual and a "normal" one is a matter of degree. All individuals talk to themselves; the schizophrenic client talks out loud to himself. All individuals daydream when frustrated; the schizophrenic hallucinates. All individuals have mood changes; the manic-depressive client has intense and frequent mood shifts. All individuals show residues of conflict on the oral level; the psychotic individual is more distrustful and has deeper and more pervasive yearnings to merge and to symbiose.

The main reason that many clinicians reject the psychotic spouse for treatment is because he shows feelings, attitudes, and behavior which most clinicians try to reject in themselves. Many a marriage counselor is frightened when he sees a psychotic spouse talking to himself, because he, the therapist, fights doing that himself. Clinicians tend to remove themselves from the client who wants to merge with his spouse because they fight this wish in themselves. Practitioners are not too pleased to work with a client who is very regressed, because when they observe him their own regressive wishes are activated. By ridding themselves of the psychotic spouse they rid themselves of their own desires to regress.

If marriage counselors and other clinicians can accept the truism that the psychotic client is not qualitatively different from other clients or from himself, he moves into the counseling situation with more empathy and optimism. If the marriage counselor can also accept the fact that he, too, has wishes to merge, symbiose, regress, and depart from reality, he does not have to reject the psychotic spouse as much. All too often marriage counselors and other practitioners send the psychotic spouse away by recommending referral to a mental hospital or by prescribing drugs and depressants. In so doing, they tacitly say to the client, "You are incapable of a human relationship and therefore I do not want to humanly relate to you."

One research situation conducted on in-patient schizophrenic clients demonstrated that the best therapists for these clients appear to be first-year social work students. The major reason for this seems to be that social work students *do not* consider clients diagnosed schizophrenic as schizophrenic. As I reported elsewhere (Strean, 1982, pp. 151–152),

> Notions like "poor ego functions," "narcissistic object relations," "narcissistic transferences," "oral fantasies," "unresolved resistances toward murder" and "hostile introjects" are not in their vocabulary and do not ever cross their minds. In contrast to the more experienced practitioner who begins treatment with a concept of a serious disease process at work which frequently ignites latent counterresistances in him, the social work student optimistically and very humanely wants to help a real person in a real situation.
>
> Unperturbed by previous therapeutic failures, unimpressed by the cautionary admonitions of his mentors, unencumbered by a bevy of therapeutic procedures swimming in his head, the social work student unconditionally regards his (client) positively and truly accepts him where he is. In contrast to experienced professionals who often unconsciously communicate their therapeutic pessimism to the client which then becomes introjected and incorporated by the latter, the student in effect says, "I want to help you and I think I can." The client seems to respond after some testing with, "Wow, no one has ever had faith in me before. That makes me love you. Let's work together." The student's benign and humane attitude seems to alter the vicious cycle and self-fulfilling prophecy that has been perpetuated by experienced professionals, who have unwittingly communicated to the client the message, "You are crazy, pathological, and perhaps even a bit unhuman. I shall move cautiously with you because your prognosis is guarded."

Mabel L., a married woman in her 50s, was hospitalized in a mental institution. She had lost contact with her husband, children, family, and friends during her seven-year hospitalization. Mabel had been the recipient of various types of therapy such as shock, insulin, vitamins, psychotherapy, and group therapy, but none of these therapies had helped her. Her conviction that she was "a horrible sinner" who deserved to be punished and killed continued regardless of the kind of treatment she received. In the hospital she sat alone and cried most of the time, bemoaning her fate. Mabel often took the position that she was born infected, probably had leprosy, and that if anyone got too near her, he would catch her leprosy and be infected by her other diseases.

Mabel was greeted by her social work intern, Ms. N., who said she wanted to get to know her. Mabel responded with, "To know me is to know a witch. You can do better things." Ms. N. said that she had "never met a witch" and even wondered if witches existed. "But," Miss N. went on to say, "I am curious." Mabel responded, "Well, here you are, dear. I am the first witch you've met."

For a number of interviews Mabel recounted how she had killed people—her mother, father, a brother, and some friends. She described taking an axe and beheading them. Furthermore, Mabel reported that there was no reason for this "horrible behavior" on her part. When Ms. N. said that though she was a very inexperienced professional and did not know about many facts of life, she was "absolutely positive that no one murders unless he is very angry."

Mabel, in succeeding interviews, was able to describe how she was neglected by her alcoholic parents and given little gratification as a child. She reasoned, early in life, that there must be something wrong with her inasmuch as she was so hated by her parents and other family members. "I started to believe that I had some infectious disease." Ms. N. told Mabel that children understandably hate their parents when they feel neglected by them and criticize themselves because they need their parents. Mabel then wept and wept. "You are a doll. You really understand. My hatred is my poison. It has infected me because I haven't let it out! I wanted to kill so badly that all these years I have believed that I have really done it."

After about six months of twice-weekly interviews with Ms. N., Mabel was able to look at her marriage with Herman. Herman was described as a man whom she thought would save her from all of her "persecutors," but she realized that she had "made him a persecutor, too." In seeing how she had distorted her perception of Herman, she expressed real regret, but did not need to punish herself too much "for past imagined transgressions." Mabel was able to contact Herman and tried to resume a relationship with him. Inasmuch as he had remarried, he was not too eager to do so. However, Mabel took his rejection in stride. With a stronger ego and a much less punitive superego, and with Ms. N.'s friendly and empathetic ear, Mabel slowly moved out of the hospital and into her own apartment. Later, she went on to a job as a teacher's aide. She began to date men and when last seen was trying to arrange to get married again and "doing it with less poison in my system."

The work with Mabel is typical of the treatment conducted by many social work students with in-patient schizophrenic clients. It demonstrates that if the practitioner begins where the psychotic spouse is, does not impose biases, relates humanely and optimistically, the psychotic spouse has a chance of enjoying a more fulfilling marriage and a more fulfilling life.

In an empirical study of psychotherapy (Truax, 1973) which examined the effective ingredients in psychotherapy in psychoanalytic, client-centered, and eclectic therapists, one of the major findings that correlates very positively with successful therapeutic results was the practitioner's style: non-possessive warmth, genuineness, and a type of empathy that conveyed the message, "I am with you." Furthermore, the research not only demonstrated that appropriate empathy or unconditional positive regard is higher for more successful cases than for less successful cases but that this relationship holds even truer for severely disturbed schizophrenic clients.

It would appear that the psychotic spouse, like all clients who are in marriage counseling, can benefit a great deal from the therapist's non-possessive warmth, genuineness, and empathy.

CHAPTER 7

Treating the Sadomasochistic Spouse

Assuming the child has been the recipient of consistent, tender love and care during the first year of life and assuming further that he has been weaned within a loving atmosphere, he is ready to take on some frustration and move toward an acceptance of the reality principle. It is frequently overlooked that for any human organism to psychologically mature the organism must be able to renounce certain gratifications. Otherwise he will remain a narcissistic infant dominated by the pleasure principle, interested solely in cultivating his Garden of Eden and insistent on being "His Majesty the Prince."

One of the reasons the second year of life has been called "the terrible twos" is that the child is acting out his enormous resentment against the demands, frustrations, and limits that are imposed upon him. The child protests as he is asked to move from the position of being essentially a passive recipient to one in which he is expected to give a little. He would prefer to continue to defecate or urinate when and where he wants to rather than be toilet-trained. Although his musculature is such that he is ready to creep and walk, in many ways he would rather be carried. His parents are recognizing that it is not helpful for him to own everything in sight and frequently say "no" to him; the youngster is angry about being limited and balks when he is frustrated. "The terrible twos" is often the time when a child is very negative. In response to the "no's" that he hears from his parents, he retaliates and frequently says "no, no" to everything his parents say to him.

When parents have not helped a child accept "no" for an answer, when they have not felt comfortable about toilet-training the child, when they have not curbed the youngster's demands and helped him learn to accede to some of their requests, the youngster becomes a very immature adult who is an extremely difficult spouse to live with. As a mate he is indignant when demands are made upon him and is furious when his own requests are not gratified immediately. Because he does not accept the fact that part and parcel of being married is absorbing frustration, he always complains that he is exploited and misunderstood. Angry that he must cooperate with the partner, he is a revengeful spouse. Similar to the two-year-old who continually says "no, no," he experiences virtually every request of his mate's as an indignity and is positive that justice is always miscarried.

Many adults who visit marriage counselors are reminiscent of two-year-olds who insist on maintaining their omnipotent positions and who refuse to accept the dictates of reality. This spouse constantly collects injustices, is contemptuous of the partner most of the time, feels horribly unloved all of the time, and never believes that he plays a role in the marital fracases. It is his partner's fault that he is always miserable. He believes that his rights are always being violated and he rarely talks about his own responsibilities.

If we review the many different ways parents and children interact during the child's second year of life and consider the impact of these interactions on the child, it helps us understand many different types of dysfunctional marital behavior. As we have already suggested, the child who has not been helped to take "no" for an answer will later not be able to take "no" for an answer from his mate without protesting angrily. There is also the child who has been trained very harshly and arbitrarily: When he did not please his tyrannical parents he was threatened, physically beaten, or verbally assaulted. This is the child whose parents could not take "no" for an answer from him—he always had to indulge them. Intimidated, frightened, and very unsure of himself, this child becomes a very compliant, intimidated, masochistic spouse who always caters to his partner and rarely considers what he wants for himself. Although he suffers from a great deal of repressed rage, this spouse treats his marital partner as if she were the tyrannical and punitive parent of his past who must be obeyed at all times.

Characteristic of the child during the learning and training period of the second year is a great deal of ambivalence; that is, he feels much love and much hate. On one hand, the child is very dependent on his parents for physical and psychological survival, and is grateful to them for what they have provided and can provide. On the other hand, he bitterly resents them for the controls they have placed on him. When parents are ambivalent about limiting their children and/or feel ambivalent toward their children in general, the latter become very conflicted spouses who hardly ever feel comfortable with their mates. At times they experience their mates as the parents who did not spontaneously love them; consequently, they do not want to cooperate with their partners. However, just as a child cannot feel comfortable with his hatred toward his parents because he fears being abandoned or punished, after a while the ambivalent spouse renounces his hatred toward his partner and tries to love her and cooperate with her. Unfortunately, when he loves and cooperates with the partner, he senses that he is submitting to a tyrannical parent and eventually feels compelled to rebel again. The ambivalent spouse, like the ambivalent child, is on a perpetual seesaw with his marital partner. He never knows where he stands with her because he feels so ambivalent; she usually feels similarly toward him.

Because the child instinctively aggresses toward his parents and often wishes to kill them when they impose limits, he frequently feels like a "bad child." It is not infrequent to observe a child at the age of 20 months or so, slapping himself or herself and saying, "bad boy" or "bad girl!" The child is developing a censor or superego and is beginning to curb his instincts. When hostile and murderous fantasies are intense but frightening and unacceptable to the child, he develops a very strict and punitive superego. The superego prevents him from feeling and/or acting upon his destructive fantasies. When a child is very much influenced by a strict superego, he avoids pleasurable situations. He rarely aggresses, infrequently asserts himself, and usually shuns any form of sexual stimulation. For example, if he masturbates and/or has erotic fantasies, he believes he should be struck dead or should be inflicted with some other severe punishment.

The child with a punitive superego becomes, of course, a spouse who cannot allow himself very much pleasure in marriage. This is the marital partner who insists that there is no joy in sex, no stimulation in communication, and no fulfillment in any part of marriage. While he might very well accuse his spouse of depriving him of pleasure in marriage, his chronic complaint that no fun is available in marriage covers his unconscious wish to stay away from pleasure because, in his mind, pleasure in marriage is a sin.

Certain sexual problems in marriage have their roots in the training period. If the child has been subjected to arbitrary and punitive training, as an adult he tends to view sex not as mutual pleasure but as "putting out" and being exploited by a tyrannical parent. In the same way as the child who refuses to defecate or urinate for his parents because he sees no pleasure in it for himself, the spouse who has been the recipient of harsh training when he was a child sees "nothing in sex for me."

Sex, if it is to be a pleasureful experience and culminate successfully, requires the individual to enjoy his sexual tensions and be pleased to gratify them through an orgasm with his partner. Often, adults equate a sexual discharge with anal or urinary discharge. This is why they feel that sex, like urine or feces, is something "dirty." It is as if they are either urinating or defecating on or in their partner or as if their partner is defecating or urinating in or on them.

When a child loves and hates his parents he feels comfortable neither near them nor away from them. On being with them he feels confined, controlled, and wants to run away. However, when he moves away from his parents he worries whether or not he has killed them. He comes running back only to feel controlled again and, therefore, he must soon leave. As an adult he may arrange to have a "lark–owl" marriage wherein he sleeps during the day and is up at night while his partner does the opposite. While the partners in this marriage often attribute their opposing sleep routines to biological factors that set the pattern of energy and fatigue in the individual (Brozan, 1982), what usually is taking place is that the partners love and hate one another. They cannot live with one another but they do not seem to be able to live without one another. Some marital partners arrange to work in different cities and try to believe that their lack of sexual and emotional intimacy is solely because of their work requirements. They do not want to acknowledge that they have arranged their lives so that they are not forced to be too intimate too often; they are not aware that each believes that too much intimacy feels like submission.

Having briefly reviewed some of the neurotic forms of marital behavior that evolve from the second year of life, we are now in a position to discuss the treatment of those spouses who manifest them.

THE REBELLIOUS SPOUSE

As we mentioned earlier the rebellious spouse is reminiscent of the youngster who feels it is beneath his dignity to be toilet-trained. As a child, the rebellious spouse frequently defecated and urinated on the floor or in his pants; as an adult he believes his partner "should take his shit" while he has no responsibility to her. The rebellious spouse constantly experiences his marital partner as the parent who is trying to dominate him. Consequently, he is forever attempting to use power to defeat her. The rebellious spouse has never forgiven his parents for frustrating him so he frequently uses his mate to derive enjoyment from frustrating her as if she is the one who deserves his retaliation (Fenichel, 1945).

The client we are discussing is one who very infrequently yields to his partner; he is extremely stubborn. It is as if he is still expressing his wish for power over his parents by not giving them what they want. To give warmly—to the rebellious spouse's mind—is to lose one's identity and autonomy. Consequently, he remains stubborn and enjoys either consciously or unconsciously "playing dirty tricks" on his mate and on others.

The rebellious spouse is also one who is constantly worried about being his partner's victim. Therefore, he tries very hard to be in the driver's seat. Frightened of being in a passive position, he strives valiantly to be a director. Worried that his mate can turn him into a slave, he works overtime to be her master (Stoller, 1975). Psychiatrist Charles Socarides (1977) has pointed out that the rebellious, sadistic spouse is a vengeful person who is forever trying to get his partner to say, "You are superior, more powerful, and I bow to your judgment and decision."

Invariably the rebellious spouse rebels against the idea of marriage counseling. When an attorney, physician, or clergyman suggests counseling to him, he experiences it as an insult—as if the referring party were deliberately trying to humiliate him. In effect, he sees treatment as he saw toilet-training and he protests vehemently against it. The therapist, if he is to involve the rebellious spouse in counseling, must stay clear of the client's battles and not get involved in the power struggles that this client sets up. If the therapist attempts to focus on the client's conflicts or marital responsibilities too early in the contact, he is experienced transferentially as the parent who is trying to get his child to submit. This becomes infuriating and humiliating to the client.

Ellen A., age 29, was referred by her attorney to Dr. Z. for marriage counseling. After her attorney listened to Ellen's marital complaints as well as to her request for help with a divorce, he felt that it might be a good idea for Ellen to discuss her problems with a marriage counselor before she finalized her decision. Although Ellen had quite a bit of resistance to seeing Dr. Z., she decided to go ahead and make an appointment to talk with him.

In her first consultation Ellen told Dr. Z. that she was not eager to go through counseling because she knew that she wanted a divorce. Insensitive to Ellen's resistance to being with him, and unaware of her obvious irritation with her attorney's referral, Dr. Z. said, "Well, it takes two to tango, tell me what's been going on in your marriage." Annoyed at Dr. Z.'s implication that she, as well as her husband, was creating the marital conflicts Ellen said, "I don't want to review how I have been victimized, abused, and destroyed. I just want out."

Dr. Z., not mindful that he was slipping into a role in which Ellen perceived him as the tyrannical parent of her past and the annoying husband of her present, told Ellen that she seemed to think that everything that had been going wrong in her marriage was her husband's fault. At this point Ellen yelled at Dr. Z. and told him, "I don't like your approach!" She then rose from her chair and left Dr. Z.'s office, never to be heard from again.

As stated in earlier chapters, it is important to find out how any client—not just the rebellious spouse—feels about being referred for treatment. If the client feels negatively about the idea, as was true with Ellen A. in the above case, the practitioner must allow the client sufficient opportunity to ventilate resentful feelings toward the referring party and to discuss the inevitable resentful feelings he has toward the therapist for accepting the referral. This issue is extremely pertinent with the rebellious spouse because this client, as we know, is extremely worried about being dominated and demeaned. If the practitioner does not help the client talk about how irritating the idea of counseling is, the client will rebel against the therapeutic process immediately and leave treatment.

We have discussed in previous chapters that the idea of having some responsibility for marital conflicts is something that most marital partners fight. Husbands blame wives and wives blame husbands for their disputes. It is important to remember that if clients were able to acknowledge their own roles in their marital conflicts they would have much better marriages and might not be clients in the first place. The rebellious spouse, perhaps more than most, strongly rebels against the idea that his attitudes and behavior contribute to the marital woes. Consequently, the therapist usually has to wait a long time before confronting the client with his role in marital problems.

Usually when the therapist neutrally listens to the rebellious spouse's complaints about the partner and neither condemns nor condones him, the client feels frustrated. To him, somebody who does not concur with his attitude and does not support his behavior is provoking him. The therapist's neutrality gets him furious and the sadism that the client feels toward his marital partner emerges in the transference relationship with the therapist. If the therapist can cope with the client's sadism without censuring him, then the client might feel a little safer to examine his own role in his marriage.

Ben B., age 40, was referred to Ms. Y., a marriage counselor, by his physician. Ben had told the doctor that he thought the reason he was always tired and had high blood pressure was because of his marital difficulties. When Ben met Ms. Y. he angrily told her that his wife was "an obsessive-compulsive" who could never make up her mind about anything. She never knew what kind of clothes to buy, what food to purchase, and what kinds of recreation she really preferred. In his first interview with Ms. Y. he recounted many incidents in which his wife Zelda was "extremely ambivalent." This, according to Ben, "drives me out of my mind." In the interview Ben spoke "non-stop," and Ms. Y. said virtually nothing.

As treatment continued on a twice-weekly basis, Ben brought in story after story in which he was furious with Zelda for her indecisiveness. After nine sessions Ben turned to Ms. Y. and asked her, "What's your reaction to all of this?" Ms. Y. asked Ben, "What have you been feeling here with me that prompts your question?" Ben immediately got very irritated with Ms. Y. and told her that just like his wife, she couldn't take a stand on anything. He bombarded her with invectives and for almost the rest of the interview told her that she was "an incompetent." To his surprise, as the session was about to close, Ms. Y. said, "I'm glad you could tell me about your dissatisfactions with me. Perhaps we can look at them more next time." As he left the session Ben said with a smile, "You are a peculiar woman!"

At his next appointment Ben candidly told Ms. Y. that he had thought she would lambast him or throw him out of the office when he had made derisive remarks about her. He went on to talk about the many fights and arguments he had had with his parents when he was a child. Ben said that he had grown up with a conviction that in a relationship, "the other guy is always your enemy." "Life is one big power struggle," Ben concluded.

As Ms. Y. and Ben looked at his conviction that part of living necessarily involved power struggles, Ben was able to recall how much he resented his parents for what he termed "their arbitrary authority." He further pointed out that in many ways his entire modus vivendi was motivated by seeking revenge on his parents and on others like them.

While Ben began to feel more positively toward Ms. Y. as he recounted his history and examined his past and present power struggles, he started to feel more positively toward Zelda. However, as he reported progress in his life and felt that the gains evolved because of his work with Ms. Y., he started to come late for his interviews with her and bounced a couple of checks that were meant for Ms. Y. When Ms. Y. brought these issues to Ben's attention, he told Ms. Y. that more and more she was reminding him of his geometry teacher in high school. Ben said, "The old bag was imposing a lot of junk on me and always wanted her own way. There was only one answer to a problem—hers—and I hated her guts for her obvious arrogance and superiority."

On Ms. Y.'s investigating with Ben what she was doing in her work with him that reminded him of the geometry teacher, Ben (after some resistive remarks) was able to tell Ms. Y. that he was quite sure that she had a hidden agenda in her work with him. That agenda was to get him to be a "compliant good boy," the way he was forced to be in school and at home. Once more he told Ms. Y. that she was his enemy because she wanted to dominate him and he was determined not to let that happen.

As Ben freely associated to his notion about being dominated, he eventually was able to see that he was conducting a futile battle with Ms. Y., Zelda, and "all the people of my past who gave me rules and regulations." He noted that he, himself, was in many ways arranging battles and "liking the fight." After a year of treatment he began to take some responsibility for his fights with Zelda. Insightfully, he pointed out that he viewed her indecisiveness as a weapon that she had over him "rather than what it really is—an emotional problem." As he saw Zelda more as she really was and not so much as the arbitrary parents of his past, their marriage improved a great deal. With more acceptance from Ben, Zelda moved into therapy for herself and examined her indecisiveness without feeling punished for it.

What is frequently overlooked in therapeutic work with the rebellious spouse is that underneath his hostile veneer hides a great deal of fragility. In many ways his rebelliousness is his manner of defending against his unacceptable passive yearnings. The rebellious spouse longs to be a dependent child but he fights against revealing these feelings. He desires love but renounces his wishes for it lest he appear weak and vulnerable. Only when the rebellious spouse feels very safe with the therapist is he able to show what lurks beneath his hostile surface.

Jill C., age 32, had been in treatment three times a week for a year-and-a-half with Dr. R., a male therapist. She sought him out because she wanted help in getting a divorce. Jill described daily battles with her husband Peter. Frequently they would physically attack each other, often to the point where one of them needed medical attention.

After Jill recapitulated her marital conflicts in the transference relationship with Dr. R. and had fantasies of maiming him, castrating him, and possibly killing him, she focused on her early family life. For the first time in 10 years she was able to cry about how excluded she felt in her family, how hurt she felt that her two older brothers received preferential treatment, and how being a girl made her feel like a second-class citizen.

When Jill was able to face some of her feelings of vulnerability and felt accepted by Dr. R. with them, she had much less need to cling to her rebellious defense. As a result she could become much more loving toward Peter. While Peter initially welcomed Jill's changes—as with many other spouses we have discussed—he began to feel uncomfortable and reacted by having some temper tantrums. Eventually he entered conjoint therapy with Jill where they both discussed their mutual anxieties when feeling intimate with one another.

THE COMPLIANT SPOUSE

As we have suggested earlier in this chapter, when a child feels intimidated by his parents and fears their disapproval, their withholding of love, or their possible abandonment, he becomes a very compliant child with a very strict superego. As a spouse he is frightened of his partner and feels obligated to cater to her lest *she* withhold love or leave him. He renounces his individuality, curbs his spontaneity and surrenders to his partner who he feels knows much more and is much more capable than himself.

As we pointed out in Chapter 2, the compliant-masochistic individual usually chooses a marital partner who is similar to his parents—exacting, demanding, and sadistic. Recapitulating his childhood in marriage, the compliant spouse works hard trying to extract love from a demanding parental figure. Usually his exacting superego is projected onto the mate and he continually anticipates punishment, scorn, and physical and mental abuse. It is not only love that the compliant spouse wants to extract but enough love to compensate for his feelings of deprivation. However, when he is loved he cannot enjoy it because he feels he does not deserve it (Strean, 1980).

What is sometimes overlooked in the assessment and treatment of the compliant spouse is that he has great amounts of repressed anger. Because he has always feared asserting himself with his strict parents, his vengeance goes underground; instead of permitting himself to voice his anger, he feels guilty just for feeling it. He flagellates himself, thinking that if he continually cries "mea culpa" his punitive mate will finally love him. In *Masochism in Modern Man,* Reik (1941) showed how the compliant masochistic spouse is really an immature child willing to undergo all kinds of suffering and deprivation in his quest for love and acceptance. This self-hating person says, in effect: "I have a great deal of anger toward my parents for all the humiliation they have made me feel. I would like to hurt them but if I do, I'll lose their love and feel lost and abandoned. So, I'll repress my anger, submit to my tyrannical superego, and suffer in the hope that some day I will be loved."

Spotnitz and Freeman (1964, p. 154) in discussing the compliant-masochistic husband state:

> The husband who lets himself be bossed around for years, then one day breaks his shell of "Yes, dears" and kills his hated wife in a moment of intolerable pressure, has hidden his wish to kill under the mask of masochism.
>
> Many masochistic husbands would like a divorce, but their need to suffer will not permit them to get one. In order for a husband who suffers

to leave his wife, he must believe he will find someone better. He must have both the incentive to give up the suffering and the vitality to take action. Sometimes a masochistic husband has all he can do just to muster the energy to walk around the house.

What Spotnitz and Freeman have said about the masochistic husband can also be applied to the masochistic wife. Literature and films are full of examples of suffering men and women who have great difficulty coping with their aggression. In W. Somerset Maugham's *Of Human Bondage,* the main character, Phillip, felt that he could not live without his sadistic partner. The more cruelly she behaved, the more attached to her he became. In the film *La Strada,* the more the leading character is abused, the happier she becomes.

The compliant-masochistic spouse yearns for his partner and others, including his therapist, to witness his pain. According to Reik, masochistic people rarely cry alone and most of the time their chief witnesses are their mates. The lambskin they wear hides a wolf. Their yielding always includes defiance and their compliance always contains opposition (Reik, 1941).

In working with the compliant spouse in marriage counseling the therapist should always bear in mind how much this client wants to use the treatment to partake in masochistic orgies. The client derives a great deal of gratification in reporting to the therapist how he is misunderstood, misjudged, and mistreated. He presents himself as a devoted spouse who is always sensitive to his mate's needs, but he is never appreciated. He will give the therapist example after example of how he was generous to his mate but she was selfish; how he spoke kindly while she yelled; how he took care of the children while she watched television, and how he was full of love and compliments while she was full of hatred and accusations.

What the therapist must be sensitive to in the treatment of this client is how much the client uses his partner as a superego to punish him for his secret hostile and sadistic fantasies. The compliant spouse, as we have noted, is unconsciously a defiant person who subtly provokes his partner to be contemptuous of him. If the client's hatred is not faced in his therapy he will continue to suffer in his marriage and will try to use his therapist to feel sorry for him and to indulge his self-pity.

It is very tempting for the practitioner when counseling the compliant spouse to align himself with the client against his seemingly cruel partner. When the client exhibits to the therapist the psychological and physical bruises that were inflicted by his mate, the therapist may be inclined to offer sympathy to the client and condemn the partner. If the client reports how he was insulted in front of his children, derided in front of his friends, and criticized in front of his in-laws, the practitioner's response might very well be, "How horrible!" Yet a too sympathetic response to this client only motivates him to bring in more stories of how he was abused and misunderstood. To achieve this kind of interchange with the counselor he will subtly provoke his partner so that he can receive more and more consoling remarks from the therapist.

Don D., age 36, was in marriage counseling with Dr. S., a male therapist. He needed treatment because he found it increasingly difficult to cope with his wife, Rose's, "constant criticisms." Don told Dr. S. that Rose always appeared like an army sergeant who made him feel like a lowly private. In story after story that Don presented to Dr. S., Don was always the unappreciated loser.

Although Dr. S. had taken a history on Don and knew that his compliance and his self-devaluation was a lifelong problem that he brought into every relationship, Dr. S.'s overidentification with Don interfered with his helping him therapeutically. Instead of waiting for Don to show his compliance and masochism in the transference relationship with him, and in lieu of linking Don's submissiveness in his marriage to his past, Dr. S. became very solicitous of Don. He asked him in the tenth session of his once-a-week treatment, "Did you ever think that perhaps Rose is a bitch?" Don laughed when he heard Rose characterized this way and began to defend her and devaluate himself. Obviously afraid of his own hostility, he protected himself by his usual self-effacing remarks and said to Dr. S., "Maybe I'm not the man she wants." To this Dr. S. replied, "Maybe she's not the woman you want!" Again, Don could not accept critical remarks about Rose and said meekly to Dr. S., "She's really not that bad."

As treatment went on Don continued to bring in more examples of how Rose derided him. Each time Don did so Dr. S. felt sorry for him and criticized Rose. And each time Dr. S. criticized Rose, Don defended her. Eventually, both Dr. S. and Don began to tire of their unproductive interchanges, and in desperation Dr. S. referred Don and his wife to another therapist for conjoint therapy.

It is easy for the therapist who works with the compliant spouse to forget that though this client has a great deal of muffled rage toward his partner, he is very frightened of it. He became a compliant masochistic person long before he was married because he was so fearful of his own aggression. Furthermore, he was compelled to marry a dominant person in order to be controlled and to help him subdue his hostile tendencies. When the therapist criticizes his partner, the client becomes upset for several reasons. First, as already suggested, the client cannot tolerate hearing critical remarks about his partner because his own revengeful fantasies, which he wants repressed, might come to the surface. Second, his partner is, in his mind, an omnipotent parent whose love he craves and feeling critical toward her might impede him from receiving her love. Finally, the compliant spouse makes his mate a superego figure. Attacking her will lead, as he sees it, to her counterattack and he becomes very worried that she will abandon him or annihilate him.

The compliant spouse also can induce another countertransference response in the therapist which is rarely discussed in the professional literature but which appears quite frequently in practice; namely, this client can provoke the therapist's sadism. Although therapists do not like to acknowledge that they can feel hostile toward a client, the compliant spouse is quite capable of inducing such a response. Just as this client unconsciously provokes his partner to dominate and abuse him, he is quite ready to repeat this pattern with the therapist. On hearing over and over again from the compliant spouse that he, the client, is a "sad-sack" who can only lead a life of misery and self-abnegation, the therapist can feel irritated by the client's persistent moans and groans and directly or indirectly tell him, "Cut it out!" Of perhaps more pertinence, the compliant spouse, as we know, harbors a great deal of unconscious resentment; therefore, he subtly tries to defeat the practitioner's efforts. Unless this is well understood by the practitioner, he can find himself angry at the client for not getting better. Under the guise of utilizing therapeutic parameters to liberate the compliant spouse's constructive aggression and help him mature, therapists can be quite sadistic to this client (Spotnitz and Meadow, 1976). When the therapist is hostile the client continues to bathe in his masochism and does not mature. At best, he forms a sadomasochistic therapeutic marriage with the counselor and becomes a little less masochistic with his partner. However, should he end treatment, he will rearrange a sadomasochistic relationship with his partner.

Mary E., age 27, was in marriage counseling with Ms. T. After about 20 sessions of once-a-week treatment in which Mary told her therapist in one way or another that she, Mary, was a poor wife, an incapable woman, and a lousy mother, Ms. T., unknown to her herself, became irritated. Under the guise of trying to help Mary stop hating herself and to start aggressing, Ms. T. told Mary that maybe she should leave her husband so that he could be free to go and get a mature wife. Mary was a little surprised and asked, "Do you think I'm that bad?" Ms. T. said, "Yes, you appear helpless and hopeless."

Instead of asserting herself more, Mary began to become more masochistic in her sessions with Ms. T. She told Ms. T. that maybe she was not a good candidate for marriage counseling and perhaps she should leave her husband, Hy, so that he could better his life. Ms. T. responded with "Perhaps."

Inasmuch as Mary was feeling very intimidated by both Ms. T. and Hy, was extremely frightened of asserting herself toward either, and worried about being rejected by each of them, she told Ms. T. that she would just have to "try harder." By "trying harder" Mary meant catering to Hy more and indulging him as much as she could. Hy felt even more contempt toward Mary when he was indulged, and Mary became more and more discouraged with herself and with her marriage. Her discouragement angered Ms. T. and—rather than examine her own countertransference problems—she referred Mary for group therapy. Mary was relieved to leave Ms. T. and accepted the referral. The group therapist, sensitive to Mary's marital and therapeutic ordeal saw her in individual treatment and helped her resolve some of her masochistic problems so that she could enjoy a better marriage with Hy.

The compliant spouse, as our case illustrations attest, is not easy to counsel. His self-accusations must be heard, but he should be neither attacked for them nor supported for them. When the client sees that the clinician maintains a neutral stance as he recapitulates his marital pain in the transference relationship, the client slowly begins to aggress toward the therapist. If the therapist does not retaliate or appear defensive when he is attacked, the client tends to spontaneously associate to his early battles with his parents and siblings. On seeing that much of his masochistic behavior is a defense against the early rage he felt, he begins to try and resolve his silent and futile battle with his marriage partner and with the rest of the world.

Arthur F., age 45, a capable and successful business executive, found himself constantly doubting his capacities, feeling inferior to colleagues, and depressed by the fact that "I can never like myself for too long." Arthur was also disturbed about his relationship with his wife of 16 years, Valerie, who alternated "between warmth, indifference, and constantly putting me down." For many years Arthur had fantasies about getting a divorce, but he found it very difficult to think about what it would be like living without Valerie and his children. One of the factors precipitating Arthur's wish to enter therapy was a growing ambivalence about his two-year extramarital affair with Roberta, a married woman in his community whom he was seeing several times a week. Arthur was worried that Valerie would find out about the affair and decide to leave him.

Arthur described his parents as strict disciplinarians. If he had not come in first in his class, been the outstanding athlete on the baseball field, or "say the right thing at the right time," he was verbally assaulted and scorned. His parents had frequently compared him unfavorably with other children whose performances were more to their taste. In one interview he told his male therapist, Mr. U., "Once I got all A's except for one B and the whole family ridiculed me."

Graduating with honors from an Ivy League college, Arthur had his choice of several jobs. Women liked him but he was particularly attracted to Valerie "because she had both feet on the ground, seemed to know the rules of the road, and wouldn't take crap from anybody."

Rather early in his three-times-a-week treatment, Arthur was able, without much help from his therapist, to recognize that Valerie was an externalization of his "ego ideal"; that is, he too would have liked to feel comfortable being in the position of "not taking crap from anyone." Arthur idealized Valerie who seemed to enjoy her dominant position with her husband telling him what to do, what not to do, and in general making him toe the line. Valerie was clearly a parental figure for Arthur. He craved her approval, rarely felt that he deserved it, and silently resented his submissive position. After about four years of marriage Arthur began to feel resentment toward Valerie for her controlling attitude and behavior. However, when he asserted himself he became frightened of his aggression and intimidated by Valerie's counterarguments.

In his transference relationship with Mr. U., Arthur assumed the role of the hard-working son. He conscientiously reported his dreams, fantasies, and history. Furthermore, he always accepted his therapist's interpretations, came for his appointments on time, paid his bills promptly, and was very deferential in his attitude toward Mr. U. After about seven months of treatment Arthur began to ask Mr. U. for advice and support. He wondered if he should break up his affair or if he should divorce Valerie. Mr. U. did not answer his queries but tried to investigate what Arthur was feeling when he asked them, and Arthur eventually became annoyed with Mr. U. Actually, it was quite difficult for Arthur to be direct in expressing his annoyance, and Mr. U. helped him look at some of the dangers in asserting himself. Arthur was able to say, "It's like with Valerie. I am afraid if I tell you what I don't like you'll yell at me. I feel like a child, I guess, with both of you."

As Arthur began to feel more comfortable being himself with Mr. U., he could aggress toward him with more freedom. Yet, in one of his dreams he wanted to yell at a man who represented Mr. U., but he lost his voice. In another dream he saw Mr. U. about to fall off a building and die, but tried to convince himself it was not really Mr. U. whom he wanted to kill.

In examining his anger toward Mr. U., Arthur began to realize that he was trying to make him the parent who would love and support him. He was able to tie this observation to the fact that he was forever trying to get Valerie to praise him. Not only was he angry that love was not forthcoming, but he was eventually able to realize that in his marriage, in his therapy, and in virtually every one of his relationships, he was perceiving people as if they were his parents who were demanding of him that he be "Mr. Superstar." As he realized that he was constantly trying to produce for everybody and hating it, he began to relax a great deal. He started to ask Valerie to do things he liked and occasionally made some legitimate demands on Mr. U., such as asking Mr. U. to give him a more convenient appointment time. When Arthur did not have to make Valerie such a punitive superego, he loved her more and dropped his affair. Valerie seemed able to adapt to Arthur's more assertive, less compliant attitude and did not seem to need treatment for herself.

It should be mentioned that an extramarital affair can provide temporary gratification for some compliant-masochistic husbands and wives. Feeling picked-on, they feel justified in seeking a lover who will treat them more lovingly than their mates do. Usually the lover they choose encourages them to voice their complaints about their partners, and if they do not feel too guilty about discussing their partner's mistreatment of them they get gratification from this. For the compliant spouse whose masochism is not very deeply entrenched, the idea of going behind mother's or father's back and doing something secret and forbidden makes it appealing to have sex in some hideaway hotel or motel. But the gratification through an affair does not sustain itself indefinitely. Guilty over his rebellious fantasies, uncomfortable about facing his resentment directly, and fearful of his partner's retaliation, the compliant spouse either begins to feel depressed about the affair, as we saw in the case of Arthur F., or else he arranges to get caught (Strean, 1980).

THE AMBIVALENT SPOUSE

When a child is handled ambivalently during his "terrible twos," he becomes an ambivalent person feeling both love and hatred toward his parents. His ambivalence is inevitably directed toward his marriage partner. He loves her for the warmth and comfort that she provides; he hates her for the demanding, controlling parent he feels she is. He also feels he is required to submit to her. However, he is comfortable with neither his love nor his hatred. When he loves, he feels he gives up his autonomy and individuality; therefore, he rebels and tries to dominate his mate. However, when he rebels and dominates, he is afraid that his aggression will become too powerful and fears his needed mate will either leave him, stop loving him, or become very harsh with him. Consequently, he starts loving her again.

The ambivalence of the spouse that we are discussing extends into virtually all of his marital activities. He cannot make up his mind about whether he should or should not have sex on a particular day and he can go back and forth 20 times within an hour as to the wisdom of the idea. He may be perplexed for weeks and months about whether he should go on a vacation with his mate or whether the children should accompany them. He is undecided about whether or not he should help with domestic chores, visit in-laws, or go to the movies by himself.

When the mate of the ambivalent spouse suggests an answer to his dilemmas, he usually opposes her. When she relents, and takes the other side of his ambivalence, he accuses her of indecisiveness. This spouse is in enormous agony most of the time because his conflicts around love, hate, dominance, and submission pervade virtually every one of his marital interactions. Nothing seems quite right to him.

It is obvious to almost any observer that the ambivalent spouse is very difficult to live with. He is unreliable, undependable, and unpredictable. Such behaviors tax his mate's patience; in her anger, she can be critical of him and/or threaten to divorce him. In response to his mate's anger, he can get furious as well, but as we have already pointed out, the ambivalent spouse cannot tolerate his hatred for too long and when threatened by it, he begins to love his mate again. However, this leads him into the vicious cycle with which he is always struggling.

The ambivalent spouse is, of course, going to be ambivalent about treatment and ambivalent toward the therapist. He is the client who tells the practitioner in the first interview that for months he has delayed calling for an appointment and now that he's made the plunge, he's not sure he wants anything to do with it. He is the client who asks many questions about the therapist's qualifications, the rationale of the treatment process, and whether or not any form of counseling really works. If the therapist explains the treatment process or gives information about his qualifications, the client shakes his head in dissatisfaction, because the ambivalent spouse is never convinced of anything for too long.

If the ambivalent spouse does stay in counseling he uses much of the time to express his enormous ambivalence about his mate. However, he sees his ambivalence as a natural and appropriate response to a mate who has many assets and many liabilities; it is not, in his mind, because of his own unconscious inner struggle. Most ambivalent spouses find it very difficult to focus on their inner lives. They rarely report fantasies, dreams, or memories. They concentrate on externals and often ask the therapist to take over and offer guidance. However, should the therapist offer direction, they feel ambivalent and may try to defeat the suggestions.

This client can induce intense countertransference reactions in the therapist. It is difficult to listen to a client who over and over again says "on the other hand" and never makes a decision on seemingly simple and mundane matters. It can be irritating for a therapist to always have the treatment process questioned and his own qualifications held suspect. It can be dull and boring to hear a client with constricted affect and limited spontaneity go back and forth for 45 minutes discussing the advantages and disadvantages of buying a clock for the kitchen.

In order to help the ambivalent spouse face his internal struggles between love and hatred and between dominance and submission the therapist should refrain from offering advice, providing direction, or appearing too authoritative. While the therapist is frequently tempted to do just this, if he gives in to his inclinations the therapy will not move for several reasons. First, the ambivalent spouse, by definition, is ambivalent toward the therapist and, therefore, if he heeds the practitioner's advice in one session, he will reject it in a later one. Second, the ambivalent spouse has a great deal of anxiety about being in a passive position and taking advice makes him feel that once again he's on the potty, having to obey an authoritarian parent. He must secretly rebel against this to avoid feeling vulnerable. Finally, and most important, if the therapist imposes his own notions on the client, the client's internal struggle does not get resolved. At best, the client covers up his own dilemmas about handling love and hate and only temporarily identifies with the therapist's way of coping.

The practitioner, to be therapeutic, must directly face—with the client—just how ambivalent the client is about his marriage and everything else. While the client probably feels ambivalent about an interpretation regarding his mixed feelings, when he sees that the practitioner does not direct but listens, does not advise but empathizes, does not take stands regarding solutions but stays neutral, the client over time, albeit usually a long time, does get to his internal conflicts which propel his intense ambivalence toward his mate.

Wendy G., age 34, was in treatment with Dr. P., a female therapist, because she was unsure what to do about her seven-year marriage to Dick. She thought Dick was a kind man who made a good living and that he was considerate of her and of the children, but he was not "strong, decisive, or sexual." She told Dr. P. that she "found it difficult to live with Dick but difficult to think about living without him." During her first consultation with Dr. P., Wendy gave many instances of her very ambivalent attitude toward Dick's interests, values, and activities. When Dr. P. empathized with her agony and how difficult it was for her to know which way to turn regarding her marriage, Wendy asked doubtfully, "Do you think just talking to you about this can help me?" Dr. P. replied, "I guess you have your doubts about me." Wendy said that Dr. P. seemed like a nice, kind person but she needed somebody who could be strong, authoritative, and firm, and she wasn't sure Dr. P. had these qualifications. Obviously, Wendy was immediately transferring her feelings toward Dick onto Dr. P. Dr. P. suggested that she might want to return for a second interview to discuss her doubts about therapy and about Dr. P. In her true ambivalent style, Wendy said, "I may do that but I'm not sure."

In her second interview Wendy resumed talking about her ambivalence toward Dick and her ambivalence toward Dr. P. After going back and forth verbalizing mixed feelings about both her husband and her therapist, she asked Dr. P. if she could tell her what to do because she was so terribly conflicted. When Dr. P. told Wendy that she realized how difficult it was to make up her mind about therapy, her marriage, and how much she would like an answer, Wendy got irritated with Dr. P. She told her that she had come to see a counselor to get direction and all she was getting were evasive responses. "I don't mean to hurt your feelings," said Wendy, "but I don't think this approach will work. I need direction." Dr. P. suggested that it might be helpful to see what was going on in her mind when she needed direction and suggested again that it might be fruitful to have another interview. Again Wendy said, "Maybe."

In succeeding interviews during her once-a-week treatment, Wendy clearly felt guilty about criticizing Dr. P. and appeared quite conciliatory. When this became clear, Dr. P. told Wendy that apparently she felt uncomfortable about having criticized her. Wendy acknowledged that this was true and told Dr. P. that she, Dr. P., seemed like such a nice, kind person and she didn't think Dr. P. deserved Wendy's "abuse." "When you criticize, do you feel you are abusing?" Dr. P. asked. Wendy said that all her life she had been frightened of asserting herself. She said this was certainly true in her marriage and was particularly true in her childhood. Wendy went on to describe her parents whom she regarded as "nice and kind but very pushy." She resented their dominating attitude, but was always frightened to say so, lest she be criticized further or punished.

Wendy did feel a little better after releasing some hostility toward Dr. P. and her parents and seemed to be a little less ambivalent toward Dick, as well. However, this improvement was short-lived. While seeming more spontaneous in her interviews and appearing to feel warmer toward Dr. P., in an interview during her fourth month of treatment Dr. P. was asked by

Wendy, "Do you think I would do better in group therapy?" Dr. P. realized that Wendy was trying to move away from her: the increased closeness that Wendy felt toward Dr. P. was making Wendy uncomfortable. However, she did not want to be manipulated into being a director or advisor and therefore Dr. P. said to Wendy, "Let's see what you are feeling these days that prompts your desire for group therapy." Wendy told Dr. P. that her question was a good one.

In exploring her wish for group therapy, Wendy told Dr. P. that lately she realized she had a deep yearning for a family and that group therapy appeared to be an opportunity to participate in a reconstituted family. When Dr. P. remained silent, Wendy appeared somewhat agitated. Dr. P. then called Wendy's expression of agitation to her attention and Wendy said, "I guess I don't want to put all my eggs in one basket." By this she meant that she did not want to rely exclusively on Dr. P. for therapeutic assistance.

When Dr. P. explored Wendy's misgivings about putting all her eggs in one basket, Wendy said that if she relied on one person, she would worry that the person would let her down. Further exploration led Wendy to talk about Dr. P. not being strong enough to help her consistently. Beneath her fear of Dr. P.'s not being strong enough was, of course, a wish of Wendy's to weaken Dr. P. When this was interpreted to Wendy, she vehemently denied it and told Dr. P. that she did not understand her. She pointed out that she wanted a strong person as a therapist, but she was entitled to have her doubts about Dr. P.

Again Wendy returned to her ambivalent position toward Dr. P. and again she felt equally ambivalent toward Dick. She pleaded with Dr. P. to give her advice about group therapy, her marriage, and whether she should stop seeing Dr. P. in treatment. Maintaining her neutrality, Dr. P. again verbalized how terribly mixed up Wendy felt these days about so many issues in her life.

On seeing that Dr. P. was once more not going to be manipulated into a role of advisor or director, Wendy became more furious than she had been in her six months of treatment. She told Dr. P. that she was a very noncommittal, indecisive person who couldn't take a stand on anything. Obviously projecting aspects of herself onto her therapist, Wendy speculated that Dr. P. probably had parents similar to her own. "You were probably held down a lot and you are fearful of asserting yourself," Wendy speculated about Dr. P. When Dr. P. did not confirm or deny Wendy's hypotheses about her own life history, the client went on to discuss the latent power struggles she consistently found herself in with her parents. She talked about her wishes to defy them but worried about being abandoned. Memories flowed, anger was released, and Wendy slowly began to see how she was recapitulating her battles with her parents in her therapy, her marriage, and practically everywhere else.

After releasing a great deal of rage, Wendy began to feel more positively toward Dick and Dr. P. While she had to stop the flow of her positive feelings toward them many times during the course of her therapy, her hatred became less and less, and her capacity to love Dick and others certainly increased.

In working with the ambivalent spouse, it is tempting—particularly at the beginning of the treatment—to advise him. When the therapist sees that the client has one foot out the door of the consultation room and seems to be ready to move the other foot out also, the therapist becomes apprehensive about losing the client. However, it is important for the practitioner to keep in mind that the ambivalent spouse is not going to leave therapy too quickly, just as he does not plan to leave his mate too quickly. To the ambivalent spouse leaving treatment or leaving the partner is equivalent to hurting the one he loves: He avoids terminating contacts to prevent this. The ambivalent spouse fears being alone, fears retribution if he is too aggressive, and fears being too direct about anything. If the therapist can remind himself that the ambivalent spouse is *not* going to terminate treatment abruptly for these reasons, he can remain neutral in the face of the client's ambivalence. The client then has a real opportunity to confront his underlying hostility, his fear of loving, and his anxiety about submitting. As we have suggested several times, giving advice to this client only strengthens his resistance to treatment, moves him further away from the therapist, and prevents him from facing his paramount problems—the struggle between loving and hating, and between dominating and submitting.

THE SPOUSE WHO THINKS SEX IS DIRTY

Sexual problems in marriage evolve from the failure of resolving one or more developmental tasks. If the child has not been helped to trust during the oral period, he will later distrust his partner's wishes for oral gratification in sex, and will be uncomfortable with his own. Furthermore, if he has strong and unacceptable symbiotic wishes, he will be frightened of being engulfed or of engulfing in sex. As he traverses later developmental journeys, if conflicts are not resolved at the oedipal period, at latency, or at adolescence, he will manifest sexual problems in marriage that are unique to these periods. In this section we will discuss sexual problems in marriage that evolve from the anal period and we will also present some therapeutic principles that seem important in counseling spouses who show these difficulties.

As we pointed out earlier, many adults equate sexual discharge with anal or urinary discharge. Consequently, they tend to regard sexual activity as something "dirty." It is as if they are urinating or defecating in or on their partners, or as if that is what is being done to them. This distortion of the sexual encounter derives from the child's toilet training when he resented defecating or urinating in a toilet bowl and wanted to urinate or defecate on his parents instead. Such expressions of children as being "pissed off" or "giving a shit" tend to illustrate the commonality of utilizing anal or urinary discharges to express resentment or spite toward parents and others.

When the child consciously or unconsciously wants to spite his parents by defecating or urinating on them, he will bring these same fantasies into the sexual relationship with his mate. However, because he loves his mate as well as hates her, he worries about messing her or getting her dirty. Many of the men who suffer from premature ejaculation or other forms of impotence are unconsciously stopping themselves from hostilely soiling, messing, or dirtying the one they also love. Women who are unable to have orgasms in sexual intercourse often suffer from the same inhibition.

Because many men and women equate sex with a bathroom affair and see it as wallowing in mud, they cannot inflict their "dirty habits" on one they respect. This fantasy explains why some men and women can only enjoy sex with one to whom they are not married. Cohabiting couples who are not married but who eventually do wed, have spoken about the diminution of their sexual desires after marriage. What therapy reveals is that living together is like playing in the mud—something not permissible within the sanctity of marriage. Also, individuals involved in extramarital affairs have pointed out that "dirty sex" is permissible with a lover but not with a wife or a husband who is unconsciously experienced as a parental figure. Many teenagers divide the opposite sex into two groups: those who are "nice" with whom sex is taboo, and those who are "not nice" with whom sex is permissible. It is permissible "to dump one's load" on someone who is not revered (Strean, 1980).

When sex is turned into a bathroom affair and the spouse does not want to dirty the partner, not only may the spouse have sexual problems such as impotence, premature ejaculation, or frigidity, but sexual relations can be avoided altogether. Many celibate couples who are clients of marriage counselors unconsciously view sex as a dirty bathroom affair but have no real awareness of why sex in marriage arouses severe inhibitions in them.

Many of the married couples who are celibate or manifest other sexual problems believe that their problems can be resolved by learning new and different sexual techniques. Occasionally clinicians have also been lulled into being convinced of this mistaken belief (Kaplan, 1974; Masters and Johnson, 1970). Dynamic psychotherapy has revealed that when married partners cannot enjoy sex with one another they are frightened by their fantasies, plagued by their doubts, and inhibited by their angers. New sexual techniques will not help these people too much; however, exploring and understanding their unresolved psychosexual conflicts will. At best, when a therapist offers sexual instruction to a client the latter can view it as receiving permission from a parental figure to have sex and may gain some partial or temporary relief.

The spouse who thinks that sex is dirty needs to examine the punitive voices of his superego. He also needs to become more aware of the childish fantasies that propel his guilt. When this spouse enters marriage counseling he is usually not aware of how much he unconsciously wants to inhibit himself sexually. He may point out that he and his partner "do not have the right chemistry" and/or that his partner does not know how to excite him. It usually takes some time for the client to become aware of his forbidden fantasies and of the forbidden voices that emanate from his punitive superego.

Jed H., age 33, was in marriage counseling with Dr. N., a male therapist, because he suffered from premature ejaculations. Although he had been capable of sustaining erections with his wife Kay prior to their marriage, he developed sexual problems soon after the wedding. While Jed pointed out that he and Kay had a smooth relationship in every other aspect, ever since he got married he suffered from premature ejaculations.

After Jed reported his history, which at first blush sounded uneventful and nontraumatic, he used his therapy sessions to think out loud about his sexual problems. What Dr. N. began to notice after about six or seven sessions with Jed is that he rarely stayed with a topic for long. He would talk about a conversation with Kay, and in the middle of it switch to another subject such as a work problem, but would not complete describing either event fully. Thinking to himself that Jed's premature termination of talking about a subject seemed similar to what happened in sex, Dr. N. decided to explore the manner in which Jed related to him in the interviews. When Jed was told by Dr. N. that it seemed difficult and perhaps unsafe to complete his thoughts in the sessions, after some intellectualizations, Jed did get to the heart of the matter. He talked about not wanting to appear like "a big shot" with Dr. N., that this would make him seem "too big" and "too aggressive."

In later sessions when Dr. N. asked Jed to associate to the term "big shot," Jed referred to being too aggressive and too mean. Eventually he was able to get in touch with wishes to dominate and demean the other person when he felt like a "big shot." Spontaneously he moved to a discussion of his relationships with his parents and older sister, with whom he felt powerless and toward whom he harbored many revengeful fantasies. He talked about wanting to "knock down," "beat up" and "destroy" his family members and "cover them with shit."

In talking in his sessions about destroying his family members and "covering them with shit," Jed began to feel more spontaneous and more potent in his sexual relations with Kay. He also became more spontaneous in his interviews with Dr. N. and did not need to change the subject as much. However, Jed soon began to come to his sessions late, had little to say, and found himself "forgetting" to pay Dr. N.'s bill. When Dr. N. confronted Jed with his resistive behavior, he was able to tell Dr. N. how much he resented the fact that Dr. N. seemed to be "the one in power" in their therapeutic relationship. Said Jed, "You control everything here. You tell me what time I should come for the appointments, when we should end them, and I have to put out for you." Here, Dr. N. said, "I seem to make you feel like a kid on a potty who has to put out for me." Although Jed laughed when he heard Dr. N.'s interpretation, he had several fantasies of reversing roles with Dr. N. in which the latter would be the patient and Jed "would be king." He further discussed his wish to castrate Dr. N. and make him suffer.

After Jed was able to talk about his sadistic fantasies toward Dr. N., he could see how he was holding these fantasies back when he had sex with Kay. He further realized that he was making her a parent of his past whom he wanted to hurt. As he more and more realized that he was making Kay, his therapist, and others omnipotent parents whom he wanted to maim, and as he recognized the self-destructive component in his battle, he began to feel more loving and more self-confident—and his sexual problems diminished.

Some married men and women in marriage counseling have reported to their therapists that although they have enjoyable sex with their partners, they find themselves arguing with their mates before and after sexual relations. What frequently occurs with these clients is that they have to punish themselves after having a "dirty" experience, which sex is to them, or else they have to punish themselves before they transgress and have the dirty experience. They feel so guilty for what to them is hostilely wallowing in the mud that they have to pay a price for their transgressions.

Sometimes arguing and fighting before sex can help certain couples discharge their "dirty" impulses through "shitting and pissing" on each other verbally. After sadistically and masochistically playing in mud and after getting punished for it by their partners through absorbing their harsh criticisms, they can then "make up" and have pleasurable sex. Yet, their constant arguments bother them and they seek a marriage counselor to help them curb these scenes.

Josephine I., age 28, told her therapist, Ms. M., that she was finding herself in constant arguments with Jerry, her husband, to whom she had been married for three years. Although Josephine and Ms. M. worked intensively and cooperatively, it took client and therapist several months before they could pinpoint that the arguments usually took place before Jerry and Josephine had sex. "After the fight is over," said Josephine, "I feel much more loving and much more receptive to Jerry."

As Josephine's history was reviewed and her interpersonal problems assessed, it became clear that she had been involved in intense power struggles all her life with both men and women. She described her parents as "always thinking they were members of a royal family and I had to submit to them." Josephine further recalled that in her constant verbal arguments with both of her parents, "after a while we would start to laugh and we did end up kissing and hugging."

After Josephine reviewed the power struggles in her family and in her marriage with Jerry, she began to experience these very same power struggles with Ms. M. She told Ms. M. that often while they talked, Ms. M. appeared to be a cold, dictatorial schoolteacher, who seemed to demand that Josephine "put out and do her homework." As Josephine began to criticize Ms. M. more and more, it appeared clear that she wanted Ms. M. to argue with her. At one point after telling Ms. M. that she used poor techniques as a therapist and that she did not know how to function in a therapeutic relationship, she ordered Ms. M. to "Defend yourself!" When Ms. M. neutrally pointed out that Josephine seemed to want an intense argument with her and that Ms. M. was not gratifying her wish, Josephine began to cry, and eventually asked Ms. M. "to forgive" her. It was becoming clear that Josephine was acting out with Ms. M. the sequence of fighting, making up, and love-making that she unconsciously arranged with Jerry and which seemed to be such an important dimension of her relationship with her original family. When this was shared with her by Ms. M., Josephine acknowledged the truth of it and began to explore the why's and wherefore's of this sequence in her therapy.

Josephine realized that she harbored a great deal of love and hatred toward her parents and toward Jerry. She told Ms. M. that her hatred always bothered her and she always wanted to get rid of it. It soon dawned on Ms. M. and on Josephine that one way of getting rid of hatred before making love with Jerry was to have an argument with him. Then she could enjoy herself.

As Josephine became more aware of her childish hatred which was constantly expressed in her marriage, she needed it less. Particularly when she saw that she was making Jerry the parents of her past toward whom she felt sadistic was she able to feel more consistently loving toward him.

When Jerry saw that Josephine was not arguing with him as much he felt much better. However he "missed" the fights and when he saw that he was starting to provoke many of them, he sought therapeutic help for himself.

As we suggested earlier, one of the etiological factors in the extramarital affair is that "dirty sex" can only be enjoyed away from the marital partner who is experienced as a revered parent. Therefore, many a husband or wife behaves like Dr. Jekyll and Mr. Hyde—as a tender, dutiful "child" with the marital partner and as a child having fun in the dirt with a lover (Strean, 1980).

Calvin J. told his male therapist, Dr. L., in his first consultation that he felt very depressed "for no accountable reason"; he suffered from migraine headaches and colitis, was frequently afraid to assert himself, and derived "little pleasure out of living."

Calvin described his wife Ida as "a good woman," a devoted mother and wife who "took her responsibilities very seriously" and always kept a "stiff upper lip." Although Calvin had a great deal of respect, admiration, and even some awe for Ida, there was little spontaneity in their relationship and almost a complete absence of physical demonstrations of affection.

It took Calvin several months before he could discuss his sex life with Dr. L. It turned out that sexual relations were very infrequent—once or twice a month—and accompanied by a ritual that both Calvin and Ida were compelled to enact. Each would take a long bath before sex "to make sure our private parts were clean" and then, after sexual relations, each would take another bath "to get rid of the dirty stuff on our private parts." Evidently both Calvin and Ida experienced sexual intercourse as a soiling experience and therefore had to take many precautions. In one treatment session Calvin exclaimed, "How can I soil such a fine woman!"

As Calvin described his sexual rituals to Dr. L. he felt extremely uncomfortable. When his discomfort was explored, he told Dr. L. that "talking about sex with you has *contaminated* our relationship." Similar to his relationship with Ida, Calvin felt that if he respected Dr. L., he could not discuss sex with him because that dirtied their relationship.

Eventually Calvin was helped to face that he had wishes to contaminate his relationship with Ida and with Dr. L. because of the hostility he felt toward both of them. He had made both of them his punitive superego and both of them reminded him of his parents. Both of his parents were described as compulsive people whose living room wall actually displayed the embroidered motto, "Cleanliness is next to godliness." As a boy Calvin had to wear clean, white, starched shirts and "never get dirty."

As Calvin's treatment moved on and he faced some of his resentments toward his parents, toward Ida, and toward Dr. L., the power of his punitive superego began to diminish. Therefore he began to loosen some of his resistance to pleasure. He joined a bowling group, tried some clay modeling, and started to go to the movies. As he permitted himself to have fun he also started to feel increased sexual yearnings and began an extramarital affair. Calvin found that he enjoyed cursing with Effie, his lover. He delighted in taking her to porno films where they had sex on occasion, "and instead of being so uptight I wear dungarees when I'm with her."

As Calvin's therapy continued, he began to get in touch with his strong anal eroticism. In one of his dreams he and Effie were children playing in a sand box. In another dream he had anal intercourse with her and "when she came she shit all over me and it was fun."

Although Calvin was in many ways very free with Effie, he continued to be a "clean boy" with Ida. It took him a long time to realize how he made Ida a virgin mother who had to be protected from his dirt. In his transference relationship with Dr. L. he saw how terribly guilty he felt for wanting "to smear with shit anybody who reminds me of a parent" and how much he punished himself for these fantasies. It took Calvin over three years in therapy before he could begin to accept some of his boyish wishes "to shit on my mother." When he stopped fighting the wishes so much, he relaxed more and began to enjoy himself with Ida.

Sometimes the Dr. Jekyll/Mr. Hyde personality can maintain two relationships indefinitely, provided that he can cope with an enormously complicated life. He stays in his marriage because of his unconscious wish for punishment. He initially seeks an affair because he wants to find tenderness and acceptance which he feels his spouse cannot (or is not permitted to) express. The extramarital affair becomes an arena in which he acts out his repressed anal eroticism (Strean, 1980).

THE LARK–OWL MARRIAGE

In Chapter 6 we pointed out that the various forms of marriage that we discussed are not mutually exclusive. It is possible to find problems with trust, dependency, and symbiotic wishes all lodged in one husband or wife. It is equally true that one spouse can suffer from sadomasochistic problems, be ambivalent most of the time in his marriage, and also view sex as a bathroom ritual which should be shunned. Often the spouse who is a member of a lark–owl dyad (Brozan, 1982) suffers from all these problems and more.

The spouse who is either "a lark" or "an owl" sleeps and works on a different schedule from his partner. Often husband and wife do not see one another for a week or more. They inevitably ascribe their emotionally distant relationship as a function of their work schedules; however, they are usually a couple who fear emotional and sexual intimacy. They are frightened that if they get close to one another they will enter a power struggle. Consequently, to avoid fighting—which they fear but feel impelled to do if they get together—they form a truce and see one another intermittently.

This dyad harbors unconscious sadistic wishes and masochistic fantasies but works hard to remain unaware of them. The "lark" or "owl" has some love for the partner and can show it providing he sees the mate infrequently. If he sees the mate for a prolonged period of time, such as on a vacation, he usually gets into arguments with her, feels controlled, and cannot wait until he gets back to work and away from the mate. In effect, this spouse works overtime to stop himself from seeing and expressing his strong sadistic rage. Furthermore, if he has sex infrequently with the mate he does not have to feel so guilty. Either he is a celibate all week long and endures enough privation so that he can permit himself some pleasure on a weekend, or else he is involved in an affair and has little to do sexually with the partner he does not want to sully.

What often puzzles the observer of the lark–owl marriage is that the partners are often overtly compatible; frequently there is an absence of tension in their relationship. However, what the clinician should keep in mind is that the reason for the absence of overt tension is that there is an absence of emotional and sexual intimacy. Both partners are usually people who must isolate their sensual desires from their tender feelings. As we have pointed out earlier in this chapter, to have sex with the one they respect and like is seen as disruptive because they unconsciously perceive sex as something dirty; consequently, they do not wish to contaminate the beloved. They feel more comfortable maintaining an adolescent platonic relationship (Strean, 1983).

When clinicians have had the opportunity to work with members of this marital dyad, they have learned that these husbands and wives had superficially pleasant relationships with their parents and family members (as in their current marriages), but there was also a lack of emotionally gratifying experiences. It is this lack that has induced intense hostility in them. However, these people have had to control their hatred, and their plight manifests itself in their abhorrence of intimacy.

The "lark" or "owl" rarely seeks marriage counseling. Just as these individuals fear the closeness and intimacy of a sexually satisfying and emotionally gratifying marriage, they shun therapists and counselors in whom they would confide and with whom they would be emotionally intimate. When they do seek out or are referred to a helping professional, it is usually for a reason other than discomfort about their marriage.

Henry K., age 39, was referred to a mental health clinic by a physician because he had migraine headaches, insomnia, and shortness of breath. A hard-working accountant, Henry was away from his wife and children most of the week and "rested and recuperated" on weekends.

Henry described his relationship with his wife, Edith, and their children as "friendly and well organized." It was clear from the beginning of his contact with his therapist, Ms. G., that Henry shunned emotional intimacy and feared spontaneity in himself and others. He described the atmosphere in the home with his parents as also "friendly and well organized."

In the tenth interview of his once-a-week treatment, Ms. G. asked Henry about his sexual relationship with Edith. Blushing and anxious, Henry responded, "We have no time for frivolity." When Ms. G. tried to discuss Henry's resistance to having sex, Henry changed the subject and started to miss sessions. Eventually, he quit the treatment altogether.

In the above case illustration we again note that the client who wants to keep away from his mate is going to want to keep away from the therapist. The therapist has to wait until a comfortable working relationship is established with the client before exploring the client's reluctance to participate in an intimate relationship. What the client avoids in his marriage, he will avoid in therapy. Consequently, the therapist has to respect the client's resistance and wait until he manifests some readiness to open the area of emotional distance for exploration.

Some marriage counselors have taken the position that the "lark–owl" dyad do better in conjoint therapy where they have to face their mutual avoidance of intimacy and their mutual fear of emotional spontaneity (Ackerman, 1958; Jackson, 1965; Zilbach, 1968). What seems to be overlooked in this point of view is that when members of a marital dyad wish to avoid emotional intimacy, they can do so regardless of the treatment modality. Very often when the emotionally distant couple is placed into the conjoint format, they unite to defeat the practitioner.

Larry and Jean L., a couple in their mid-thirties, were referred for marriage counseling by their family physician, Dr. A. The physician told Larry and Jean that many of their physical problems (insomnia, headaches, tiredness) were due to stress in their marriage. Larry worked at night, Jean worked during the day, and it was Dr. A.'s opinion that this arrangement caused both of them stress.

The L.'s were very reluctant to accept Dr. A.'s prescription for marriage counseling and they kept postponing their call to the mental health clinic Dr. A. had recommended. Finally, because of Dr. A.'s persistent urging, the L.'s contacted the B. clinic.

Because of their different schedules, it took the L.'s about two months before they could find a mutually convenient time for a consultation. They arrived 15 minutes late for their first appointment. When Mr. C., the therapist, asked them if they had some difficulty finding the clinic, Jean—with Larry agreeing—said that they really didn't feel much like coming for an appointment and they did it just to please Dr. A. When Mr. C. recognized how irritated they were to be referred to the B. clinic and were further irritated to be with him, the L.'s relaxed a bit and talked about their hectic work schedules. However, they both agreed that their schedules could not be changed and that they both "had to adjust to them."

Although Mr. C. continued to respect the L.'s reluctance to be counseled and their resistance to be with him, and although the L.'s seemed to feel safer with him as time went on, during their tenth interview they resolved together that they were "not going to have any more of this." They began to accuse Mr. C. of trying "to trap us into a closer relationship" and said that they were "comfortable the way we are." They terminated treatment and never returned for further help.

Members of the "lark–owl" dyad, in addition to their anal problems, often regress and show problems on the trust-mistrust level. Inasmuch as they distrust the therapist, it is difficult to involve them in treatment. However, as we suggested in Chapter 6, when the client manifests a lot of difficulty with trust, it does seem advisable to provide him with a one-to-one relationship where the trust problem is best resolved.

THE PSYCHOPATHIC SPOUSE

The terms "psychopath," "sociopath," and "antisocial personality" are reserved for individuals who are basically unsocialized and whose behavior patterns bring them repeatedly into conflict with society. These people often appear to be incapable of significant loyalty to individuals, groups, or social values. They appear grossly selfish, callous, irresponsible and impulsive. Frustration tolerance is low and they tend to blame others or offer plausible rationalizations for their behavior (Diagnostic and Statistical Manual of Mental Disorders II, 1964).

The individual diagnosed as psychopathic frequently demonstrates superior intelligence and succeeds brilliantly for a while at work, studies, and human relationships. However, inevitably and repeatedly, he fails by losing his job, alienating his spouse, or provoking his family or friends. Seldom does this person find adequate motivation to explain why, in the midst of success, he grossly shirks his responsibilities and abandons his work at the behest of impulses that seem no more compelling than a trivial whim (Cleckley, 1959). Unreliability, untruthfulness, and insincerity are his distinguishing defenses. When the psychopath demonstrates no remorse or guilt and is confronted with the facts of his behavior, he is usually quite skillful at projecting blame on others (Fenichel, 1945; Freedman, Kaplan, Sadock, 1976; Glover, 1949).

Virtually every writer who has explored the problem of psychopathy has referred to the client's lack of remorse and guilt and has emphasized the apparent lacunae in his superego (Fenichel, 1945; Freedman, Kaplan, Sadock, 1976; Gaylin, 1976). Although there is much unanimity among writers that the psychopath is devoid of guilt feelings and has a weak, fragmented superego, certain phenomena that the typical psychopath exhibits makes this inference a questionable one (Strean, 1982).

Many clients who are diagnosed as psychopathic seem to have a wish to be punished. The psychopathic gambler may eventually be ruined, the arsonist caught, and the thief incarcerated. One of the dynamics that has been consistently observed in clients who have been assessed as "criminal psychopaths" is their feeling of relief when they are caught and punished. As an example of this, Freud described the "criminal out of a sense of guilt" (Freud, 1916). This is an individual who is so oppressed by a tyrannical superego that by becoming involved in provocative and illegal acts he finds comfort in being incarcerated. His punishment dissipates his guilt which almost always has an unconscious origin.

Many spouses are really "criminals out of a sense of guilt." They act out all kinds of hostility toward their marital partners with the hope that they will be punished. They are like angry children who wish to violate every rule that their parents impose, but they feel guilty about their antisocial behavior and unconsciously arrange to be reprimanded severely.

Recent psychobiographers, particularly those who are psychodynamically oriented, have agreed that many well known public figures in history who have been described as dishonest, callous, and ruthless have also harbored a strong sense of guilt. In the case of President Nixon, he acknowledged that the death of his brothers during his childhood left him with a strong sense of guilt and with a need to punish himself for harboring hostile and rivalrous feelings toward them (Johnson, 1979). In Nixon's book, *Six Crises,* he describes how he felt after incriminating Alger Hiss, a member of the United States State Department (Nixon, 1962, p. 37):

I should have been elated. However, I experienced a sense of let-down which is difficult to describe or even understand . . . There was also a sense of shock and sadness that a man like Hiss could have fallen so low: *I imagined myself in his place* . . . I realized that Hiss stood before us completely unmasked—our hearing had saved one life, but had ruined another. (Italics mine)

The quotation above seems to refer to Nixon's feeling of sadness, depression, and *guilt* after exposing Hiss. Some 25 years later, Nixon stood "unmasked" and "ruined" after he unconsciously arranged to expose his own guilt by producing tapes that revealed his own activities.

It would appear that the presence of guilt and the existence of a punitive superego has been overlooked and/or underestimated in the diagnosis and treatment of psychopathic clients. Actually the psychopathic client may be described as an individual who is at war with a strong, sadistic, punitive superego that constantly dominates him. He is similar to the child who feels overpowered by aggressively demanding parents and wants to rebel against their strict and punitive controls. His asocial, aggressive, callous, and impulsive behavior may be viewed as a defensive operation, that is, a rebellion against his punitive superego which he projects onto mate, family, colleagues, and society in general. Because the psychopath has an unloving superego, he feels that he must be punished for his antisocial activity; that is why he inevitably leaves traces of his misdeeds for others to see (Strean, 1982).

Mel H., age 30, was referred for therapy by a criminal court judge who felt that Mel's constant thefts, illegal manipulations, and sadistic assaults reflected "deep psychological problems." Mel, an attorney, initially showed no remorse when he discussed the fact that he had stolen money from his clients, was promiscuous and sadistic with women, neglected his wife, made false promises to colleagues, and abused his children. However, after 15 sessions of counseling, he asked his male therapist Dr. T., "Aren't you ready to throw me out for my lousy behavior?" When the meaning of Mel's question was explored with him by Dr. T., Mel pointed out that "in some peculiar way, I'd feel better if you thought little of me and *punished me for my sins*. When I am not punished I feel *a sense of uncertainty*."

Later in Mel's treatment he was able to identify the feeling of "constant guilt" for "gypping my brothers and father and being my mother's favorite"; "seducing teachers and fooling the other children"; and "being number one in my crowd, without deserving it." As Mel became aware of his oppressive superego which he used to punish himself for childhood fantasies and childhood deeds, he realized "how guilty I feel and have to do things to relieve it."

Although the psychopathic spouse very frequently enters the counseling situation in a state of defiance, this defiance has to be well understood by the therapist and related to empathically. The defiance is almost always an expression of rebellion against the therapist who is usually experienced as the client's punitive superego. If the therapist does not take the client's provocative remarks too literally or defensively, but instead helps the client see how he is asking for punishment, the client can involve himself in the counseling process.

Sally D., age 31, came for counseling because of severe marital problems, sexual promiscuity, difficulties with her children, constant arguments with parents, friends, and colleagues, stealing in stores, frigidity, obesity, and hay fever. In her initial consultation interview with Dr. H., a male therapist, she told the latter that she had been sexually seduced by three of her former male therapists. "I really try to do the therapeutic work. But, something happens and they want me sexually. I know it's of no help to screw your 'shrink', but they get to me," Sally lamented.

For her first six sessions, Sally seemed to take her therapy seriously. She examined fantasies, dreams, and history but did not make any references to Dr. H. In her seventh session she told him that she experienced him as cold, "just like my father." She asked, "Couldn't you be a little warmer? Couldn't you show some love?" When Dr. H. asked Sally what she was feeling that made her want some warmth from him, Sally raged, "That is a stupid question. It's like asking somebody who is thirsty why he wants water. You are a cold potato," she bellowed and walked out of the office.

In her next session, Sally apologized for her "performance" and "realized that you want to help me." She went on for several sessions to talk about how she always missed approval and warmth from her father "who was always out with the boys." In her thirteenth session of her once-a-week treatment—after telling Dr. H. how she still yearned for a father—she asked him to hold her for a brief moment "for some reassurance." On Dr. H.'s asking Sally what she was feeling and thinking that made her want some physical reassurance, Sally left the office immediately and said, "I'm leaving forever!"

Sally did not come for her next three sessions but did call Dr. H.'s office to curse him on his phone machine. During one of these calls, Dr. H. picked up the phone and, after a silence, Sally asked, "Will you still see me?" Dr. H. responded that he had been keeping Sally's hours open and would see her.

Sally came for her next appointment with a proposal. She would like to stop the counseling with Dr. H. because she was "not ripe for it." She would go into group therapy with another practitioner and become the therapist's friend. On being asked by Dr. H. what bothered her about being in counseling with him, Sally said, "I believe that I'm so beneath you. I can't stand your power over me. You seem like a big prick and I feel like a nothing that has been wiped out."

As Sally began to see how she was projecting her own ego ideal on to Dr. H.—an omnipotent phallus—and hating him for it, her sexual provocativeness decreased and she began to examine her rivalry with her husband, with Dr. H., and with men in general. It took her several years to resolve these problems but her marriage improved tremendously and virtually all of her presenting problems abated.

The psychopathic spouse is reminiscent of the rebellious spouse that we discussed at the beginning of this chapter. While both spouses rebel, the psychopathic spouse has a much more punitive superego and resorts to extreme antisocial behavior in order to cope with it. This client often alienates the therapist because his provocativeness is so intense. However, if the clinician keeps in mind that this client is behaving provocatively in order to be punished and eventually shows in his demeanor that he understands this dynamic—as Dr. H. did in the above case—the psychopathic spouse has a chance of enhancing his marriage.

All too often the psychopathic client is declared untreatable. This would appear to be a countertransference reaction that emanates from the therapist's anger and helplessness. Like a spouse with sadomasochistic problems, he can respond positively to an empathetic ear and a demeanor which says, "I want to understand you."

CHAPTER 8

Treating the Sexually Conflicted Spouse

No child escapes the Oedipus conflict; the "family romance" influences the love life of every adult in every society (Malinowski, 1963). By naming the central conflict of childhood after a Greek tragedy, Freud (1905) emphasized the universality of the Oedipus complex. While the theme of this developmental conflict is not always palatable to laymen and not always acceptable to professionals, ample verification of its existence is available by observing children's play (particularly children in play therapy), and by listening to adults' fantasies, dreams, and memories.

Fairy tales with oedipal themes have delighted the imaginations and gratified the wishes of children for generations (Marasse and Hart, 1975). Jack chopped down the beanstalk, killed the giant, and for many years afterward lived alone with his mother and relished being her conquering hero. Both Cinderella and Snow White were able to compete successfully with their stepmothers and marry handsome princes. A song that has been popular for many decades is "I Want a Girl Just Like the Girl that Married Dear Old Dad."

Resolving the Oedipus complex is not an easy task. On one hand, the child is drawn to the parent of the opposite sex and has strong yearnings to marry and have a child with that parent. On the other hand, as ubiquitous as oedipal wishes are, the incest taboo appears to be close to a universal phenomenon. In all 250 societies studied by the anthropologist George Murdock (1949), and in 200 of the societies examined by anthropologists Ford and Beach (1951), sexual intercourse and marriage are strictly forbidden between parents and children.

Compounding the impact of cultural restrictions on incestuous fantasies, most children are very fearful that they will be severely punished for their aggressive desires toward the parent of the same sex. Small children who want to wipe out their gigantic opponents are convinced that they will be destroyed for their hostile fantasies. Many childhood phobias are attributable to the child's fear of retaliation for his competitive desires. For example, children fear that a burglar will beat them, an animal hurt them, or a policeman incarcerate them.

In Freud's presentation of his five-year-old patient Little Hans (Freud, 1909), Hans was convinced that if he went out into the streets a horse would trample him to death. In love with his mother whom he wanted to penetrate with his "widdler," and in strong competition with his father whom he wanted to butt against the chest with his head and eventually annihilate, Hans found himself in a perplexing dilemma. He was in this dilemma because he also loved his father and feared his father's retaliation and withdrawal of love if the latter knew about Hans' hostile desires. Furthermore, Hans felt guilty about his incestuous desires toward his mother and was sure that these wishes also antagonized his father. Hans repressed his hostile feelings toward Father, displaced them onto horses, and feared the horses' retaliation. Because Hans had to avoid horses he also had to stop himself from going outdoors altogether because the streets of 1909 Vienna had horses everywhere. While he stayed at home he received the tender ministrations of his attractive mother and thereby gratified some of his incestuous desires.

Long before the advent of psychoanalytic theory, punishment for oedipal wishes was discussed in several places. In Sophocles' *Oedipus Rex* young Oedipus was punished for seducing his mother and killing his father; he was blinded for his transgressions. In the Old Testament there is frequent reference to the principle: "An eye for an eye and a tooth for a tooth." A common dream reported by children and adults for many centuries is one in which the dreamer has his teeth forcibly extracted—or if not forcibly extracted, they spontaneously fall out. When this type of dream is analyzed the dreamer inevitably feels deserving of punishment for sexual and aggressive wishes.

Many of the sexual, emotional, and interpersonal problems that husbands and wives bring to marriage counselors emanate from their unresolved oedipal conflicts. As we have implied in previous chapters, virtually every married person ascribes some parental qualities to the partner. When the partner is unconsciously experienced as a parent of the opposite sex, this activates many anxieties and many marital conflicts. If a man experiences his wife as his mother or a woman experiences her husband as her father, these individuals feel like guilty children each time they have sex with their partners. Many spouses who are celibate, impotent, or unable to achieve orgasm in sexual intercourse are punishing themselves for their incestuous wishes. Often, when there is a great deal of emotional distance between marital partners, the couple is working hard to prevent incestuous fantasies from erupting into consciousness.

As was have implied in earlier chapters, many who are in miserable marriages have experienced their wedding ceremony as an oedipal triumph. Their marital misery is their punishment for the damage they feel they have done. When men or women are chosen as "the one" they can unconsciously turn their successful wooing of their partners into a defeat of all their real and imagined rivals. Fantasizing that they have murdered, they have to wipe themselves out for their "evil deed." This is another reason why some cohabiting couples enjoy their relationship only until they get married. Marriage, when experienced by them as an oedipal triumph, has to be denigrated.

In previous chapters we have presented several vignettes in which the spouses were indulged as children. We pointed out that when a child is indulged he expects to be catered to by everybody, including his marital partner when he grows up. The son whose mother dotes over him and neglects her husband feels like an oedipal winner and later insists that his wife dote on him and pay little or no attention to anybody else. Similarly, when a father indulges his daughter she later expects indulgence from her husband; she becomes furious with him if he abdicates his responsibility to pay constant homage to "Her Majesty the Queen" (Neubauer, 1960).

In Chapter 3 we noted that when boys and girls experience considerable guilt over their oedipal desires there is a tendency to regress into a latent homosexual position. While this is a universal phenomenon, it is a temporary solution for most youngsters. However, when the anxiety emanating from forbidden oedipal wishes is strong, children can remain fixated in the latent homosexual position. As adults they question their sexual identities and in marriage they frequently need reassurance and support to buttress their shaky self-images. Many marital arguments take place because husbands and wives feel insufficiently appreciated by their partners. They feel their spouses do not provide them with enough reinforcement to minimize their doubts.

Although the extramarital affair and other forms of swinging and switching can be caused by one or more psychosexual conflicts, many couples use their affairs to cope with their oedipal conflicts. For example, if a man experiences his wife as a mother, he feels a lot more comfortable having sex with a woman who is not so reminiscent of "home and mother" (Strean, 1980).

Men and women who have not resolved their oedipal conflicts usually suffer from a great deal of anxiety for which they cannot account. Inasmuch as their competitive and incestuous fantasies are often unconscious, they do not relate their fears of impending doom, abandonment, mutilation or death to anything specific. They do, however, always prepare for something to go wrong.

Doug A., age 28, was in marriage counseling because he continually felt that his wife was going to leave him even though she had never threatened to do so. Furthermore, the fear of being rejected or abandoned also existed in Doug's work relationships; here, too, he had never been threatened with being fired.

It took Doug over two years of three-times-a-week therapy to realize that his conviction that some kind of disaster would inevitably befall him was related to his strong but unconscious competitive desires toward his father, for which he felt very guilty. Every time Doug enjoyed himself with his wife or anytime he achieved something worthwhile, he expected to be mutilated: That was what he fantasied doing to his father. When he focused on his competition more directly, his fear of impending doom diminished a great deal and he was able to derive more pleasure from his marriage.

Adults who have unresolved oedipal conflicts usually remain in a state of intense excitement. Although they are not consciously aware of it, they are in constant pursuit of the parent of the opposite sex and are in battle with the parent of the same sex. Inasmuch as these people frequently experience considerable anxiety and guilt, they spend much of their time placating others, ingratiating themselves, and trying to appear lovable. To compensate for their feelings of being "bad," "perverse," and "oversexed," they develop charm, imagination, and sensitivity. Their rich fantasy life serves as a refuge for their unpleasant reality which is devoid of real pleasure. Because these people are imaginative and full of fantasies, they are colorful conversationalists (Austin, 1958). Their many real strengths and abilities, combined with a defensive capacity to simulate more adequacy than they feel, often enable them to conceal their feelings of inferiority (Abraham, 1927).

In working therapeutically with husbands and wives with oedipal conflicts it is important for the therapist to recognize that underneath the current distress are feelings of vulnerable and anxious children. While these clients may give live and convincing examples of how their marital partners are insufficiently appreciative of them, the sensitive clinician is aware that their utterances emanate from fears of intimacy and inability to cope with success. Adult clients with oedipal conflicts turn their childhood phobias into sexual and interpersonal inhibitions in their marriages. Instead of worrying about a burglar beating them or an animal hurting them, they resist sexual and interpersonal closeness because the fantasies attached to these experiences are, in their minds, forbidden and punishable.

As the clinician works with "the child" in the clients under discussion, it is also important for him to avoid being seduced by their childish charm.

It is not difficult for the therapist to form a love-and-be-loved parent-child relationship with these clients that offers support and reassurance to them but does not help them resolve their marital conflicts.

Betty B., age 27, was in marriage counseling with Dr. Z., a female therapist. In a convincing manner Betty told Dr. Z. of many instances in which she was "very giving" to her husband Chuck who she described as "a cold potato." Not recognizing that underneath Betty's chronic complaint was a wish to have a cold husband, Dr. Z. overidentified with Betty and oversympathized with her plight. After just three or four sessions with her, Dr. Z. told Betty that she realized how discouraging it was to be ready and able to have an intimate relationship with Chuck while he was so very unwilling to do the same.

Dr. Z.'s stance added fuel to Betty's fire and she used Dr. Z.'s statements to continue to criticize Chuck. She told him that her therapist agreed that he was "a cold potato." This only antagonized Chuck further and he withdrew more and more. When Chuck threatened to leave Betty, she became very frightened and left Dr. Z. to go into conjoint therapy under another practitioner.

It is, of course, a frequent happenstance for a client to use the therapist against the marital partner. When the therapist notes that this is occurring, he has two tasks to perform. First, he must ask himself if anything in his own attitude prompted the client to use him as a weapon against the partner. If this is so, the therapist must analyze his own countertransference problems so that he can adopt a more neutral attitude and be more therapeutically helpful. Second, the therapist must investigate what the client is feeling in the marriage and in the transference relationship with the therapist that activates the client's self-destructive behavior.

Barry C., age 32, was in treatment with Mr. Y. Each week he reported to Mr. Y. that after their sessions he felt stronger and more capable of dealing with his wife Karen. Since this became a habitual pattern of Barry's, Mr. Y. felt that it had some latent meaning. Therefore, Mr. Y. asked Barry "What do you suppose is taking place between you and me that makes you feel stronger and more capable after each appointment?" Barry had an interesting response. Animatedly he told Mr. Y. that his conception of marriage counseling was "to gain an ally to fight the enemy." Barry said triumphantly, "You are my ally and Karen is the enemy!"

In further therapy sessions it became clear that Barry wanted very little else from his marriage other than to fight successfully with Karen.

He compared Karen to his "enveloping mother" who "intimidated" him. With Mr. Y.'s help Barry was eventually able to see that he was fighting an old battle with his mother. He later realized that he was as afraid to love Karen as he had been about his erotic feelings toward his mother. His fighting was a defense against intimacy.

Mr. Y. avoided siding with Barry against Karen. Instead, he helped him to see *why* he wanted to fight with her and *why* he wanted his therapist to join him in the fight. Therefore, Barry was able to enhance his relationship with Karen rather than try to defeat it.

Many clients tend to view marriage counseling as an opportunity to find an ally to help them fight their partners and/or get permission to divorce them rather than as an opportunity to understand themselves and their marital interactions better. This tends to occur more often with husbands and wives who have oedipal conflicts. Like Barry C. in the above illustration, these clients are frightened to love their partners. In addition, many of them have witnessed fighting between their own parents with whom they have unconsciously identified. Particularly when clients were members of a divorced or separated family do they feel that marriage counseling provides an arena to mobilize for their own divorce or separation. As we have pointed out several times, the empathetic and responsible clinician rarely prescribes divorce or separation. He tries to help his clients make their own decisions and choose their own life-styles through helping them increase their own self-awareness.

Harry and Sadie D., a couple in their early forties, applied for conjoint therapy because they both wanted a divorce but were afraid of the impact it would have on their two children, ages five and six. In their intake interview with Ms. W. at a mental hygiene clinic, Harry and Sadie mentioned that both of them were products of broken homes and both had suffered when their own parents had divorced. On Ms. W.'s empathizing with their plight and pointing out that although they both wanted a divorce they both seemed frightened of the consequences, Harry—and later Sadie—verbalized a great deal of surprise. They were both sure that divorce was the only solution to their marital conflicts; they were pleased that they could examine their mixed feelings about it with one another and Ms. W. and come to a decision later. After a year-and-a-half of marriage counseling, they decided to remain together.

On the other hand, some couples—because divorce is such a terribly painful idea to them—think marriage counseling exists solely to cement relationships and prevent divorce. The disciplined therapist should help his clients consider all their alternatives and all their fantasies without taking a stand himself.

Matt and Emily E., a couple in their mid-thirties who were also products of broken homes, sought marriage counseling because they were busily fighting with each other almost daily. Their fracases were both verbal and physical.

When Mr. V., their therapist, asked them in their sixth session if they had ever fantasied divorce, they responded with a long silence. As the meaning of their silence was explored it turned out that both Matt and Emily had each fantasied divorce many times but were frightened to admit it to themselves and to each other. Mr. V., in effect, gave them permission to look at their feelings and fantasies about divorce. As a result they both became freer in communicating with each other and with Mr. V.

After two years of marriage counseling in which the E.'s examined a number of alternatives and many of their thoughts, feelings, fantasies, and memories, they mutually decided to divorce amicably. In the process, Mr. V. did not encourage them or discourage them to take a particular path. His neutrality helped them make a decision which appeared correct to them.

As in previous chapters, we will look at some of the therapeutic principles involved in treating different forms of marital distress now under consideration. There are several forms of marital dysfunctioning that oedipal conflicts take. Let us first look at perhaps the most common problem, the spouse who has to fail—that is, the oedipal loser—and discuss some therapeutic issues that are pertinent to counseling him.

THE OEDIPAL LOSER

As we have already indicated many men and women cannot stand success of any kind. To them, success is unconsciously equated with the destruction of someone; in marriage it means that they have hostilely triumphed over the parent of the same sex. They would prefer to destroy their own marriage rather than feel destructive toward their parents.

When clients want to be losers in marriage and elsewhere they try to lose, albeit unconsciously, in their therapy. On hearing about a modus vivendi from their clients in which initiative is inhibited, success is shunned, and defeat is ever-present, the practitioner can legitimately hypothesize that these clients will unconsciously strive to make therapy a failure.

The oedipal loser is not one who comes in overtly competing with or denigrating the therapist. On the contrary, this client appears compliant, cooperative, and conciliatory. There is even a tendency on his part to idealize the therapist. However, he rarely seems to make much progress in bettering his marriage. The same sexual problems recur, the same marital arguments ensue, and the same overall discouragement prevails.

If we recall Erikson's notion that the oedipal loser resists taking initiative but is more comfortable feeling inferior (Erikson, 1950), it should not surprise us that the oedipal loser unconsciously strives to feel inferior in both therapy and marriage. To take in the therapist's interpretations and enhance his life is a crime. He must maintain his defeated position.

Unless the therapist helps the client see how he sabotages his therapy, little progress can ensue.

Gloria F., age 37, had been in treatment with Dr. R., a female practitioner, for over two years on a twice-weekly basis. She entered treatment because she felt very depressed about her relationship with her husband, Erik. "We don't communicate well, we don't enjoy sex with each other, and our life is quite mundane," Gloria lamented. She also pointed out that while she and Erik had had an enjoyable courtship, their 12-year marriage could be characterized by "dullness and a lack of vitality."

In reviewing her history, Gloria was able to recognize strong loving feelings toward her father and a subtle but real competition with her mother. Yet despite the fact that she was able to see that she kept punishing herself for her oedipal conflicts in marriage and elsewhere, and although she recognized that this conflict emerged in her life prior to her marriage, she seemed to stay fixed in her misery.

Dr. R. was sensitive to the fact that when a client does not make therapeutic progress there is always a transference issue that is not being faced. Consequently, Dr. R. suggested to Gloria, "There must be something going on between you and me that stops you from feeling better and functioning better." Gloria denied that there "was anything negative" going on between her and Dr. R. As a matter of fact, she began to extol Dr. R. and told her what a wonderful person she was, that she was sensitive, kind, and very humane.

When Dr. R. remained silent after Gloria verbalized these compliments, Gloria began to cry. She felt very sad that she couldn't "please" Dr. R. and demeaned herself, saying that she was a poor patient. As Gloria proceeded to demean herself more and more it became clear to Dr. R. that Gloria was also seeking some reassurance and hoping that Dr. R. would tell her that she wasn't such a bad client after all. However, when the reassurance was not forthcoming Gloria, for the first time in her therapy, began to express some irritation with Dr. R. She told Dr. R. that she was starting to remind her of her mother whose love she wanted but never received. She felt that her therapy was becoming more and more reminiscent of her childhood years when she tried hard "to be a compliant girl and did not get sufficiently reinforced."

As Gloria began to take some initiative with Dr. R., aggress toward her at times, and compete with her occasionally, her self-esteem rose. Inasmuch as Dr. R. did not retaliate or become defensive as Gloria attacked her, Gloria felt quite safe with her newfound strengths. Slowly she began to have fantasies of competing with Dr. R. for men. She began to consider how, in some ways, she was superior to Dr. R. and could even acknowledge that at times she thought she looked more attractive than her therapist and that she dressed more stylishly.

The more Dr. R. helped Gloria feel freer to feel like a winner with her, the less Gloria had to be a loser in her marriage and elsewhere. When she faced her oedipal conflicts in her transference relationship with Dr. R. her marriage improved.

Dr. R., in reviewing her work with Gloria, realized that in the initial stages of the marriage counseling she had enjoyed basking in Gloria's love and admiration. This prevented Gloria's latent hostility toward a mother figure from emerging. As a result the loved-and-be-loved therapeutic relationship prevented Gloria from taking initiative with Dr. R., and sustained her conviction that she was an inferior client.

If the client's oedipal conflicts make him feel like a loser in marriage, then his feeling of inferiority next to the therapist will be a paramount issue in his treatment. Some practitioners mistakenly believe that the way to help the client overcome his feelings of inferiority is to compliment him, support him, and encourage him. This approach does not help the client. He feels inferior because he punishes himself for his hostile and murderous thoughts. Because of his guilt, he has to denigrate himself. If he is complimented he feels worse because it is his conviction that he does not deserve praise.

When a client arranges to be an oedipal loser, nothing will help him more than to face his hostility and competition in the transference relationship with the therapist and to see that being the therapist's equal does not mean the end of the world. If the therapist does not help the client aggress toward him it may mean the end of treatment.

Boris G., age 34, had been in treatment with Dr. P., a male therapist, for about a year on a twice-weekly basis. Boris sought treatment because he saw himself as "a scapegoat" in his marriage, at work, and in most of his friendships. His history revealed that in his own family he felt inferior to his older brothers and like "a cast-off" as far as his parents were concerned. Sensing his deep feelings of inferiority and his low self-esteem, Dr. P. felt that Boris needed "ego-supportive therapy." Dr. P. tried to sensitize himself to Boris's strengths. When he found something that Boris did well, he praised him. While at first Boris responded positively to Dr. P.'s approach, after a few months of treatment he began to feel uncomfortable and questioned Dr. P.'s approach.

Instead of helping Boris disagree with him and aggress toward him by listening to his questions (which contained latent criticisms), Dr. P. told Boris that he was so accustomed to feeling rejected by his wife and others that he found it difficult to accept Dr. P.'s praise. While Boris acknowledged that Dr. P. "may have a point," he felt quite strongly that Dr. P. really did not understand him. Feeling more and more misunderstood, he finally left Dr. P. and went to another therapist.

The rejected, inferior status that the oedipal loser assigns to himself protects him against wishes to reject others and to surpass them. Unless this issue is directly faced in his treatment, the oedipal loser feels misunderstood by the practitioner and has to leave therapy.

Inasmuch as the oedipal loser is so frightened of his aggression, he is prone to take a very passive role with the therapist. He is the client who often asks for advice, poses questions, and wants reassurance. To answer his questions or reinforce his decisions only strengthens his passive, inferior position and does not help him resolve his marital conflicts. The client will be able to overcome his dysfunctional adaptation to his marriage and to the rest of the world only if the therapist withholds gratification of his requests and helps him look at why he is making the therapist the dominating boss.

Harriet H., age 40, was in marriage counseling with Dr. O., a male therapist. She sought help because she found herself feeling "empty" in her marriage, "unfulfilled" in her work, and "uncomfortable" in her relationships with her friends. She also found it burdensome to cope with her two daughters, ages 7 and 10.

In reviewing her history, Harriet talked a great deal about not feeling accepted by either of her parents. In addition, she often felt that her older sister was favored by them. However, as treatment went on it turned out that her parents had indulged Harriet a great deal and that her father had constantly referred to her as "my favorite princess." Father and Harriet seemed to have a mini-love affair going on well into her late adolescence. However, when Harriet was 17, her father suddenly died of a heart attack. Harriet withdrew, became very depressed, and consciously wondered if she had done something to cause her father's death.

From the age of 17 on, Harriet was quite unassertive, passive, and phobic. She felt as if any form of assertiveness or initiative on her part could lead to something disastrous—like her father's death. Consequently, she became very passive in all of her interpersonal relationships. She dated boys only if they sought her out, but she had to keep herself almost hidden most of the time. She married Ike because he seemed to "take the lead in relationships" and she thought he would be "a good guide."

In her treatment with Dr. O. Harriet constantly sought reassurance and advice. When Dr. O. encouraged Harriet to examine what she was feeling and thinking when she wanted him to be her guide and to take the lead, she became more and more helpless and more and more depressed. She lost sleep, started to stammer, and showed directly and indirectly that since she had begun counseling with Dr. O., she had been feeling and functioning much worse.

On Dr. O.'s pointing out to Harriet that there must be something upsetting to her about their work, Harriet's initial response was to deny that she was reacting negatively to Dr. O. and to the treatment. However, when Dr. O. remained silent in the face of Harriet's efforts to placate him, Harriet's tone changed. She began to realize that the depressed feeling that she was currently experiencing was similar to the one she felt when her father had died. "But," she said to Dr. O., "You are not dead. Yet, I'm responding to you as if you were." With a little help from Dr. O. Harriet could talk about wanting to arrange for Dr. O.'s death in the same way that she had secretly wanted her father dead at times. The reason for her wanting Father and Dr. O. dead was because with both men she thought she could be their princess "but neither of you came through for me."

As Harriet faced some of her death wishes she did not need to maintain her passivity so much. As a result she did not have to be as inhibited in her marriage and began to enjoy Ike more.

Unless the clinician is willing to withhold answers to questions and refrain from offering advice, reassurance, praise, and support, the oedipal loser will remain a loser in his marriage, in his therapy, and in his life. He needs to have an experience in the treatment encounter where his passivity, lack of initiative, indecisiveness, and compliant attitude get little or no reinforcement. When the therapist maintains his neutrality and does not become a directing parent, the oedipal loser slowly begins to take initiative and starts to assert himself in his marriage and out of it.

THE OEDIPAL WINNER

Although we live in a society in which winners are admired and are supposed to live happily ever after, oedipal winners—like oedipal losers—do have difficulties in marriage. The oedipal winner is the son or daughter who was mother's or father's favorite. However, in contrast to the oedipal loser, his or her position of being "the one and only" was rarely challenged. Often the son and the mother or the daughter and the father did such things together in the absence of the other parent as going to the movies, shopping, going out to dinner, or talking together for hours at a time. Inevitably the love affair between the young person and the parent of the opposite sex involved discussions in which the other parent was criticized, derided, and demeaned. In many instances the oedipal winner turns out to be an individual who has lived alone with the parent of the opposite sex because either the other parent died or the parents divorced.

When children get many of their oedipal fantasies gratified they can become omnipotent, narcissistic individuals who are highly motivated to compete and win. They are usually unable to tolerate a loss or a defeat of any kind. If they get less than an A in an examination, they are indignant and will point out to the examiner that the latter has clearly erred. In his teenage years, and later years as well, the oedipal winner is drawn to triangles—relationships with the opposite sex where there is always a rival to be bested. Very often the marital partner of the oedipal winner is one who was very much involved in a relationship with someone else but whom the oedipal winner pursued until he vanquished his opponent and won the prize.

The oedipal winner, accustomed to participating in psychological duels and winning them, is far from the easiest spouse with whom to live. He is a difficult marital partner for several reasons. First, oedipal winners are so used to being treated as "His Majesty" or "Her Majesty" that they find it very uncomfortable to be in any situation with their mates unless most of the attention is heaped upon them. If their mate or someone else is the center of attention they become very angry or very depressed. Second, oedipal winners experience much discomfort in taking care of domestic chores. This is much too humiliating an activity for people who want to be treated as royalty. Finally, because oedipal winners are motivated to compete and to win battles, they often tire of their marriages and look for new competitors to best and new partners to woo.

The oedipal winner rarely seeks marriage counseling on his own. If he becomes a client it is usually because a physician or an attorney has insisted on it. As far as the oedipal winner is concerned, he has no neurotic problems of his own; his marital tension exists because his partner is not capable of meeting the legitimate needs of an outstanding person.

Inasmuch as the oedipal winner appears quite arrogant, belittling, and self-sufficient, he can induce strong countertransference reactions in the practitioner. Feeling demeaned by him, some practitioners cope with their anxiety by directly or indirectly trying to put the client in his place—which is off the throne and on to a chair that is for all people, not one that's just fit for a king or queen. This attitude, while understandable, only compounds the oedipal winner's resistance to counseling and only strengthens his narcissistic orientation to his mate and to the therapist.

Scott I., age 36, was referred by his physician to Ms. N. for marriage counseling. His physician had actually responded to Scott's wife Bernice, who had pleaded for help. Scott was physically beating Bernice frequently, going out with other women constantly, and almost always neglecting his family responsibilities.

When Scott met Ms. N. he immediately denied his need for therapeutic help and told her that "it was very clear that Bernice was in dire need of help because of her severe pathology and her powerful immaturity." Ms. N., not realizing how threatened Scott felt because his narcissism had been punctured by the referral and not understanding why he had to project the marital problems onto Bernice, seemed to respond solely to Scott's overt smugness and said to him, "But why do you think your doctor wanted *you* to see me?" Calmly Scott stated, "So that you can get a full picture of Bernice from the person who knows her better than anyone else."

Feeling frustrated by his denials, projections, and refusals to take any responsibility for his marital problems, and under the guise of showing Scott some reality, Ms. N. attacked him. She told him that she was aware of his beating his wife physically and verbally. She also mentioned that she was aware of his extramarital affairs and she knew that Scott neglected his family. To these remarks of Ms. N., Scott said, "You seem very upset, Ms. N. What do you suppose is bothering you?" Feeling even more infuriated now, Ms. N. could hardly control herself from yelling at her client. What she did say was, "You seem to be more concerned about other people's problems than looking at your own." Scott answered, "No, you are in error, Ms. N. That's clearly your problem. I realize that Bernice will need someone else to help her. You lack the competence and maturity that she needs." He then left the interview and never returned.

From the above case of Scott I. we see that the oedipal winner can be a very frustrating client. Unready and unwilling to be in any position other than the dominant one, he does not want to talk about his own problems. He is only ready to look at his partner's psychological difficulties or his therapist's countertransference problems. He seems to require enormous patience and tolerance. Otherwise, he will have nothing to do with therapy or the therapist.

As we have suggested several times in earlier chapters, a client's resistance to treatment—no matter what form it takes—must be respected by the clinician. Otherwise his anxiety intensifies, and he leaves therapy to lessen his discomfort. Oedipal winners, because they are very narcissistic individuals, need someone who will listen to them without challenging their defenses. If they wish to talk about what is wrong with their mates, or what is wrong with their therapists, the sensitive and helpful clinician permits them to do so. Only through this kind of an attitude will a therapeutic alliance be formed and only through this kind of a perspective will the client eventually accept some help.

Mary J., age 26, was referred to Dr. M., a male therapist, by her attorney. Mary had sought an attorney because she needed his help in effecting a divorce. The attorney, quite convinced that Mary was an immature individual, thought it would be a good idea for Mary to talk over her feelings with Dr. M. before going through with the legal work. To motivate Mary to see Dr. M.—which she was quite reluctant to do—he told her that it had been his experience that if one talked through feelings first a divorce was easier to arrange and easier to cope with.

When Mary met Dr. M. she appeared very attractive and very charming. Clearly eager to have Dr. M. as an ally she told him that he'd probably met a lot of women who had been victimized and that her story was not a new one to him. On Dr. M.'s asking how Mary had been victimized, Mary evaded his question. She went on to describe how her husband of two years, Ned, was insufficiently appreciative of her. "He only gets me flowers once a week," lamented Mary and continued with further complaints: "He compliments me very rarely—maybe once a day . . . We go out for dinner once in a blue moon—maybe once every two weeks."

As Dr. M. listened to Mary without commenting too much, Mary eventually asked him if her "expectations from marriage were too high." Dr. M. did not give her a direct answer but asked, "As we've been talking about your marriage, have you had that impression?" Here, Mary got quite annoyed with Dr. M. and told him that she had heard and read about "Freudian shrinks" who answer questions with questions. She further told Dr. M. that as far as "expectations from a therapist are concerned," she certainly believed that she had "a right to hear his impressions." Here Dr. M. said, "I'm like your husband. I don't give you enough. I let you down." Mary agreed and said that ever since she got married she had been running into a lot of bad luck. First she got a lousy husband and then a lousy therapist.

Mary contrasted the treatment she was receiving from Dr. M. with the way her father had treated her during her childhood and adolescence.

Stated Mary, "He gave me everything I wanted. He never frustrated me. I was his favorite." On Dr. M. pointing out that it must infuriate her that he, Dr. M., was not always available to her—that he had other clients— and that Ned was busy at work much of the time, Mary agreed. She brought out that because her father had owned a restaurant near her home she had seen him almost anytime she had wanted. Furthermore, whenever Mary had entered her father's restaurant her father stopped whatever he was doing and spent time with her.

While Mary was talking about her love affair with her father and simultaneously relating to her own sexual and interpersonal dissatisfactions with her husband, she became seductive with Dr. M. She told Dr. M. after six months of once-a-week counseling that after reviewing her history and after thinking about her marriage she needed someone like Dr. M. to hug her and to hold her. When Dr. M. did not gratify Mary's wishes but tried to explore what she was feeling and thinking that prompted her requests, Mary became very indignant. She told Dr. M. that he was just like Ned—always frustrating her and never appreciating her needs. Just as she threatened to break up her marriage, she threatened to end the therapy.

As Dr. M. listened to Mary's vitriolic accusations without retaliating, and as he listened to her wishes to be held and to be hugged without gratifying her, Mary slowly began to realize how much she was trying to be "Daddy's little girl" and that anything else felt "so second best." Eventually she could see that indeed her expectations about marriage and therapy were very high and unrealistic. But her omnipotent, narcissistic attitude often taxed Dr. M.'s patience. It took over three years of treatment before Mary really considered giving up her extreme demandingness. On many occasions Dr. M. felt like telling Mary that she was a spoiled brat. However, he controlled himself, realizing that her demands were ones he had to renounce in himself and that made him envious of her from time to time. The more he realized that what he could not tolerate in Mary was something in himself that was hard to face, the more he could compassionately relate to Mary's sexual and emotional problems and eventually help her to enjoy her marriage.

Oedipal winners are very competitive people. As we have observed in some of the cases we have discussed in this section, they are going to compete with their therapists, particularly if their therapists are members of the same sex. Counseling frequently becomes an overt battle for oedipal winners. If they think that treatment is helping them they feel humiliated and destroyed by a therapist who has been triumphant and victorious. Therefore, the oedipal winner wants his therapist to become a loser.

Some therapists respond to the oedipal winner's competitiveness by becoming intimidated. They end up feeling defeated. Other clinicians who are more openly competitive themselves can get into an intense power struggle with the client. This seemed to be the issue, to some extent, with Ms. N. in the case of Scott I., presented earlier in this chapter.

It is difficult but necessary for the clinician to remain neutral in the face of the oedipal winner's efforts to defeat him and the therapy. If the clinician submits to the client's provocations, the client will end up feeling contemptuous of him and will leave treatment. If the therapist engages the client in verbal battles, the client will also leave treatment and use his termination of therapy as a major weapon to render the therapist impotent.

The oedipal winner needs a therapist who confronts him with his wish to compete without competing. In effect, he should be a parental figure who says to his symbolic child, "I know you want to fight with me and perhaps even want to destroy me. However, I will not retaliate. Instead, I will try to help you understand why you want to hold on to your feverish desire to engage in feverish battles."

Fred K., age 32, was in marriage counseling with Dr. L., a male therapist. From the initiation of their contact, Fred made Dr. L. his enemy and Fred's wish to do battle with and defeat Dr. L. took many forms. In the early part of treatment Fred constantly questioned Dr. L.'s orientation to therapy and told him that he questioned his approach to counseling because there were so many different types of treatment. "How do I know I'm with the right guy?" Fred constantly asked. Dr. L. suggested to Fred that he seemed to have many doubts about him and the way he conducted treatment. He asked Fred what his doubts were, and Fred became very sarcastic, saying to Dr. L., "You won't admit that you are a fraud, will you, Freud?" On saying that Fred thought there was something fraudulent about him and asked what it was, Fred told Dr. L., "The main thing is you won't admit that you are a fraud. Why don't you come out with it?" Again, Dr. L. tried to get Fred to say what he felt was fraudulent about him and again Fred said, "Come up with it; you know." Here, Dr. L. said, "Maybe you know what's fraudulent about me?" To this Fred said that what seemed to be fraudulent about Dr. L. was his never getting angry. "I'm suspicious of you because behind your friendly mask is an angry, pompous ass," Fred bellowed in his twentieth session of once-a-week treatment.

Realizing that Fred was projecting his own arrogance and grandiosity on to him, Dr. L. felt it would be helpful to have Fred analyze Dr. L.'s "pomposity." Fred told Dr. L. that he seemed "to be a guy who always had his own way." He critically told him, "All your life you've wanted to be on top. Whenever you meet a challenger like me, you get very upset. You know damn well you'd like to fight back but you are scared I'll put you down!"

When Dr. L. suggested that what might be fraudulent about him was not only his wish to fight but his refusal to admit that he was frightened of being defeated, Fred laughed with pleasure. "Now you got it, you S.O.B.! You are frightened of me. Admit it! Admit it!" When Dr. L. asked what it would do for Fred if he admitted he was frightened of him, Fred became very pensive. Reluctantly he admitted that he, himself, was frightened of ever being a loser and assumed Dr. L. felt the same way. Eventually he was able to talk about his relationships with his father and other men toward whom he always felt "smug" but also worried that maybe they could put him down.

While it took three years of treatment for Fred to recognize that almost every day he was reenacting a childhood wish to defeat every father figure around him and therefore was always having to "stand guard," he was able to integrate this understanding into his marriage and into the rest of his life. As his own wish to fight and destroy receded, he had more energy available to enjoy his wife and children. At the end of his treatment he thanked Dr. L. by saying, "You never fought with me. You were never cowered by me. You hung in there and that's what I needed."

The oedipal winner, if marriage counseling is to be effective for him, must get in touch with the fact that he is devoting so much effort to fighting that he has little energy remaining to enjoy his marriage and to take pleasure from the rest of life. The therapist should not try to puncture his narcissism but should try to stay outside his battle and help the client see why he needs to fight so much. This is what seemed to help Fred F. in the case above.

THE SPOUSE WITH IDENTITY PROBLEMS

In Chapter 3 we saw that children can become very frightened of their oedipal wishes and regress. One way of coping with the anxiety that incestuous and murderous wishes provoke is to submit to the parent of the same sex and renounce erotic yearnings toward the parent of the opposite sex. While submission to the parent of the same sex wards off anxiety and limits fears of retaliation, it is uncomfortable for most youngsters to face their homosexual fantasies. For example, when a boy renounces his competition toward his father and wants to be his lover instead, or a girl does the same thing with her mother, these youngsters are not that comfortable when they feel forced to repress and deny their heterosexuality (Jacobson, 1956).

If youngsters are unable to overcome their regressed state and need to maintain their latent homosexual orientation, they become anxious adults. They are constantly preoccupied with the fear of being exposed as inadequate males or inadequate females. The male Don Juan and the woman who is sexually promiscuous are frequently individuals who are trying to buttress their shaky sexual identities (Fenichel, 1945). When these individuals marry they need enormous reassurance from their partners that, indeed, they are full-fledged men and women.

What complicates the marital interaction of a spouse who has a shaky sexual identity is that frequently he is married to someone who has a similar problem (Kubie, 1956). As we have pointed out in Chapter 2 and reiterated several times throughout this text, individuals with similar psychological conflicts and with similar levels of maturational development are attracted to one another and often marry—for better or for worse. What seems to worsen the marriages of couples who have uncertainties about their sexuality is that they constantly reprimand one another for not appreciating their virtues and competencies as men or women. Husbands accuse wives of being too castrating and wives accuse husbands of being unsupportive and unappreciative of their femininity. Neither seems able to face his own self-doubts.

When the spouse that we are discussing enters marriage counseling, he is very quick to center the discussion on his mate's inadequacies. He tells the counselor that his lack of sexual desire, his chronic anger, his depression, and his feeling of emptiness is due to his mate's uncompromising and unloving attitude. Because he experiences himself as a victim of circumstances, he is prone to ask the practitioner to manipulate his environment. He may demand that in lieu of himself his mate should be seen for counseling; he may suggest that a different treatment modality be considered, or he may ask for advice on how to get better emotional responses from his mate.

In work with the spouse with a shaky sexual identity, it is important for the clinician to once again remind himself that beneath this client's chronic complaints are unconscious wishes to keep the mate just the way he or she is described. The husband who describes his wife as castrating needs such a wife. A warm, responsive, sexual woman would activate his forbidden incestuous desires and his frightening competitive wishes. The wife who complains that her husband lacks tenderness needs such a man. If he behaved warmly and tenderly, she would feel anxious and guilty. Consequently, in helping this tormented spouse, the therapist must not be too ready to comply with the client's demands nor be too influenced by the client's complaints. Rather, the clinician is most helpful to this client if he empathically listens and waits until the client's marital complaints are brought into the transference relationship with the therapist. When the client begins to see that his dissatisfactions with his mate and with his therapist are similar, he may begin to acknowledge that his marital problems are in many ways internal. He may then be able to see them as part and parcel of his neurotic modus vivendi which took form long before he was married.

Moe L., age 40, was referred for treatment by his physician. Moe had ulcers, headaches, a lack of sexual desire, and insomnia. In talking to his physician about his difficulties he mentioned that he found himself in constant arguments with his wife, Bessie. Therefore, the physician referred him to Dr. K., a male therapist.

During his first few sessions with Dr. K., Moe complained a great deal about Bessie. He talked about her coldness, her derogatory attitude, and her lack of interest in sex. When Dr. K. patiently listened to Moe without supporting him in his complaints or criticizing him for them, Moe became restless and anxious in the interviews. He wondered whether it would not be better for Dr. K. "to try a different approach." On being asked by Dr. K. what he thought would be a better approach, Moe told Dr. K. that he should interview Bessie. He said that she "needs to be dressed down and told what a bitch she is." Dr. K. said, "I guess you'd like me to tell her off," and Moe agreed.

As therapist and client explored how it would help Moe if Dr. K. told Bessie off, Moe again became quite anxious. He stated that he himself had tried to tell her off on frequent occasions but "it didn't work too well." Moe went on to say that he was now feeling very helpless with Dr. K. and as he thought about it, it was the same uncomfortable feeling that he often had with Bessie. After a few moments of silence he said to Dr. K., "I guess I need some reassurance from you. I believe I need to be told I'm not a sad sack. Tell me I'm your equal." Here Dr. K. pointed out that what Moe wanted from him seemed to be almost the same as what he so frequently desired from his wife.

Moe, after two months of twice-a-week treatment, began to talk about those doubts which activated his wish for reassurance. He realized that he "never felt like a potent man." He started to recall "bitter arguments" with his father that always ended up with Moe feeling "remorseful and like a loser with my tail between my legs."

As Moe examined his relationship with his father he became sensitive to his own ambivalence toward him. In one interview during his eighth month of treatment Moe said, "I hated my father but I also loved him. I got scared of my hatred and started to lick his ass instead. But that idea didn't make me feel very good so I tried arguing some more. I think I should write a play, 'Life Without Father—A Vicious Cycle.' "

On feeling and expressing his intense ambivalence toward his father, Moe began to feel the same ambivalence in his relationship with Dr. K. From time to time he wanted to argue with Dr. K., and he did try it a few times. On one occasion he told Dr. K. that he thought therapy was like a religion and that a therapist was a guru; he elaborated on that theme in several sessions. Of course Dr. K. did not argue back but did point out to Moe that the notion of therapy being a religion and of the therapist being a guru sounded similar to the way he felt he had to relate to his father, that is, submit to a god. While Moe agreed with Dr. K.'s interpretation, he also was worried about hurting Dr. K. with his criticisms. Because he was still frightened of his aggression, Moe had to placate Dr. K. He went back and forth for several months in feeling positively and negatively toward the therapist. Sometimes he would have fantasies of hugging and kissing Dr. K. and sometimes he would dream of maiming him. As Moe accepted both parts of himself with less anxiety, he began to feel stronger and started discussing his sexual feelings toward women, particularly toward Bessie and toward his mother.

As Dr. K. anticipated, Moe had a great deal of guilt about his erotic feelings toward Bessie and toward other women because he unconsciously made them his mother. However, as he could share his incestuous feelings with Dr. K. in an atmosphere of safety, he slowly began to feel more comfortable with Bessie. As we have seen in other cases, Bessie became quite threatened by Moe's more potent demeanor and tried to undo it. However, with Dr. K.'s help Moe saw Bessie more objectively and helped her get therapeutic help for herself.

Moe's therapy took four years and Bessie's two before both of them felt more loving toward each other as man and woman.

When husbands and wives with conflicted sexual identities are in treatment with a therapist of the opposite sex, they may try to use the therapist as a sexual object who will reassure them of their doubts by falling in love with them. Sometimes therapists become convinced that the way to help clients who can't like themselves as men and women is to show interest in them sexually. If, for example, a woman in marriage counseling does not think she is attractive, it is recommended by some clinicians that it would be therapeutic for a male therapist to tell her that she is attractive. And, as we indicated earlier, some therapists have gone so far as to prescribe sexual relations between therapist and client as a means of enhancing the client's self-esteem and buttressing the client's sexual identity.

What is sometimes difficult for some clients and some therapists to understand is that when somebody has doubts about his or her sexual identity, all of the compliments and all of the reassurance in the world will not alleviate these doubts. As soon as the reassurer leaves the scene for a moment, the client's doubts reappear.

It should also be borne in mind that when clients have serious questions about how really adequate they are as men and women, they become extremely dubious about the sincerity and the competency of one who flatters them, expresses sexual interest in them, or has sex with them. Usually this form of treatment ends up with the client feeling betrayed (Freeman and Roy, 1976).

Rose M., age 32, was in marriage counseling with Dr. J., a male therapist. Rose sought therapeutic help for several reasons: She was completely uninterested in sex with her husband to whom she was married for four years; she felt "depressed," "empty," and "disgusting" most of the time; she went on eating binges from time to time and then felt guilty afterwards.

In talking about her history Rose described intensely ambivalent relationships with both of her parents and with her older brother. She told Dr. J. that throughout her childhood and adolescence she always questioned how lovable she was and never felt genuinely accepted by family members or friends.

After Rose had been seeing Dr. J. for two months on a twice-a-week basis, she told him how much she appreciated his interest in her and how much better she was feeling since she had begun counseling with him. She said that she had not gone on one eating binge, was feeling much less depressed, and was feeling much less empty. However, she also told Dr. J. that she could not seem to get interested in sex.

As Rose went on to discuss her inability to enjoy sex, she smiled at Dr. J. and eyed him amorously. Dr. J. clearly felt narcissistically gratified by Rose's therapeutic improvement as well as with her obvious sexual interest in him. Under the guise of "exploring the transference," Dr. J. asked Rose how she thought sex with him might be. Rose blushed, laughed nervously, and blurted out, "I think it would be wonderful!" At the end of the session as Rose left Dr. J.'s office, she affectionately patted him on the shoulder.

Continuing to rationalize his sexual interest in Rose by "exploring the transference further," Dr. J. asked her to describe her sexual fantasies toward him. Rose used this opportunity to tell Dr. J. what a perfect lover she thought he would be and "how great" it would make her feel to know that someone "as masculine, as attractive, as brilliant, as tender, and as sensitive" as Dr. J. could appreciate her. Failing to recognize how stimulating Rose's remarks were to him, and unaware that he was really trying to buttress his own shaky sexual identity, Dr. J. made a proposal to Rose. He thought it would be "a corrective emotional experience" for her to have sex with him. He said, "All your life you have not been able to enjoy yourself sexually nor appreciate yourself as a sexual woman. Inasmuch as you trust me and like me, it will help you to have sex with me." Rose thought that Dr. J.'s idea was "splendid." She further admired him for his "deep sensitivity" because he also told her that she would have an opportunity to discuss all of her reactions to sex with him. This reassured Rose that he was "not exploiting" her but was "trying to help" her.

At first Rose was in ecstasy. She had found a man whom she loved and admired and he appreciated her sexually. Her self-esteem grew by leaps and bounds, her symptoms vanished, and Rose felt the euphoria of one who had fallen in love. She even found that she felt friendlier toward her husband.

Rose continued to see Dr. J. twice a week for her regularly scheduled appointments of 45 minutes. Rose and Dr. J. had sex and then Rose would discuss her reactions—her fantasies, feelings, and thoughts before, during, and after sex. The sex "got better and better" and Rose "felt better and better" in her day-to-day living. However, as happens in most love affairs, Rose wanted more from Dr. J. and began to find the twice-a-week appointments of 45 minutes much too limiting and wanted to be with Dr. J. more than the time allotted to her. She started to become more demanding of Dr. J. and asked to be taken out to dinner, to go for walks with him, or to attend a play. Dr. J. tried to tell Rose that these "extratherapeutic contacts" would not be helpful for her treatment and he had to say, "No." Rose became more and more furious, began to call Dr. J. "a teaser and a tantalizer," and threatened to call his wife and professional societies in order to inform them about Dr. J.'s "indiscretions."

With Rose's anger mounting at a feverish pace, she began to lose her sexual interest in Dr. J. Eventually she stopped their contact altogether and entered treatment with another therapist. It took Rose several years to overcome her rage toward Dr. J. and almost as much time before she trusted another therapist.

While therapists can rationalize their "therapeutic interventions," sex with a client is almost *always* used to gratify the therapist and almost *never* resolves the client's doubts regarding his or her sexual identity. At best, it offers some temporary reassurance to a client who wants bolstering and some gratification to a therapist who has difficulties that mirror the client's. Most of the time it interferes with the growth of the client.

Although the therapist who wants to help clients resolve their marital conflicts and enhance their lives should abstain from having sex with them, this does not mean that verbalization of sexual fantasies of clients toward therapists should be discouraged. On the contrary; when clients explore their sexual fantasies toward their therapists they usually discover some of the neurotic components and some of the childish dimensions in their marital interactions. If the therapist is not overly stimulated by the client's sexual feelings toward him, these feelings can be utilized to help the client resolve marital conflicts.

Joel M., age 26, was in marital counseling with Ms. I. He sought therapeutic help because he found himself constantly arguing with his wife Shirley to whom he had been married for over two years. In addition to being upset about his constant fracases with Shirley, Joel found himself sexually impotent on occasion and depressed frequently.

Describing his relationship with his parents and younger brother as "superficially friendly," Joel pointed out that he had never had an enjoyable and fulfilling relationship with anyone. In both high school and college he had been "a social isolate" and he believed he had married Shirley because "she was the only woman I had ever met who would have me."

Joel welcomed the opportunity of being in counseling with Ms. I. He told her after the tenth interview of once-a-week treatment that "talking to you always makes me feel better. I'm functioning better at work and better with Shirley." Joel, a few sessions later, told Ms. I. how "kind" she was and if she were a few years younger he would love to date her.

As treatment moved on with Joel constantly extolling Ms. I., and reporting dreams and fantasies of having sexual liaisons with her, Ms. I. asked him to try to fantasy specifically what would transpire between them on a date. Interestingly, Joel fantasied Ms. I. as a maternal figure with whom he would have a lot of foreplay but *not* intercourse. On Ms. I.'s recognizing with Joel that there was something frightening to him about intercourse, Joel was eventually able to tell her about fantasies of being overwhelmed, engulfed and eventually castrated. At times he fantasied Ms. I. as a witch on a broomstick who would penetrate him anally with her broomstick and then rape him.

It was clear from Joel's fantasies that he wanted to reverse sexual roles with Ms. I. He gave her, in his fantasies, a big penis in the form of a broomstick while he was penetrated by her. When his wish to reverse roles was interpreted to him, Joel spent a lot of time talking about intense oedipal fantasies that frightened him. He remembered experiencing both of his parents as "tyrants" and recalled feeling a compulsion to submit to them and placate them on many occasions. As he realized how protective the submissive role was for him in his earlier life, he began to see how he was continuing the same psychological interaction with Shirley and Ms. I. that he had had with his parents. Slowly he experimented in taking more initiative with Ms. I. in their interviews and with Shirley at home.

While it took over four years for Joel to complete his treatment, he referred to the process as "turning me into a new man." He described Ms. I. as "a person who only had one thing in mind—to help me become a full-fledged man."

OVERT SEXUAL PROBLEMS OF OEDIPAL WINNERS AND OEDIPAL LOSERS

In almost every dysfunctional marriage both partners are sexually unsatisfied. The reason for this is because sex is an interpersonal experience and can never be divorced from the individual's feelings, fantasies, and memories. When men and women are preoccupied with angry thoughts, distrust, and guilty feelings, they will not be able to combine and enjoy tender and erotic desires. While there are some unhappy couples who can enjoy themselves with each other sexually, they argue either before or after having sex and their battles have to be considered part and parcel of their total sexual relationship.

As we have pointed out in previous chapters, sexual problems can arise when any maturational task has been unresolved. Unresolved symbiotic yearnings, intense oral fantasies, and problems with trust can cause impotency or frigidity. Similarly unsolved tasks related to limits, controls, masochism, and sadism can create similar sexual difficulties. Perhaps the majority of sexual problems that come to marriage counselors are caused by oedipal conflicts. Unresolved oedipal conflicts can turn sex into a murderous triumph or a forbidden incestuous act. As we have already noted in previous chapters, marital partners frequently turn each other into parental figures; consequently, many husbands and wives cannot freely fuse tender and erotic feelings without feeling anxious and guilty.

POTENCY DISTURBANCES

One of the sexual problems that confronts virtually every marriage counselor is impotence in the husband. Unless due to a chemical, hormonal, or some other physical dysfunction, impotence evolves from one or more unresolved maturational problems. While physical anomalies should be ruled out first, successful treatment of this marital problem—like all others—involves helping the client face forbidden infantile desires such as incestuous wishes, oedipal competition, or homosexual fantasies. From time to time impotence can be an overdetermined symptom when conflicts on several levels of psychosexual development contribute to it.

For the man, the average duration of sexual intercourse is from one to five minutes from the act of insertion until the completion of orgasm. In most instances, ejaculation is achieved after some 30 to 50 thrusts, lasting about three to four minutes. Yet, there are wide individual variations; some men perform active coitus form 10 to 20 minutes before they ejaculate. Ejaculation which takes place in less than one minute should be considered premature (Eisenstein, 1956).

Impotence can take many forms. It may be partial or vary in frequency. It may manifest itself in *ejaculatio praecox* (premature ejaculation) or *ejaculatio retardata* (late ejaculation), in which erection is maintained within the vagina for a half an hour or more without ejaculation being achieved. In complete impotence, there is inability to attain or maintain an erection during an attempt at sexual intercourse. Finally, a less discussed form of impotence is one in which the husband can sustain an erection and ejaculate at the appropriate time but receive almost no pleasure from his ejaculation. In effect he has no orgasm and may not even realize that he has ejaculated.

The most common etiological source of impotence is based on the persistence of an unconscious sensual attachment to the mother. Inasmuch as the husband unconsciously arranges for his wife to be a mother, he "castrates" himself for his incestuous act. The client has the unconscious conviction that sex is dangerous, and the defensive forces that demand avoidance of the sexual act are sustained and assured by interference with the physical reflexes (Fenichel, 1945).

It is extremely easy for the impotent husband to believe that the cause of his impotence is his wife. He may point out that prior to his marriage he was quite potent with other women, yet with his wife he is impotent. If he is engaged in one or more extramarital affairs, he can point to the fact that he is potent with his mistresses. Finally, he can say that when he was courting his wife he was potent with her. After marriage she changed and that is why he is impotent.

Inasmuch as all of the aforementioned disclaimers are correct, at times they may be convincing to the practitioner. Furthermore, the wife of an impotent man is frequently an unhappy woman and may, in fact, be "castrating" in her behavior with him. Nonetheless, the impotent husband in over 90 percent of cases coming to the marriage counselor unconsciously wants to be impotent. Potency for him, as we have pointed out, is dangerous because he is unconsciously committing something close to a crime. To be potent before or away from the marital bedroom is or was not a crime because he did not have to worry about having sex "at home with mother." Now that he is with "wife-mother," he feels guilty in bed with her.

While the impotent husband's complaints about his wife should not, of course, be refuted by the clinician but listened to, as the client goes on complaining without rebuttal he can slowly take some responsibility for his malady. When he sees that the therapist neither condemns nor condones him, he slowly begins to experience his psychological conflicts in the transference relationship with his therapist; that is, he feels impotent in treatment. As the client is afforded the opportunity to examine carefully his impotent feeling with the therapist, the genetic and dynamic forces that give rise to his impotence become clarified.

Mel N.,* age 33, went into treatment with Mr. H. because of sexual impotence. He had been married to Bertha for over a year, and with the exception of one or two successful performances was impotent virtually all of the time. Prior to the marriage, Mel had been potent with Bertha and with other female sexual partners. "It's only since I got married that I'm in trouble," Mel lamented.

In their interpersonal relationship Mel was quite submissive to Bertha. She made the major decisions and Mel consulted her about everything from his business affairs to his wardrobe. He acknowledged in his early interviews with Mr. H. that he felt quite intimidated by his wife who sometimes reminded him of his "tyrannical mother."

Mel's mother, in addition to being described as tyrannical and prone to many temper tantrums, was also quite seductive with Mel. When he was a young boy she had frequently asked him to zip and unzip her clothes, and "to hug me and show me how much you love me." Mel's father was described as authoritarian, strict, and distant. When Mel was 13, his father died unexpectedly, and Mel became "the man of the house," and "took care" of his mother and younger sister.

Initially in the treatment situation Mel was very cooperative with Mr. H. and was glad to find a father figure with whom he could share his troubles. The "honeymoon stage" of treatment strengthened Mel, and some of his sexual potency was restored. "As long as I have you, I feel stronger and more erect," he told Mr. H.

As the treatment went on and Mel looked more deeply at his relationship with Bertha, he got in touch with his incestuous wishes and his oedipal conflicts. While doing so he began to cancel some appointments and come late for others. When his resistive behavior was pointed out to him by Mr. H., he at first offered many rationalizations, such as pressure at busi-

* A shorter version of this case is reported in *The Sexual Dimension*, Herbert S. Strean, Free Press, New York, 1983, p. 133.

ness and subway delays. However, after a while he began to say that he felt "very weak, perhaps impotent" in his interviews with Mr. H. He also told Mr. H. that his impotence had returned with Bertha.

When Mr. H. suggested that Mel was feeling very uncomfortable with him and perhaps they could look at this together, Mel told Mr. H. that he found it very difficult to discuss his sexual life with him. He said in one interview, "It's as if I'm talking about screwing my mother and telling my father all about it. It is disgusting." In a later interview Mel confided, "Sometimes when I think of having sex with Bertha, I see an image of you. Sometimes you look as if you'll hit me and at other times I think you and I should have the sex."

Mel's fantasy of having Mr. H. present in the marital bedroom occupied quite a bit of therapeutic discussion. It became clear that Mel was re-enacting his childhood oedipal conflicts with Mr. H. Either Mr. H. was made the oedipal father who would punish and castrate or else he was made the father to whom Mel would submit sexually.

When it became clear that Mel was making Mr. H. his father, Mel talked more about his relationship with his father and said there had been much love and hatred in their interaction. Mel spoke about fantasies of hugging, kissing, and merging with his father; these were followed by fantasies of maiming and killing his father. Mel was able to recognize that one of the reasons he took his father's death extremely hard is because he had had wishes to kill him and his father's actual death had made him feel that, indeed, he was a killer.

After about two years of twice-weekly treatment, Mel was able to have conscious fantasies in which he wanted to destroy Mr. H. When Mel's hostile and competitive expressions were not criticized or refuted, Mel's sexual anxiety was reduced and his potency increased. Although Mel found it difficult to believe that Mr. H. would not be angry, would not disappear, and would not die in response to his hostile fantasies, Mel was able to say, "The fact that you are here after each one of my tirades means to me I'm not that destructive."

One of Mel's fantasies about his mother that emerged near the end of his treatment was that she took his father away from him. He had strong sadistic fantasies toward her which, when discharged and better understood, also contributed to more pleasurable sex with Bertha.

Impotence evolves if the unconscious meaning of the sexual act causes the husband guilt or anxiety. Treatment should be aimed at freeing the client's childish incestuous and oedipal fantasies so that his sexual energy is not sapped by anxiety and maladaptive defenses. As we saw in the case of Mel N. described above, impotence can be an overdetermined symptom.

The man can suffer from guilt and anxiety over incestuous desires and oedipal competition as well as from sadism and distrust.

The impotent husband very much needs a therapist who relates to his whole person, not just to his impotence. The client's fears, anxieties, forbidden sexual fantasies, and history need a great deal of attention, particularly as they are expressed in the transference relationship with the therapist. Although intensive psychotherapy may take longer to treat sexual impotence than do the more conventional sexual therapies, as Karasu and Socarides (1979) point out, psychotherapy seems to sustain potency for longer periods of time and usually is more effective in enhancing the marital interaction of the client.

FRIGIDITY, OR ANORGASMIA

By frigidity, or anorgasmia, we are referring to the inability of the woman to have sexual pleasure; usually this inability exists in relation to any marital partner. Some clinicians and researchers still subscribe to a rather narrow definition of frigidity, maintaining that it should refer to the woman's inability to attain orgasm from coitus.

A woman may on one occasion suffer from near-total frigidity and on another have an almost complete orgasm. Some women can experience sexual excitement during foreplay but lose their desire during coitus. There are others whose lack of vaginal pleasure is manifest even in the absence of lubricating glandular secretions in the vagina during sexual stimulation. In very intense degrees of frigidity, anxiety produces painful intercourse in which the vaginal sphincter muscle closes so tightly that it is virtually impossible for the penis to enter the vagina. In all types of frigidity sexual excitement may be felt, particularly in the clitoris; however, pleasurable vaginal sensations end before the involuntary contractions of the vagina, characteristic of true orgasm, can be achieved (Eisenstein, 1956).

As is true of impotence there are many causes of frigidity and anorgasmic women can suffer from one or all of them. Frigidity may have unconscious oral or anal significance such as fear of symbiosis and engulfment or fear of losing control during orgasm which may be equated with fear of losing urinary or sphincter control. However, one of the most common etiological factors in frigidity is the unconscious comparison of the husband with the woman's father. When a husband is unconsciously made an incestuous object, the wife—out of guilt and anxiety—holds herself back sexually. On making her husband a father figure, a wife is usually in active competition with her mother, albeit unconsciously; consequently, sexual excitement leading to orgasm is equated with destroying her mother. To avoid feeling destructive the woman inhibits her excitement.

Many wives in marriage counseling who have orgastic problems have reported that they perceived their own mothers as anorgasmic. Not only does it turn out that these clients are identifying with their mothers, in the same way that some impotent men identify with their fathers, but for these women to become orgasmic is to surpass their mothers. For many women the act of surpassing Mother is distorted into the mistaken belief that Mother is being destroyed. To expiate for unconscious wishes to kill Mother the woman inhibits herself sexually.

Another common source of anorgasmia is the woman's rejection of her own vagina. In our still existing patriarchal culture in which the male is idealized, many women tend to depreciate their own genitals and unconsciously—sometimes even consciously—idealize the penis. When the penis is idealized there is inevitably unconscious resentment toward it. Therefore frigidity may be an expression of anxiety connected with sadism, jealousy, and envy. Rather than castrate the man for having the prized penis, the woman punishes herself for her revengeful wishes toward it by becoming anorgasmic. Some women who subscribe to the belief of the principle, "an eye for an eye and a tooth for a tooth," anticipate being injured during intercourse; therefore, they cannot relax and enjoy themselves (Fenichel, 1945).

When oedipal wishes cause anxiety and/or phallic competition induces guilt and fear of retaliation, the married woman may regress and unconsciously turn her husband into a mother figure. Then, the activation of homosexual fantasies can create anxiety in her, and she inhibits her sexual excitement and orgasms.

Usually anorgasmia cannot be resolved by changing marital partners. In some cases, when a wife unconsciously equates her husband with a parental figure she can become orgasmic with an extramarital partner. However, should the lover become her husband or even talk about wanting to become her husband, she will become anorgasmic with him also (Strean, 1980).

Frigidity, like impotence and other psychosexual problems in marriage, requires treatment of the whole person. When a wife cannot enjoy herself with her husband sexually, she and the therapist have to look at her hatreds, childish fantasies, maladaptive defenses, history, and other facets of her character, particularly as they emerge in the transference relationship with the therapist.

Adrian O., age 37, came for marriage counseling because throughout her 10-year marriage, she had been completely anorgasmic. Her inability to derive sexual pleasure in her marriage was not relegated to intercourse. She found herself consistently inhibited during foreplay, as well.

Adrian described her husband Alex as a warm, gentle man who she respected a great deal, found attractive in many ways, but a man with whom she couldn't feel sexually stimulated. While Adrian was "turned on" to Alex before they were married, she did not feel sexually fulfilled then, either.

Adrian told her therapist, Ms. G., that she always idealized her "daddy" and felt "a cold distance coming from my mother." She also mentioned that her older brother was her parents' favorite and she "just accepted that that was the way it was and that was the way it had to be."

In the early stages of her three-times-a-week therapy, Adrian was very deferential toward Ms. G. and very compliant in general. Frequently she would nod her head in agreement with Ms. G. without even fully hearing what Ms. G. had to say. She was so eager to please Ms. G. that from time to time she would come to a session and ask her what she should talk about. On other occasions she ended sentences with a question, "Do you suppose I was right?"

When Adrian's extreme submissiveness was pointed out to her by Ms. G., Adrian experienced her therapist's comment as a criticism and began to cry. She told Ms. G. that she was "trying very hard to be a good patient and now I feel that I'm not good enough." As Adrian talked more and more of feeling like an inadequate client, she was eventually able to recall that that was how she had felt so frequently next to her mother during her childhood and teenage years. When Ms. G. explored this feeling toward her mother further with her, Adrian was eventually able to release hostility toward her mother. "I always felt that she acted like a queen, like a know-it-all, and I had to serve her," said Adrian in her fifth month of treatment.

Adrian's release of anger toward her mother helped make her feel freer with Alex and in the rest of her life, as well. This was only for a brief period, however. After about two weeks of liking herself Adrian returned to her self-hating, masochistic, depressed stance. Her therapy revealed that she felt very guilty for expressing anger toward her mother. She felt like "a bad girl who should be punished." When Ms. G. pointed out to Adrian that apparently she equated the expression of angry feelings with destructive acts and felt like a criminal, this interpretation helped Adrian a great deal. She realized that a great deal of her energy was spent hating herself and punishing herself for thoughts and feelings—"as if feeling and thinking were the same as dropping atomic bombs."

When Adrian felt safer with Ms. G. in expressing her anger toward her mother, she was able to bring some of her oedipal conflicts into her trans-

The Experimenting Spouse   179

ference relationship with Ms. G. In one of her dreams she yelled at Ms. G. "for being so high and mighty." In another one she turned Ms. G. into a competitor at a high school dance and took away Ms. G.'s dancing partner from her so that she could dance with him.

Inasmuch as Ms. G. made it safe for Adrian to compete with her, Adrian was able to bring into treatment many erotic fantasies toward her father and toward father figures, including men that she thought were in Ms. G.'s life. As she became more accepting of her incestuous fantasies, she could see how she had turned Alex into her father and had felt guilty about having sex with "my father-husband."

While becoming aware of her oedipal conflicts and feeling them in the transference relationship helped Adrian feel a lot more relaxed in her sexual and interpersonal relationship with Alex, it did not relieve her anxiety completely. She needed to examine her envy of her brother and her resentment toward her father before she could feel completely free sexually. As she expressed her fantasies to castrate and destroy her brother and father, she did not have to act them out as much with Alex. After four years of treatment she was not only fully orgasmic, but her therapy had also helped her to become a less constricted, less hateful, and more loving and communicative woman and wife.

As we observed with impotence in the male, frigidity has many possible etiological sources that can all exist in the same woman: unresolved oedipal wishes, incestuous desires, penis envy, and fears of dependence. As the client becomes able to unearth these conflicts and experience them in a benign and understanding therapeutic relationship, the frigidity is less likely to be needed as protection.

THE EXPERIMENTING SPOUSE

Many clinicians, if not most, agree with anthropologist Margaret Mead (1967) that monogamous heterosexual love is probably one of the most difficult, complex, and demanding of human relationships. As was pointed out in Chapter 1, marriage challenges our mature ego functions—frustration tolerance, impulse control, acceptance of reality, empathy with others, and so on. These are demands that most married individuals resent in an age of sexual freedom and narcissism. Therefore, many individuals seek escape from marriage by becoming a workaholic or by compulsively engaging in travel, organizational activities, or hobbies.

An increasingly common means of escaping from the difficulties of marriage is through the extramarital affair. The percentage of married people engaged in prolonged affairs keeps rising, with the current rate about 60 percent for married men and over 40 percent for married women (Strean, 1980). In an extramarital affair, the individual has two part-time mates, both of which are important to him or her. To those involved in "open marriages" (O'Neill and O'Neill, 1972), one intimate, monogamous relationship feels frightening, demanding, frustrating or boring.

Any practitioner who has worked with husbands and wives involved in prolonged extramarital affairs comes to recognize that these are unhappy people who need two part-time relationships. A single mutually loving relationship frightens them, although they are the last to acknowledge it. They choose the route of an affair and tell themselves that they need greater sexual enjoyment. What they do not want to face is that they cannot enjoy sex in marriage. As we have suggested in earlier chapters, when psychosexual tasks are resolved, one can enjoy a monogamous marriage and cope with its frustrations, but when these tasks are not mastered there is a neurotic choice of mate, the marital relationship induces anxiety, and the individual seeks to escape from it one way or another.

Husbands and wives are involved in prolonged affairs for one or more reasons: They may be escaping from an overwhelming fear of a symbiosis; they may be running away from a parental figure who appears like a punitive superego and seems too controlling; or they may be trying to seek reassurance regarding their sexual identity. Yet, the most common reason for an affair is an unresolved oedipal conflict. When the marital partner is ascribed the role of parent, as we have seen in several cases, sex takes on incestuous connotations and has to be avoided. Many men experience their wives as "virgin mothers" who must be avoided sexually while they turn their girlfriends into "whores" who excite them. While these men rationalize their sexual inhibitions, dissatisfactions, and frequent impotence with their wives, they unconsciously feel that they are little boys with big mothers. The same may be said for the many women who unconsciously turn their husbands into fathers and must avoid them sexually and seek out another partner.

Those writers who have researched the extramarital affair (Bartusis, 1978; Block, 1978; Hunt, 1969; Strean, 1980) have all pointed out that in most instances married individuals involved in affairs do not marry each other. The reasons for this are several: first, one reason the couple is attracted to one another at the start is because they relate to one another away from the marital bedroom without its incestuous connotations; second, individuals involved in extramarital affairs frequently experience their own mates as parental figures whom they wish to defy—the affair affords them the opportunity to spite their "superego-parent-spouse"; third, men and women involved in extramarital affairs are usually quite attached to their own mates—they can't live comfortably with them but they can't live comfortably without them; and, finally, men and women involved in affairs fear the intimacy of a monogamous relationship. They are much more comfortable with two part-time relationships.

In Chapter 3, we discussed the case of Jack M., a man who was impotent with his wife but very potent with his girlfriend. As we recall he became impotent with his girlfriend when they went away for a week, thus demonstrating that the man or woman involved in an affair cannot cope with incestuous feelings toward the mate who is unconsciously being made a parent. The following case demonstrates the same phenomenon with a woman client.

Paula P., age 40, came for treatment for several reasons: She had difficulty getting along with an aged mother and wondered how much time she should spend with her; she felt unsure of herself on the job as a librarian; she often got involved in sadomasochistic quarrels in her social and professional relationships. In her marriage, she had a lot of resentment toward her husband Martin whom she said was a "know-it-all," "considers me beneath him" and "screws like a naive boy."

In her treatment, as Paula began to voice more resentment toward Martin for being "a bossy know-it-all"—whom, of course, in her mind she had to castrate by making him "a naive boy"—she moved into an affair with a married man. In contrast to her husband, her lover, Larry, was not "a know-it-all" but "a man of the world." Larry was described as "a great lover" who "turns me on." She contrasted Larry to her husband who "turns me off."

When Paula and Larry, after knowing each other about a year, went on a camping trip for several days the relationship "cooled." The couple argued incessantly and the love and bliss which previously characterized their relationship broke down. Paula declared after returning from the sojourn with her lover, "When I was with him over time, everything lost its glamor."

For individuals involved in extramarital affairs, sex with their mates is experienced as if they are little children with big parents. That is why it is described by many of them as "overwhelming," "controlling," and "debilitating." Because they do not have to live with their extramarital partners on a sustained basis, they can enjoy them sexually and interpersonally. When the extramarital partner appears like a spouse the relationship deteriorates.

In working with the spouse who is involved in an extramarital affair, it is extremely important for the clinician to neither condemn nor condone the affair. The client, in almost every instance, is conflicted and ambivalent and needs an opportunity to look at all the aspects of his affair as well as all the aspects of his marriage. In a neutral atmosphere the client's internal conflicts emerge in the transference relationship with the therapist where they can be explored in depth.

Howard Q., age 36, was in treatment with Ms. F. He found himself very turned off sexually to his wife, Becky, particularly after she gave birth to their son (when they had been married for five years). It was at that time that Howard started an affair with a married woman, Louise.

Howard, at the beginning of treatment, felt that his affair with Louise did not present a conflict for him. Within about a month of his twice-weekly treatment, he began to realize that many of his symptoms—insomnia, depression, gastrointestinal disorders, lack of concentration on the job—were expressions of his guilt and anxiety over the affair. After six weeks of treatment, he asked Ms. F., "In view of the fact that my symptoms come from my affair with Louise, do you think I should stop the affair?" When Ms. F. asked Howard if that was something he was considering these days, Howard responded, "Yes and no." He brought out that Becky was "a warm friend," "a maternal person who is kind," but who "upsets me sexually." "Louise," he said, "really turns me on."

As Howard felt freer to discuss his marital and extramarital conflicts with Ms. F., he began to feel much closer to Ms. F. and told her so. Although not realizing it, he described Ms. F. in the same terms he used to describe Becky: "warm," "friendly," "kind," and "maternal." However, as Howard began to experience Ms. F. as a mother figure, he started to arrive late for his appointments, cancelled several, and wondered if he should go into treatment with another therapist.

On Ms. F.'s pointing out to Howard that apparently she seemed to be a lot like Becky and therefore she had to be avoided, Howard denied the connection at first. However, upon further reflection, he was able to say, "Yes, you are both good mothers."

Recognizing that he had made his wife and his therapist mothers, Howard began to examine his relationship with his own mother. He described her as "a very attractive woman" who alternated between being seductive and punitive. At times she could be warm and giving but she could also be cold and withholding.

As Howard got more in tune with his erotic feelings toward his mother, he realized how frightened he was of them and that it was the reason he had to move away from Becky and Ms. F. "Louise, who is less maternal, is easier for me," Howard insightfully said during the beginning of his second year of treatment.

Facing incestuous fantasies was helpful to Howard in understanding his marital conflicts, but other issues were at work too. As he confronted erotic feelings toward his mother he also uncovered many competitive and hostile fantasies toward his father which frightened him. He recalled being very intimidated by his father and in interviews with Ms. F. told her that he often felt like "a sissy and a coward."

A factor that contributed to Howard's affair was his need to defend against feeling like a "sissy and coward." As he got in touch with his latent homosexuality and understood it better, and as he resolved many of his oedipal conflicts, he had much less of a compulsive need for an affair and enjoyed Becky more.

The extramarital affair, although considered a legitimate modus vivendi by many men and women in several, if not most, societies, is also an expression of a conflicted marriage and of a conflicted spouse. The unfaithful spouse is one who usually experiences the marital partner as a superego figure who must be defied, an incestuous object who must be avoided, or one who activates homosexual anxiety and should be shunned.

The client in an extramarital affair needs help, not so much with whether he should or should not have an affair, but with the anxieties and doubts about his sexuality which cripple him.

CHAPTER 9

Treating the Latent
Heterosexual Spouse

As noted in Chapter 3, the ages from 6 to 10 are frequently referred to as "the latency period." The term "latency" derives from the fact that during this time children expend a great deal of energy controlling themselves from overtly expressing their sexual and aggressive impulses; they try to keep them beneath the surface in *latent* form.

To prevent the possible eruption of sadistic, erotic, or competitive yearnings latency children utilize a variety of defenses (Sarnoff, 1976), one of which is the development of rituals. As an example, latency youngsters avoid stepping on the cracks of sidewalks so they will not hurt people. The popular saying goes, "If you step on a crack, you'll break your mother's back." This statement reveals the child's sadistic wish toward Mother; it also suggests how unacceptable the thought is to the child and how he must bend over backwards so that the impulse will not be acted out.

Latency youngsters are extremely preoccupied with rules and regulations. "Fair," "unfair," "good," "bad," and "cheater" are popular words in their vocabularies. The tremendous concern with rules and regulations is used as a defense against the temptation to break them. Every latency child fantasizes living a life of nonconformity but is afraid to acknowledge it (A. Freud, 1965).

The main reason latency youngsters are so obsessed with rituals, rules, and regulations is that they are working overtime trying to handle their oedipal desires. They still believe that it is "unfair" for their parents to have a special relationship that excludes them, and they are still tempted to barge into the bedroom to disrupt their parents' sexual life. They also resent the privileges and pleasures that exist in the adult world and they would like to switch positions with their parents. However, they regard their own id wishes as "wrong" and "unfair" and feel *they* would be "cheaters" if they gave in to them. They repress and suppress their aggressive and erotic wishes and find it much easier to project their own "bad" impulses onto peers and siblings, accusing others of breaking the rules.

Latency is a time for the consolidation of the superego and therefore a time when youngsters must cope with a lot of guilt. They feel guilty for wanting to vanquish the parent of the same sex; they feel guilty for their desires to get rid of their siblings, schoolmates, and peers, and they feel guilty for wanting to be kings and queens and turn everybody else into slaves.

The voices of a child's superego cause his guilt; his guilty feelings make him erect all his defensive rituals and compulsive rules. Usually the voices in a child's superego are much more powerful and punitive than any parent's admonitions. Children with powerful and punitive superegos do not necessarily have mean parents; these children have erotic and sadistic fantasies for which they feel guilty. Often when a child feels guilty, he provokes his parents to punish him. Many husbands and wives do the same thing with their mates—they provoke them to lash out at them to appease the guilt they suffer from their unacceptable fantasies.

Because latency children are working overtime to renounce their sexual wishes toward the opposite sex, they frequently avoid contact with members of the opposite gender. They tend to socialize only with members of their own sex. This defensive operation is often referred to as "latent homosexuality"; however, inasmuch as the youngsters are renouncing burgeoning and dangerous heterosexual wishes, a more apt term to describe their psychological state might be "latent heterosexuality."

Both boys and girls feel unsure of their sexual identities during the latency years; therefore, they accentuate their virility and femininity—boys boast about their athletic feats and girls brag about their capacity to give birth to babies. Girls match their "Wonder Woman" abilities while boys compete with each other regarding their "Superman" qualities.

Another dynamic that is subtly expressed during latency is the envy that each sex has toward the other. Boys want to be girls in many ways and girls secretly admire boys. This manifests itself when they shift traditional roles in games such as "playing doctor" or "playing house."

Unresolved latency conflicts emerge in many marriages and take various forms. A client who frequently appears in the marriage counselor's office is one who is so preoccupied with business affairs or organizational work that he or she has little or no time for the mate. This spouse, like the latency child, is so fearful of a close, intimate relationship that he or she escapes into activity. The mate of this spouse (most often the wife) appears even more frequently in the counselor's office. She berates herself for not being attractive or lovable enough to keep her husband at home and wants to learn how to do so.

Fear of heterosexual intimacy deriving from latency takes other forms in marriage. Men and women who are frightened by one-to-one closeness constantly need contact with other men and women for stimulation and reaffirmation. When their friends are not available they feel very restless and uncomfortable with each other and frequently end up fighting. These are also the couples to whom we referred in Chapter 8—men and women who have considerable anxiety about their homosexual fantasies and want a great deal of buttressing and reassurance from each other. Sometimes in their anxiety they resort to swinging, switching, Don Juanism, or promiscuity.

Another client who is a frequent visitor at the marriage counselor's office is the man or woman who can be compared to the overcontrolled latency youngster. Pressured by a very rigid and punitive superego, this husband or wife is angry that the mate is not following all of the rules and regulations of marriage. The client complains that the partner is not doing his share, is not fulfilling his role, or is not conforming in one way or another to what is deemed appropriate behavior. Of course the mate of this spouse feels tyrannized and often asks for therapeutic help.

Let us look at some of these unhappy spouses in more detail and consider some of the therapeutic principles in marriage counseling with them.

AWAY AT THE OFFICE

Many men and women escape marriage through business activity. While they rationalize their overactivity by saying that they must attend an emergency business meeting or must be away on a trip, these individuals cannot tolerate spending time alone with their mates. Their mates are unconsciously experienced as parental figures and they escape the possibility of having forbidden sex with them by remaining busy at a distance. When their mates complain to them about their absence from home, they become indignant and feel misunderstood. If the partner tries to entice them to stay home by being entertaining or seductive, their anxiety heightens and they may retreat into more work.

Usually the client who must be away at the office is one who must stay away from the therapist. He is rarely one who seeks help on his own. Rather, he comes for a consultation because his mate has threatened divorce or ascribes her depression to his inattentiveness. Just as he feels his mate is a pest, he tends to view therapy as coming to a pest and wants "out" as soon as he is in the door. The therapist needs to respect his strong resistances and should not try to coax him into treatment. If the client feels pressured he leaves the therapist's office and goes back to his own office quickly.

Tom A., age 40 and a successful businessman, came to see Dr. Z. because his physician told him that his frequent absences from his home were inducing a powerful depression in his wife Betty. It took months before Tom was willing to listen to his physician's advice and many more weeks after accepting the physician's advice before Tom called Dr. Z.

Tom arrived 20 minutes late for his appointment at Dr. Z.'s office. He immediately went on the offensive and told Dr. Z. that it could be seen from his tardiness that he was a very busy man and that he didn't really have time for "trivia." He knew his wife was upset with him but he could not really understand it. She had a car, a dog, a nice house, two lovely kids, and there were loads of things for her to do. "As a matter of fact," Tom proposed, "let her come here and talk 'trivia' to you."

Obviously irritated by Tom's calling his work trivia Dr. Z. asked, "You mean that a depressed wife is a trivial matter and you and I shouldn't discuss it?" Tom became very annoyed by Dr. Z.'s question and told him that he was doing stuff that belonged to "the women's world" and he didn't have time "for such nonsense."

When Dr. Z. interpreted Tom's resistance to him by telling Tom that he was running away from treatment in the same way he was running away from his wife, Tom moaned, appeared very aggravated, and said that he did not think it was worth his while to take time away from his busy schedule to come to a place where he was "going to be accused." Tom left Dr. Z.'s office prior to the formal ending of the consultation; he never returned.

We have constantly reiterated throughout this text how very important it is for the practitioner to respect the resistances of the client and not to try to remove them prematurely. Resistances exist to ward off pain and anxiety, and the client holds on to them for protection. The spouse who must be at his office is extremely frightened to be at home; otherwise he would not be so involved in compulsive activity away from his home. Furthermore, this client has strong doubts about his adequacy; a challenge to his way of coping with his vulnerabilities punctures his narcissism, strengthens his anxiety, and makes him doubt his sexual adequacy all the more.

In the case above the therapist's interpretation regarding Tom's running away from treatment was correct but premature. A client like Tom needs time to talk about his work at the office and how important it is to him. When the practitioner accepts the client the way he is, he has more of a chance to be experienced as an ally; and, involving the client in treatment becomes more of a possibility.

Bill B., age 32, was referred to Dr. Y., a female therapist, by his employer. Bill's wife, Susan, had spoken to Bill's boss several times about the fact that Bill seemed to spend so much time at his law firm that he was neglecting his wife and children. The boss, Mr. X., was extremely sympathetic to Susan's plight, told her that he had reduced Bill's workload on several occasions, but that Bill just seemed to want to work after hours. Finally, after much persuasion, Bill agreed to Mr. X.'s idea that he receive therapy.

Upon meeting her, Bill told Dr. Y. that he realized both his boss and his wife felt he was "overworking." He thought neither of them appreciated "the magnitude" of his workload and neither realized that his legal work required so much thought and research. Dr. Y., sensitive to the fact that Bill might be using his work as an escape but aware that he needed his work as a defense, asked Bill to tell her about "the magnitude" of his tasks and the rigorous work that was required doing his legal research. Brightening up, Bill proudly told Dr. Y. how arduously he worked, how meticulous he was in going over details, and how successful he was with his clients. As Dr. Y. quietly listened to Bill's proud exhibition of his talents, Bill smiled more and more, and at the end of the interview told Dr. Y. that he thought she understood him and that he might be able to find some time to see her again because he "enjoyed our chat."

Bill continued to see Dr. Y. on a weekly basis to discuss his work at the office, really using the time to show off his talents, and to justify his "laboring" for long hours. As their relationship continued it became quite clear that Bill was beginning to feel affectionate toward Dr. Y. He told her that, like himself, she seemed "empathetic, kind, and responsive." However, with the intensity of his warm feelings mounting, Bill started to cancel sessions with Dr. Y. and to become more distant in his interviews.

Dr. Y. recognized that Bill was moving away from her at a time when he was feeling affectionate. She asked him what bothered him about her lately, inasmuch as he didn't seem to want to have as much to do with her. At first Bill ascribed his cancelling of appointments to his increased workload, but on Dr. Y.'s telling him that he seemed to get busier around the time he started liking her more, Bill flushed with embarrassment. In his fifth month of treatment he told Dr. Y. that he found it difficult to get "too close emotionally to anyone." Dr. Y. calmly nodded and asked him about what upset him regarding closeness.

Bill spent several weeks talking about fears of rejection, anxiety about overwhelming others with his own needs, and "fears of appearing too seductive." Eventually he was able to talk about his mother. He recalled feeling very close to her as a boy, but also felt guilty about his desires. As he shared some of his erotic fantasies toward his mother with Dr. Y., Bill began to feel some of them in his transference relationship with her. This was very difficult for him to talk about, but as he himself said, "I'm determined to hang in there."

As Bill saw how frightened he was of his own erotic feelings toward his mother and Dr. Y., he began to see how he resisted Susan. Slowly he began to spend more time with his wife and started to have sex with her more often. Susan responded very positively to Bill's change of attitude but, as we have seen in so many of our case illustrations, she became frightened of the increased intimacy and needed some help herself to accommodate Bill's therapeutic gains.

While the mate of the workaholic spouse usually complains a great deal about her husband's business activities and points out how she is realistically neglected, as is true in every marital interaction this mate unconsciously receives some protection and gratification from his overwork. This frequent happenstance reaffirms the notion that behind every chronic complaint is an unconscious wish.

Because the mate of the workaholic *needs* a partner who provides her with some distance it is important that the practitioner avoids providing this person with advice on how to bring her partner closer. Some practitioners—in their zeal to foster better communication between husbands and wives, and in their enthusiasm to bring them closer to each other—prescribe exercises to achieve this. This understandable position only leads to negative therapeutic reactions and to more anxiety between the marital partners. If a wife complains that her husband overworks she will resist attempts of the practitioner to foster closeness with her husband because, on the deepest level, closeness terrifies her. Also, even if she goes along with the therapist's advice and does things to entice her husband, he will become terrified of her seductiveness and stay at the office for longer periods of time.

Beatrice C., age 34 and married for four years, sought marriage counseling because it seemed her husband, Hy, never wanted to have anything to do with her. She was becoming more and more depressed and even had some suicidal thoughts. She knew he was a dedicated businessman but she felt that he had enough assistance at his firm that he did not need to spend so much time away from home.

In her work with Ms. W., Beatrice said that maybe she wasn't a sufficiently good conversationalist or a responsive enough sexual partner. She confessed that she stopped trying to initiate sex and found herself wanting to withdraw from conversations with him.

Ms. W. told Beatrice that one of the problems in her marriage was that Hy was feeling rejected by her. If she was withdrawing from sex and from conversation, Hy had no alternative but to work harder. She should try to talk to him more and to have sex with him more. Beatrice responded to Ms. W.'s advice by saying that she didn't know what to talk about and she didn't know how to seduce Hy. Ms. W. came to her aid. She told her that she should talk to Hy about his business and that she should buy some sexy clothes—particularly sexy underwear and sexy nightgowns. While Beatrice initially resisted Ms. W.'s advice, she finally relented and tried "to test the waters."

Hy laughed at Beatrice's attempts. He told her to leave his business affairs to him. He also told her to have an extramarital affair if she was feeling so turned on. When Beatrice told Ms. W. that none of her attempts were succeeding, Ms. W. told her that she was giving up much too quickly and that she should try harder. Once more Beatrice complied with Ms. W.'s advice and once more Hy resisted her, even more forcefully. Eventually Beatrice left treatment feeling like a failure.

It takes time for the marriage counselor to become firmly convinced that advice rarely helps dysfunctional marriages become more functional. Not only do clients resist the advice because they are being forced to give up necessary resistances prematurely, but clients resent advice for another important reason. For many if not most clients, advice feels demeaning. They are placed in a position where they are told, in effect, that they don't have sufficient resources within themselves. As we saw in the case of Beatrice C.—who felt like a failure in the first place—taking advice lowered her self-esteem, increased her anger, and caused her to seek revenge on her therapist by quitting treatment and turning her counselor into a failure.

The seemingly helpless masochistic husband or wife often arouses in the therapist a wish to take over. However, this spouse—as we have shown in previous chapters—is an angry person underneath his or her lambskin (Reik, 1941). Angry clients need to defeat their therapists even if they appear on the surface to be compliant and self-effacing.

Even when couples acknowledge that they are both contributing to the marital estrangement and even when they both ask for advice on how to communicate better, if the therapist complies with their requests, he will be defeated.

Arnold and Barbara D., a couple in their mid-thirties, were in counseling with Dr. V., a male therapist. Arnold pointed out that he realized he spent a lot of time away from home in organizational work and playing golf and that Barbara "had a legitimate beef." Barbara acknowledged that she got much too angry with Arnold and this probably infuriated him all the more; therefore, she could understand his wish to stay away from home. Both Arnold and Barbara agreed that they needed to communicate better so that they could resolve their marital impasses. They also agreed that each time they did talk to one another the arguments ended in disaster. Tempers flared, mutual understanding diminished, and each felt more and more alienated and depressed.

Dr. V. told the D.'s that he would like to help them communicate better. Without getting any history from Arnold and Barbara on their six-year-old marriage and without getting any personal histories from either of them, he launched into his task. He told Barbara and Arnold to simulate a situation in front of him. "Pretend," said Dr. V., "that Arnold has just come home from golf and he's tired and wants to go to sleep. Pretend that Barbara is angry because she has been left for hours alone all by her lonesome." The couple tried to talk it out in front of Dr. V. in a mature fashion. However, after showing mutual respect toward one another for about five minutes, an argument ensued and Arnold and Barbara were insulting one another. Dr. V. told them with an accepting smile that he saw what happens to them and that this was helpful to him. Now he could give them some advice on how to communicate better. He advised both of them to "stay with the issues and not use their disagreement to fight." He further added, "Say what you want from each other, say what you are dissatisfied about, without insulting one another." The couple did this with a little more success in their second try at "peaceful communication."

The exercises continued and Dr. V. tried to show the D.'s when they were getting away from the issues and how they were undermining their own efforts to better their communication and to achieve more matrimonial harmony. For four months the couple dutifully came for weekly sessions and cooperated with Dr. V. However, during the fifth month of counseling they both agreed that they could not resist insulting one another and that they needed another form of therapy. Despite Dr. V.'s efforts, he could not persuade the V.'s to remain in marriage counseling with him.

When a married couple is fighting, all the communication skills in the world are not going to help them to appreciably reduce the intensity of their fights or the frequency of them. The knowledgeable marriage counselor is aware of the fact that when a husband and wife are fighting, they need and want to do so. The counselor's job is to help them understand what gratification and what protection they derive from their battles.

Gail and Ed E., a couple in their forties, went into conjoint marriage counseling. Ed was very angry that Gail spent so much time at her job and in community work and that she had no time or energy for him. Gail, defensive about her active business and social life, acknowledged that she was away from home a great deal of the time, but said, "Ed should learn to accept this."

Ms. U., the therapist, after getting a history on their 10-year marriage and personal histories on Gail and Ed, pointed out to the E.'s that both Ed and Gail had a lot of anger toward one another and that this should be understood better by each of them. She learned that neither had ever had a close relationship with anybody and she felt that both were unconsciously sustaining a distant relationship in their marriage.

In their conjoint therapy, each time one of them got close to the other, an argument between Ed and Gail would ensue in which each would belittle the other and each would end up feeling misunderstood. For example, if Gail said to Ed, "I'd like to understand your depressed feeling better," Ed would rebuff her and say, "No, you don't!" If Ed said to Gail, "I'd like to see if I can understand why being with your women friends is more fun than being with me," Gail would reply, "You couldn't empathize with that!"

On Ms. U.'s pointing out to the E.'s that it seemed frightening to both of them to reveal themselves to one another, both Ed and Gail acknowledged that from their conjoint therapy they were learning that each of them was "a very private person." Both also realized that they got angry when the other wanted to know more.

The fear of revealing feelings consumed much of the E.'s weekly treatment for several months. Each of the partners talked about feeling very vulnerable when it came to loving and being loved. They talked about actually having a lot in common in that they both came from families where tenderness, warmth, and mutual concern were things to be repudiated. As Ms. U. empathized with their mutual fear of self-revelation and explained how anger was an understandable defense against it, the E.'s began to feel a lot more comfortable in their sessions and at home with one another. After two years of conjoint treatment, they trusted one another more with their feelings and began to spend more time together enjoying intimacy.

THE RITUALISTIC SPOUSE

Sooner or later every marriage counselor has to face a very difficult client; namely, the husband or wife who is dominated by a rigid code of ethics, rules, and regulations. This spouse often reminds one of a religious or political fanatic who steadfastly maintains that anyone who does not adhere to his creed is a hostile infidel who should be admonished and ostracized.

This obsessive-compulsive spouse has rules about sex, domestic chores, entertainment, and so on, and his mate and the other family members must comply to them. If the mate does not comply she cannot offer any reasons for her refusal to do so, because the ritualistic spouse—like the latency child who is dominated by harsh regulations—merely throws the rule book in the mate's face and says or implies, "You must obey!"

The marital partner of the ritualistic spouse is one who frequently feels as intimidated and agonized as if she lived in a prison. However, little compassion is offered by her mate because as far as he is concerned she is a hostile violator of a sacred creed: She should know better.

The reason the ritualistic spouse is a difficult client is that he has rigid rules about how therapy should be conducted. He arrives armed with an agenda for each session and the therapist is supposed to be a dutiful committee member who follows "The Client's Rules of Order." Usually such a controlling client induces frustration and irritation in the practitioner; but if the practitioner questions the client's rules he is labeled a heretic. If the practitioner complies with the client's agenda, the client does not grow but remains a tyrannical boss in and out of his marriage.

To avoid a power struggle with this client is most difficult; to comply is also not easy to avoid. It often seems impossible to counsel this client—involving him in a process where he must reveal feelings and thoughts spontaneously is like asking a member of the clergy to give up his sacred religion.

While the client we are discussing taxes the patience of most counselors, and while there is much temptation to get rid of him, sensitizing ourselves to his dynamics can be of help in our work with him. This client needs his rituals because they ward off sadistic, erotic, and usually murderous fantasies. Actually, this client is in considerable pain because he derives little joy from living. Any potential pleasure in his mind is a sin and his rules and regulations are arranged and maintained so that he will not commit transgressions.

As we noted in Chapter 3, the client with a rigid superego chooses a mate who personifies his own unacceptable id. When he criticizes his mate's behavior, he is really trying to repudiate his own id wishes. It is this dynamic truth which can be utilized in his therapy.

If the clinician recognizes that the ritualistic spouse is really criticizing his own id—that is, himself—there is a chance to help him. Instead of focusing on the ritualistic spouse's internal dynamics, the therapist is well advised to listen patiently to the client's analysis of his mate's transgressions, which this client is so willing to talk about. Inasmuch as an analysis of his mate is really an analysis of himself, if this is done in a calm, accepting atmosphere, the client may begin to accept with more calmness his *own* id impulses. In effect, the counselor should permit this client to project as long as he needs to do so. When the client sees that the therapist is not thrown by a discussion of id wishes, the client may be less thrown by it himself.

Marilyn F., age 40, decided to consult her husband Roger's therapist, Mr. T. Her husband had been in treatment for about a year on a twice-weekly basis because he found himself depressed, lacking self-confidence, and feeling very intimidated by Marilyn. Although Marilyn did not want to ask Roger if it was all right with him for her to see Mr. T., the latter felt that it would be appropriate for both Marilyn and himself to do so before they got together. Roger did not have any objections to Marilyn's having an interview with Mr. T.

Marilyn arrived with a long agenda. She had a yellow pad with reams of notes on it, full of complaints about Roger. Reading from her notes, Marilyn pointed out that she knew Roger had "serious emotional problems"; consequently, she felt that his being in therapy was well-advised. However, she "regretted" to report that since Roger had been in treatment his condition had deteriorated. Prior to his initiation of treatment, he had only been "moderately belligerent"; now he seemed "quite belligerent." Before treatment he had been "oversexed"; now he seemed to be "obsessed" with it. And, up until he met Mr. T. he had "some resistance to cooperating"; now "the resistance had increased."

Marilyn went on for about half-an-hour calmly presenting her report. It seemed clear to Mr. T. that Marilyn was anxious from Roger's changes and it also seemed clear to him that underneath her calm exterior, she was furious with Mr. T. for being an instrument in Roger's changes. Therefore Mr. T. said to Marilyn, "I guess I've disappointed you. You hoped that I would help Roger be a husband that would make life easier for you; instead, he seems to be more bothersome." Marilyn responded by saying that she was not concerned about Roger's "decline in mental health." Mr. T. suggested that perhaps it would be a good idea for Marilyn and Mr. T. to get together again so that this issue could be further discussed. Marilyn agreed.

In her next and succeeding interviews Marilyn further described that Roger was becoming more "animal-like." He seemed to curse more, wanted a more variegated sex life, and was "dominated by seeking pleasure." Realizing that Marilyn was projecting her own unacceptable id impulses onto Roger, Mr. T. asked Marilyn, "Have you given any thought to what is happening to Roger internally when he wants to gratify himself?" Marilyn felt that this "was an interesting concept" about which she hadn't thought. However, she had occasionally wondered if Roger had been deprived as a child—"perhaps he had insufficient care as a youngster." She further hypothesized that Roger was really turning her into "a mother figure" and trying "to gratify infantile urges." She thought that with more treatment he had "become more perverse."

As Marilyn talked more and more about Roger's "perversions," she occasionally tried to get Mr. T. to join with her in condemning Roger. For example, in her fourth month of contact with Mr. T. she asked, "Don't you think a man of 42 should quiet down his sexual urges?" When Mr. T. did not answer her question directly but asked, "Do you?" Marilyn became a bit irritated with him and said, "Yes, I think so. I was brought up to be clean in thought, word, and deed!"

Marilyn's annoyance with Mr. T. began to mount. Frustrated in her attempts to have him as an ally in her derogation of Roger, she told Mr. T. in her sixth month of weekly interviews with him, "I'm beginning to feel that you are not the right therapist for my husband. I think that deep down you are a sex-pot. Underneath your professional demeanor, you are a voyeur." Recognizing that Marilyn was now projecting her sexual wishes on to Mr. T. and condemning him for them, Mr. T. tried to be as non-defensive as possible. He asked Marilyn, "What do you think makes me want to be a voyeur?" Marilyn told Mr. T. that he was probably squelched as a child much the same way that Roger was, and that Roger and he were having "a verbal homosexual affair with each other."

As Mr. T. continued to subject himself to Marilyn's examination, she continued to talk about his constricted background and his "depraved" condition. However, by the tenth month of their relationship she started to talk about her *own* life, particularly about her own parents. Slowly she revealed how she was forced to inhibit her own sexual curiosity and her own spontaneity. On asking Mr. T. whether he thought her parents were "too rigid," Mr. T. answered "Sometimes I wonder whether you have some doubts about that." Marilyn slowly began to question her parents' "rules and regulations." By her sixteenth month of contact with Mr. T. she started to talk about her own childhood fantasies to play doctor, to read books which had sex pictures, and to ask questions about sex.

It took Marilyn over two years to diminish her own sexual inhibitions and to lessen the severity of her own superego. This required enormous patience on Mr. T.'s part and induced much pain and anxiety in Marilyn. However, Marilyn did become a much less ritualistic spouse and Roger and Marilyn were eventually able to have a more pleasureful marriage.

Just as the mate of the ritualistic spouse is the embodiment of her id, the ritualistic spouse is the superego of her marital partner. While the latter enters therapy feeling controlled, demeaned, and derogated, it is important for the practitioner to realize that beneath his complaints he wants to be punished for his id wishes. As we have learned from discussions and case analyses in earlier chapters, the therapeutic task of the counselor with the spouse who feels massacred is to expose his wish to be so treated.

Just as it is tempting to debate with the ritualistic spouse about the necessity of rules and regulations, it is also tempting to feel sorry for the husband or wife who feels constantly criticized and forever tyrannized. However, expressing pity for somebody who feels guilty only makes him feel more guilty. It is like telling a latency-aged child who has hostile feelings toward his parents but feels guilty about them that it is perfectly okay to try to feel better. This just makes the child feel all the more sinful. What the mate of the ritualistic spouse needs is to see why he wants so much criticism.

Hank G., age 38, sought marriage counseling from Dr. S., a male therapist. In his initial interview with Dr. S. Hank reported that he was very depressed, had gastrointestinal problems and other psychosomatic complaints, insomnia, and irritability. He ascribed his problems to his "very frustrating marriage" with his wife Sylvia. Hank complained, "She's always ordering me around and is never satisfied with anything I do." Married to Sylvia for over 10 years, he found himself constantly feeling "like a guilty boy" with her. He pointed out, "I have to hide when I smoke or drink because otherwise all hell will break loose. She'll yell, scream, and be awfully punitive with me. And I can't stand that." He also mentioned that if he ever cursed in front of Sylvia, she rebuked him. Finally, Sylvia didn't seem to have very much interest in sex and months would go by without any sexual contact between them.

Hank handled his relationship with Dr. S. the same way he related to Sylvia. Just as he daily reported all his business activities to Sylvia and waited for her approval or disapproval, he reported all his activities to Dr. S. and waited for his comments. When Dr. S. did not offer any rewards or punishments to Hank, Hank began to feel very uncomfortable. He told Dr. S. after three months of treatment that "the stuff we are doing isn't working—my marriage is just as bad, my depression is worse, and all the stuff I came here with is still there."

When Dr. S. asked Hank what he thought was lacking in their relationship that prevented Hank from progressing, Hank told Dr. S., "You say very little. You offer so little of yourself. I'd really like to know your reactions and you never tell me much. I feel lost." Dr. S. helped Hank verbalize more about his dissatisfactions with therapy. Hank was finally able to tell Dr. S., "I need validation. You have to tell me whether I'm right or wrong when it comes to Sylvia!"

As it became clearer and clearer to Hank that he was trying to get Dr. S. to be his superego and to function in the same way that Sylvia did with him, he began to realize that "all my life I've been a compliant good boy always scared of my own shadow." In his sixth month of his twice-weekly treatment he was able to talk about how he always felt dominated by both of his parents. "I was scared to tell them off and I know this is the way I feel with you and with Sylvia," Hank was able to say in an interview toward the beginning of his seventh month of treatment.

The more Hank realized how intimidated he felt by his parents, by his wife, and by his therapist, he began to experiment with asserting himself. In one of his interviews with Dr. S. Hank said that he was "sick and tired of acting like a compliant boy who obeyed every letter of the law." In the interviews he began to curse a little and became critical of Dr. S.'s clothes, speech, and lack of humor. When Dr. S. did not become defensive or retaliative Hank tried to assert himself with Sylvia. Instead of reporting every detail of his life to her each day he began to ask her about her activities. Instead of apologizing for cursing he told Sylvia that maybe she had a problem with "strong language," and instead of waiting for Sylvia "to permit sex," he started to take some initiative in bed.

Sylvia responded with intense rage when Hank became less compliant and less masochistic. She experienced his increased assertiveness as assaults and told him he was becoming a sadist. She started to have temper tantrums and told Hank that ever since he started to see "that stupid Freudian charlatan," he had become a renegade. Hank tried to enlist Dr. S.'s support against Sylvia by asking him to reaffirm his own notion that "Sylvia is acting like a crazy bitch." When Dr. S. asked Hank what his doubts were about, inasmuch as he seemed to want some reassurance, Hank said, "I guess it's hard for me to believe that Sylvia is not the Supreme Law of the Land. When I feel as strong as Sylvia or maybe stronger, I feel like a kid who is toppling over his parents. Then I feel guilty and want your support."

When Hank saw that Dr. S. was not going to treat him like a child, Hank began to make more and more of his own decisions. He was able, after one year of treatment, to let Sylvia know that he had waited a long time to tell her that her rules and regulations had always infuriated him and now he didn't think they were so necessary. He also told Sylvia that he felt she needed her rules because otherwise she'd be very anxious. While Sylvia continued to fight Hank's notions, as he became more sure of himself, she eventually took his advice and went into treatment for herself.

THE GROUP-MINDED SPOUSE

A latency child who cannot tolerate the closeness and intimacy of family interactions relies instead exclusively on his group relationships. There are many husbands and wives who, like latency children, cannot tolerate being alone with each other and rely excessively on groups. These are the couples who may spend three or four nights a week at church meetings or similar events. They are "needed" by the political party, theater group, or philanthropic society almost daily. Sometimes their compulsive group activity is directly social; the couples drink, dance, and converse several times a week with each other. In some groups, there is swinging, swapping, and other forms of group sex.

Many of the couples involved in compulsive group activity feel reasonably happy within themselves and with one another provided the social or political group outlets are constantly available. However, should a social group dissolve or a political group fragment, these husbands and wives become restless, irritable, and argumentative. Because they feel threatened by a one-to-one relationship in marriage their anxiety is expressed in ways that keep them apart.

Inasmuch as the group-minded spouse cannot tolerate emotional closeness, this husband or wife is not going to feel comfortable in a one-to-one relationship with a therapist and is going to feel almost as uncomfortable in conjoint therapy where the focus will be on the marriage. Because this couple feels safest in a group, when they experience marital stress they usually seek out a group experience with other couples. This couple's choice of therapeutic modality should be respected. To try to convince them of individual or conjoint treatment usually proves disastrous.

Seymour and Diane H., a couple in their mid-thirties, were forced to move into a new community because of Seymour's job change. The H.'s had lived in a small town, Y., all of their lives. They grew up there, they met in high school, their families knew each other well, and their friends in high school and in their local college were their close friends during their seven-year marriage. As Seymour said, "We've always been part of a close-knit group."

Both Seymour and Diane came from large families; each had four siblings and both described their families as if they were organizations in which all of the members had fixed roles. It had been extremely difficult for Seymour and Diane to move from community Y. to X. Neither of them had been out-of-town before and all of their contacts resided in the Y. community.

Upon moving to X. with their two children, ages three and four, the H.'s were very lonely. They told their minister about their deep sense of estrangement and feelings of isolation. After an interview with them he sent them to a family agency in the X. community to discuss their situation.

In their intake interview with Ms. R., a social worker, Seymour and

Diane described in detail their "wonderful" community of Y., their "close" friends, and their current sadness and loneliness. After Diane said (with Seymour agreeing) that "this was a nice chat but we miss our friends," Ms. R. responded by asking the H.'s how they would feel about being members of a married couples group that met in the agency. Immediately, the faces of Seymour and Diane brightened, and they both obviously welcomed the idea. Ms. R. told them that she was the leader of the group, would mention their interest to the group members, and they could attend their first meeting in about two weeks.

Just the idea of being in a group cheered the H.'s. They found themselves feeling closer to one another even before they attended their first meeting. At their first meeting the four other couples welcomed them warmly and asked them to talk about their backgrounds. Seymour and Diane found this easy to do and the group members experienced them as delightful people.

As the group sessions moved on with Ms. R. and the group members studying the interactions of each couple, Seymour and Diane began to learn some things about themselves. One of the issues that became a topic for study in the group was that neither of them talked to the other, but spent a lot of time relating to the other members and to Ms. R. Each seemed to want approval and validation from the other group members but not as a couple. Slowly each was able to share with the group and with Ms. R. how isolated they felt in their respective families and how the best way to get along was to be a hard-working family member who looked to others as judges who would validate them. They were further able to discuss how they each feared rejection from the other, were frightened of being spontaneous, and how emotional inhibition seemed to be a modus vivendi for both of them.

Facing their own way of relating to one another in the group was very helpful to the H.'s. They began to experiment at home and in the group confronting one another, and while anxiety-provoking at first, they were able to get some gratification from one another.

When the H.'s could rely on one another more, they moved into conjoint marital therapy. While inhibited at first, they were able to overcome their shyness and began to discuss their fear of anger, their reluctance to express their sexual desires, and other issues which they had never discussed before. The group had, in many ways, helped them to find themselves.

In Chapter 5 we stressed the importance of matching the therapeutic modality to the client's dynamics, history, and unique resistances. While we have attempted to demonstrate that individual treatment lasting many months or longer seems to help resolve marital conflicts for many—if not most—husbands and wives, it is important to reiterate that no treatment modality is a panacea for all married couples. The marriage counselor has to keep an open mind and to be flexible. Group treatment seems to be the therapeutic modality of choice for couples who have strong resistances to individual treatment, who fear conjoint therapy, but who feel comfortable in a group—at least at the initiation of counseling.

THE CHILD ORIENTED SPOUSE

There is a marked tendency on the part of parents to relive their own childhoods through their offspring. At each stage of their children's development they tend to recapitulate their prior transactions with their own parents (A. Freud, 1965; Strean, 1979). For example, if a woman received tender love and care from her mother during the oral period, she will be inclined to provide the same for her own child. Similarly, if she was the recipient of inconsistent responses from her mother, despite her best conscious intentions she will respond the same way to her own youngster. This principle will also hold during other developmental periods of her children. Her own childhood experiences during her anal and oedipal periods will be part of her inner script that will govern her transactions with her children. Fathers as well as mothers recapitulate their own childhoods with their children, and, as we have observed several times in our case analyses, spouses tend to relive their childhood pasts with one another in both their marital interactions as well as in their total family life.

When parents have unresolved problems with their latency experiences, one way of coping with these problems is to turn their family into a rigid group. Certain families tend to appear like committees in which individual autonomy is squelched and group cohesiveness is perenially championed. Anything, whether it be church attendance, entertainment, or reading, must be brought before the family council. This arrangement can offer many gratifications and present much security for all the family members. However, there is an inevitable crisis should any family member desire some independence. The familial symbiosis becomes torn and anxiety, anger and depression become rampant.

When a husband and wife have participated in a family symbiosis for many years, one time that can be very upsetting for them is when the children wish to go to an out-of-town college. The reason this is a particularly difficult time is that their child's departure is a lengthy and very visible one. It is not the same as their youngster going off to camp or visiting relatives. The cord is untied and parents can feel very cut off. They often handle their distress by fighting with one another and/or fighting with their child.

Usually the husband and wife who feel an enormous sense of loss when their child wants to go to an out-of-town college want family therapy if they seek therapeutic help at all. Through this modality they feel they have a chance to keep the family intact and they hope that the therapist will convince their youngster to attend college near their home.

On meeting a husband and wife who want family therapy so that they will not lose their child, the therapist has to be aware of two potential common countertransference reactions. First, there is a tendency to over-identify with the child, promote his independence, and feel critical of the parents. This attitude, while understandable, ignores the child's inevitable ambivalence about going away and it compounds the parents' sense of loss. Second, and related to the first countertransference problem, there is a wish to see the parents by themselves in conjoint therapy and to try to convince them that they are being selfish and not acting in the best interests of their child. Of course this posture alienates the parents who are seeking an ally and it also intensifies their child's ambivalence.

As stressed throughout this book, when a couple is very symbiotic, individual treatment is usually contraindicated. By the same token, when a family is symbiotic, family therapy seems indicated, at least at the beginning of the therapeutic contact. In this way resistances are respected, anxieties are not compounded, and the therapist appears to be more of a friend than an enemy. As Williams (1968, p. 389) has suggested with regard to respecting a family's resistance and their unique modus vivendi:

> If (a family's) resistance is not recognized and dealt with, the therapist may push patients to express certain affects prematurely and, in so doing, may provoke an even more rigid maintenance of the psycho-pathological homeostasis in both the individual and the family.

Byron and Laurie I., a couple in their mid-40s, called Dr. P., a male therapist, over the phone. With each of them on separate phones, they told him in their three-way conversation that their 18-year-old daughter, Betty, wanted to go out-of-town to college and that she was "clearly not ready for the experience." The I.'s mentioned further that Betty was upsetting not only her parents but "is creating havoc" for her younger sister Elaine as well. On Dr. P.'s asking the I.'s if they would like a face-to-face consultation with him, the I.'s readily accepted. Byron said, "We'll bring in the whole gang and maybe you can straighten things out."

All of the I.'s came for the consultation and all greeted Dr. P. enthusiastically. Soon both Byron and Laurie looked angrily at Betty and said, "We don't know what's gotten into her. She wants to go far away. We've always been a close family and now she wants to disrupt things." After a silence Dr. P. turned to Betty and asked what she was feeling as she heard this. Betty responded by crying and said how "horrible" she felt, that she was sorry that everybody was so upset, and that she didn't really want to upset the family. At this Elaine, the 14-year-old sister, perked up, put her arm around Betty and remarked, "Don't feel bad! Just don't go away and everything will be O.K.!" Byron and Laurie smiled and agreed with Elaine saying that they felt sorry that Betty was upset but all would be well for everybody if Betty would go to college in the area. Betty then said, "O.K. if you want me to stay, I'll stay," and started to leave the office. At this Dr. P. pointed out to Betty, "You'll stay at home but you want to get away now." Betty laughed and said, "Part of me does want to get away." On hearing this Laurie began to cry and said, "That hurts me!" Byron then put his arm around Laurie and looking at Betty said, "See what you are doing to your mother!" Betty remarked sarcastically, "Yeah, I'm a villain."

The I.'s agreed to return for more family interviews and continued the same type of interaction that they showed in their first interview. During their sixth session Dr. P. remarked, "I see that you have always been a close family and that you all have a lot of loving feelings toward each other. I also see that if one member of the family wants some independence, it is very upsetting for all of you." With that remark Byron and Laurie both became very indignant. Byron said, with Laurie concurring, "Of course, independence of one family member upsets us and why shouldn't it? A family is supposed to be together all the time. If I didn't have to work, I'd be with them all the time and I'm sure Laurie feels the same way." When Dr. P. remained silent, Betty said, "You all feel I'm doing something cruel. All I want is my own life—at least to some extent." To this Laurie said, "You are being cruel. You want to kill us!"

Recognizing that the I.'s were experiencing Betty's desire for independence as her wish to kill them, Dr. P. said, "I see where the trouble is. You feel that Betty is throwing a bomb at you and wants to destroy you!" The family members all related to this theme. They brought out that anger was a forbidden topic in their conversations, that independence was experienced as a death warrant, and that their joint quest for "togetherness" helped them avoid conflict. During the fourth month of therapy Betty said, "Look, I'll continue to see you, be in touch with you, and be a member of the family." This remark offered some reassurance to the rest of the family and Laurie, Byron, and Elaine seemed almost ready to accept Betty's decision to go away to college. Betty, however, began to look more and more uncomfortable in the family sessions. Dr. P. remarked about this and Betty—with some help from Dr. P.—was eventually able to acknowledge that at times she did fantasy killing the family members and that, indeed, she too felt that her going off to college was a way of saying "drop dead" to them.

Although Betty was extremely upset as she made her confession, the rest of the family members—after expressing dismay and surprise—came out with their own confessions. Each was able to acknowledge death wishes toward the other family members at various times. While this was painful for everybody, it was also very relieving. The I.'s began to laugh at themselves and each other and to make jokes about their "killing instincts."

As all of the I.'s could more directly discuss their murderous fantasies, they were all able to accept Betty's departure for college with more equanimity. The rest of the family stayed in therapy for the first few months of Betty's absence. They mourned her for a while but eventually accepted her autonomy with more grace. Laurie and Byron stayed in conjoint therapy for a while to work out some of their own problems around autonomy and independence.

MARRYING INTO A FAMILY

A very common childhood wish that expresses itself during latency is the desire for a perfect family. Many children during this time have the fantasy that they are adopted and their natural parents, if found, would provide them with the joy and bliss that are absent from their current life.

Inasmuch as latency is a frustrating time—the child has many responsibilities and is trying to renounce infantile wishes—the wish for different parents is understandable. Children frequently believe that all their discontents are caused by their parents; consequently, if they had different parents all would be well. Many fairytales that involve wicked witches and sinister father figures attest to the latency child's anger at their parents; stories such as Cinderella and Snow White, where the child is rescued, illustrate the universal childhood fantasy of being rescued by warm, loving, and attentive parental figures.

As we know, the wish for a perfect family life can be very much part of a man or woman's marital choice. Many individuals select their mates not so much because of the mate's characteristics but because they are really in love with the mate's parents. It is many a man who has selected his wife because he will be part of his father-in-law's business and be in daily contact with a man whom he thinks is the benign father for whom he always yearned. It is many a woman who marries a man because she experiences his mother as the maternal figure who will answer her prayers. And it is many men and women who feel that their in-laws are so much like the people they imagined were their real parents when they were children.

The notion that one has moved into the family of his dreams can lead to a feeling of ecstasy for a while; however, like any honeymoon, fantasies get punctured and the realistic limitations of the in-laws soon become apparent. Then the man or woman who thought he or she was a member of a perfect family becomes disillusioned and feels angry and deprived. The hostility that follows can be taken out on the mate and battles-royal can ensue.

Even when a spouse continues to feel that his in-laws are great people who provide much pleasure and security, this positive feeling can be diminished greatly by life events. In-laws get ill and die, they give up the family business, or they withdraw interest for a variety of their own reasons which may have nothing to do with their son-in-law or daughter-in-law. When the stable family network is dislodged, the disappointed spouse—without consciously realizing the cause—can lose interest in the mate and marital discord can erupt.

Howard J., age 45, sought treatment from Mr. N. because he had been depressed for over a year. He had lost sexual interest in his wife, Marjorie, and found himself irritable with her constantly. He had many fantasies of divorce and was seriously considering having an extramarital affair after 15 years of marriage. Howard told Mr. N. in their initial interview that he had not felt this way before. He had always loved his wife, enjoyed their children, and could not figure out what had happened to him.

A review of Howard's history revealed that he was the middle of three brothers. He described his parents as rather distant people who seemed more involved with their business and communal activities than with their family life. Howard brought out that he derived a lot of satisfaction from his relationships in clubs, centers, Y's, and at church. He also mentioned that he often felt closer to his friends' parents than he did to his own. During the course of presenting his background Howard brought out that as a young boy he sometimes fantasized that one of his friend's parents would adopt him because he spent so much time having fun at their home.

Howard was a good student and was graduated from college with honors. After trying his hand at a variety of jobs he "got a permanent wife and a permanent job at the same time." While dating Marjorie he found himself spending a lot of time at her parents' home and particularly enjoyed having "warm and friendly chats" with her father. There was much mutual warmth between the two of them and Marjorie's father asked

Howard to become his associate in his business. Howard loved the idea and a month after he started work for Marjorie's father Howard and Marjorie got married.

Inasmuch as Howard emphasized that his life had been going well until a year before he came into treatment, Mr. N. said, "Let's see what happened in your life one year ago." After many denials and rationalizations, Howard was able to say that a year ago his father-in-law began to talk about his own retirement and was planning to make his own son the president of the company. When Mr. N. commented on the fact that Howard must have had and probably still had a lot of feeling about his father-in-law's plans, Howard became teary-eyed. He talked about the fact that his father-in-law was "like a real father to me" and not only was he moving away from Howard "but he was showing a preference for his son." To Howard this was a powerful rejection and a deep humiliation. "I feel deserted, abandoned, and robbed," exclaimed Howard.

As Howard talked about how disturbed he was with his father-in-law's plans, he began to have memories of feeling rejected by his own father who he often thought preferred his two brothers. In an interview during his sixth month of his twice-a-week therapy, Howard said with considerable emotion, "My oldest brother was loved for being the first-born and my younger brother was adored because he was the baby of the family. I was ignored because I was in the middle." He described many instances of feeling "like a second-class citizen" in his family and realized how similarly he felt at his job and in general.

In talking very animatedly to Mr. N. about his feeling rejected by his father-in-law and father, Howard began to feel less depressed and started to feel more warmly toward Marjorie. However, soon after reporting this to Mr. N., his old feelings of dejection returned. As this sequence of events was explored it became clear that Howard was feeling warmly toward Mr. N. but was frightened of his feelings. He worried that if he began to like Mr. N., Mr. N. would disappoint him the same way his father and father-in-law had. "I'm convinced," said Howard, "if I trust you, you'll get disgusted with me."

On investigating with Howard what about his behavior would be disgusting to Mr. N., Howard was able to bring out many fantasies of being Mr. N.'s little son. Howard wanted to climb on Mr. N.'s lap and be stroked. He wanted hugging and he wanted compliments. He wanted to be told over and over again that he was loved. With embarrassment he shared some homosexual fantasies with Mr. N. He wanted to suck Mr. N.'s penis and have anal intercourse with him.

Sharing his wishes with Mr. N. to be loved by him again helped Howard feel and function better but again his "up" feeling did not sustain itself for long. He again felt depressed and again lost interest in Marjorie emotionally and sexually. Mr. N. noted that Howard's depressed feeling followed his telling Mr. N. how much love he wanted from him, and Mr. N. asked Howard about this. Here, Howard was able to report that he must have disgusted Mr. N. with his homosexual fantasies and that Mr. N. couldn't want to be with him very much knowing what "a pervert" he was.

It became clear that just as Howard thought that Mr. N. would want to reject him for his homosexual fantasies he started to realize that he was interpreting his father-in-law's retirement plans the same way. In a dream Howard had after a year of treatment, Howard's father-in-law and Mr. N. were both admonishing him for wanting so much love and for wanting homosexual contact. Howard was able to interpret the dream himself, recognizing that he was arranging to be punished for his strong wishes to love and be loved by father-figures.

The more Howard could accept his wishes to love and be loved by a father figure, the less depressed he was and the more he could love Marjorie. Eventually he shared his distress about his father-in-law with her, and she was very supportive and understanding. Feeling loved by his wife and understood by his therapist, Howard left his father-in-law's business and started one of his own. It took him about two years of therapy before he could emotionally separate from his father-in-law and be his own man. With a more secure feeling about his own strengths he became much more loving and intimate with Marjorie.

In this case, Howard J. had a rather positive relationship with Marjorie and though more involved with his father-in-law than with her, he never seriously considered divorce. In some cases where the relationship between the spouses is not strong, a disruption in the relationship with the in-law can lead to a serious consideration of divorce. This is particularly true when the in-law dies.

Bella K., age 42, sought marriage counseling from Ms. M. Married for 17 years to Ray, she told Ms. M. in her first consultation interview that she needed help "to feel more confident about arranging a divorce." For the past two years she had "stopped loving Ray," was uninterested in him sexually, and did not even feel like talking to him most of the time. What bothered Bella about getting divorced was the fact that her two daughters, aged 10 and 12, would be very upset about it.

In examining her marriage to Ray, Bella brought out that they had always seemed "to get along" with each other and did not have much conflict. "We were a normal family for a long time—but now I just want to try it alone," said Bella.

Reviewing her history, Bella brought out that when she was four years old her mother died of cancer. She didn't recall any specific reactions to her mother's death, but she did remember spending a great deal of time by herself afterward. She was an only child, her father was away from home a lot, but she did "get some care from her maternal grandmother." In talking about her mother's death and her father's absences, Bella was devoid of affect and seemed to talk about these traumas in a matter-of-fact fashion.

Bella told Ms. M. that one of the things she remembered about her courtship with Ray was the close family atmosphere that existed in Ray's home. She became very close to her mother-in-law and after Bella and Ray were married, Bella spoke on the phone at least once a day to her mother-in-law and saw her at least once a week. The close relationship between Bella and her mother-in-law continued until the mother-in-law's death about two years prior to Bella seeking therapy.

It became clear to Ms. M. that Bella's turning away from Ray took place around the same time that Ray's mother died. Ms. M. felt that it was important to help Bella talk more about her mother-in-law's death. When Ms. M. asked Bella how she felt in response to her mother-in-law's death, Bella again seemed devoid of affect and spoke about the details of the death in a matter-of-fact manner. On seeing that Bella reacted to her mother-in-law's death in the same manner that she coped with her mother's death, Ms. M. said, "You know, the death of a mother is very rough to a four-year-old girl and the death of a mother-in-law who was a mother to you can be equally as rough." To this, Bella responded with a tone of resignation and merely remarked, "That's life."

After Ms. M.'s intervention Bella began to cancel sessions and come late for others. She did not give any reason for her behavior. However, when Ms. M. suggested that Bella began to withdraw from her right after Ms. M. talked about her mother and mother-in-law's deaths, Bella became irritated with Ms. M. She told her that she seemed to be trying to get her to be upset and she wasn't going to succeed. "I came here for help in getting a divorce and you are trying to talk about my mother-in-law!" bellowed Bella in her fourth month of counseling. She further pointed out that she was going to leave treatment if Ms. M. was not going to do her job properly.

Bella's sessions with Ms. M. got stormier. She began to accuse Ms. M. of "not being available" to her, of not "meeting" (her) emotional needs, and of "being in another world." When the intensity of her anger diminished a bit, Ms. M. said, "I get the feeling that you feel very let down by me in the same way that you felt let down by your mother and mother-in-law. We've all angered you." For the first time in their contact Bella was able to accept Ms. M.'s interpretation and went on to talk about how she had always squelched her anger, repressed her dependency yearnings, and tried her best to cope no matter how upset she was. Slowly she realized how revengeful she had been feeling toward her mother and her mother-in-law and wished "there was a way of getting even with them." Eventually, she was able to see that her desire to leave Ray was her unconscious attempt to put him in the same position in which she had been placed by her mother and by her mother-in-law—abandoned and helpless.

On recognizing her revengeful feelings, Bella's warmth and sexuality toward Ray returned. With this she also began to feel more positively toward Ms. M. She started to have fantasies of being rocked and fed by Ms. M. and clearly demonstrated her deep yearning to have a consistently warm and nurturing mother. From a position of being a pseudo-independent rather affectless woman, Bella began to dress up for her interviews with Ms. M. and tried to charm her. When Ms. M. would occasionally compliment Bella on her clothes and on her good taste, Bella would cry. She stated with much emotion, "That's what I always wanted from a mother."

It took Bella four years of therapy to resolve her revengeful feelings, acknowledge her dependency, and face how she displaced much of her distress onto Ray. At the end of her therapy, she was able to resume a very positive relationship with Ray and divorce seemed entirely out of the question.

One of the reasons that both Howard J. and Bella K., the clients in the last two vignettes, were able to use help profitably is that both yearned for parental figures. In both cases the therapists were experienced as the parental figures for whom they were pining. Although they felt a great deal of revenge toward their own parents, in-laws, and therapists, their unconscious wishes for a parental figure were stronger than their revenge. Sometimes a client's revenge is so powerful that he has to defeat his mate and his therapist, and despite the therapist's best efforts the client's wish to defeat him remains so strong that he leaves treatment prematurely.

Dot L., age 36, sought help from Dr. K. because she wanted to experiment with a trial separation from her husband Peter. Married for 10 years, Dot told Dr. K. that she found Peter to be very unresponsive, ungiving, and boring during most of their marriage, particularly since their daughter's birth five years before. Dot was an adopted girl and both of her parents had died when she was in her early teens. She had spent a lot of time in various foster homes and when she went off to college, she was essentially on her own. She had been graduated from college with good grades, gone on to a school of social work, and practiced social work since graduation. She met Peter soon after she began working, liked his "keen mind," and felt "very much at home" with his parents, brother, and sister.

In thinking about the deterioration of her marriage, Dot felt that Peter had become withdrawn when his parents had moved far away to retire. After Dot spoke at length about Peter's inability to face his parents' departure, Dr. K. asked her how she felt when her in-laws moved away. Dot became irritated with Dr. K. and told him that he was trying to make her a client and trying to get to her feelings. When Dr. K. acknowledged that he was attempting to understand her better Dot became even angrier. She told him that he was trying "to trap" her "into a relationship" and that this would not work. Dot further told Dr. K., "All my life I've taken care of myself and you won't win." On Dr. K.'s suggesting that his wish to talk with her about her feelings seemed to make her think that they were in a contest, Dot acknowledged this was true and she would not enter into one.

Dot began to cancel sessions, insisting that she had to spend time with her own clients and didn't want to be a client herself. Attempts on Dr. K.'s part to point out that his continued wish to talk to her made her feel trapped, were to no avail. In her last interview with Dr. K. she said, "I'm angry at you, angry at my husband, angry at the world and I intend to keep it that way. I'll help others but no one is going to help me."

BROTHER–SISTER MARRIAGES

During latency, when children are trying to renounce their attachment to the parent of the opposite sex, one way they cope is by displacing their romantic interests onto a sibling of the opposite sex. Brothers and sisters play house, play doctor, and sometimes have sex-play with each other. Many a sister and brother remain so firmly attached to each other that they do not move away from their close relationship and remain unmarried. Some of them do get married, but make their sibling their number one love: this induces jealous reactions in their mates and evokes marital discord.

A not uncommon marriage is where the spouses unconsciously make each other their siblings. Their interaction is often amicable and they both derive gratification from the relationship. However, because the incest taboo between brothers and sisters is part of everyone's superego, the brother–sister marriage has its difficulties. The couple cannot easily feel sexually intimate with one another; often, the husband becomes impotent and/or the wife is unable to derive pleasure from sex. As is true in many marriages, husband and wife blame one another for their marital difficulties. Eventually their tempers flare, they frequently insult one another, and they consider getting divorced.

When the brother–sister dyad experience a lot of marital difficulty and consider divorce, they find it extremely difficult to cope with their fantasies of separation. On one hand, they feel unsatisfied, unfulfilled, and angry enough to end the marriage. On the other hand, they are like a pair of loving siblings who cannot tolerate the break. Fantasies of murder—which are usually unconsciously present during a time when divorce is being considered—are extremely terrifying to these spouses. To want to hurt, destroy, or kill a spouse is a horrible thought. Consequently, these mates waver back and forth, threatening divorce, reconciling and then reconsidering divorce. Nothing seems right.

Inasmuch as spouses who make one another siblings are unaware that they are doing this, the marriage counselor may not recognize that this is a dynamic factor present in their interaction. Fortunately, there is usually evidence when the brother–sister marriage is at work. Often the mates describe themselves as "buddies" or "pals." They can equally participate with much respect toward one another when it comes to such matters as domestic chores, entertainment, child-bearing, and so on. Sometimes they may be engaged in the same business and work well together. Yet, what is conspicuously absent in their relationship is an erotic, intimate flavor. Not only do they have sexual difficulties, but they find it difficult to use endearing terms toward one another and find it even more difficult to kiss and hug one another. Occasionally these mates refer to one another in slang terms such as "Buster," "Pal," or "Chum." Yet, as already mentioned, both members of the dyad feel unfulfilled and angry. When they do seek marriage counseling, they usually want to be seen conjointly.

Bob and Alice M., a couple in their mid-forties who had been married for close to 20 years, sought marriage counseling at a family agency. Their social worker, Ms. K., was told by them during their intake interview that they were both unhappy, depressed, and very angry. They had not had sex with one another for over a year and instead were arguing about many things. Bob and Alice agreed that what they argued about seemed inconsequential, but they both "needed to fight."

A review of their marital interaction uncovered that Bob and Alice always felt like "good friends." They found it rather easy to do things for and with one another and identified with one another's achievements. Both of them were schoolteachers and shared their experiences and ideas, deriving much satisfaction and support from one another.

When it came to sex, Bob and Alice were able to acknowledge that neither of them had derived much satisfaction, but that both tried "to please" the other. "Sex," Bob said, with Alice agreeing, "seems to have been different from other parts of our marriage. We haven't had much fun."

On pursuing the issue that their sexual relationship was "sterile," Ms. K. asked Bob and Alice to discuss what came to their minds when they thought about sex. After many statements involving "going through the motions" and "not being turned on," Bob and Alice were able to acknowledge that they felt that there was something "forbidden" about having sex with one another. They even agreed that they might be more "turned on" by others. While this notion hurt both of them and induced quite a bit of anger in them when they talked about it, Bob was able to say, "Sometimes I think you make me your brother." In anger, Alice responded, "Sometimes I think you make me your sister."

Ms. K. confronted Bob and Alice with the fact that they both felt they were being treated as siblings. After some defensive remarks, Alice talked about her close relationship with her older brother and Bob discussed elements of his relationship with his younger sister. It took the M.'s a long time to share with one another and with Ms. K. that they had both been involved in a lot of "forbidden" sex-play with their real siblings. On making these confessions, they were able to see how their own sexual life had become "forbidden."

After about a year of once-a-week counseling Bob and Alice began to joke in their conjoint sessions and occasionally called one another "Sis" and "Bro." With more acceptance of their incestuous feelings, they talked about using their real siblings as parental substitutes. As each of them could face more and more their *own wishes* to be a sibling and their *own wishes* to make the other a sibling, sex became less dangerous and less forbidden. They began to enjoy one another much more and upon the resumption of a more fulfilling sexual life their arguments diminished a great deal.

During latency when sibling relationships are very strong between brother and sister (or between sister and sister or brother and brother), each feels a tremendous obligation toward the other to share all of their possessions. There are many individuals who cannot enjoy their married life because they feel that their brother or sister is being short-changed. In the mind of these individuals a happy marriage is experienced as depriving and hurting their sibling and they unconsciously have to wreck their own marital happiness. They unconsciously reason, "If I'm having a good time, my sibling is suffering." This distortion derives from the wish of the child who would like to be "the one and only," deprive or destroy the sibling, but feels enormous guilt for his imaginary evil deeds.

Janet N., age 26, had been married one year to a man she very much loved. However, "without any explicable reason" she began to feel less and less sexually responsive toward her husband and found herself criticizing him constantly.

As Janet and her therapist, Dr. J., a male, explored her life, it became quite clear that she had a strong symbiotic attachment to her two unmarried sisters. As she was able to discuss with Dr. J. how important it was for her "to share everything" with her sisters, she was eventually able to get in touch with her strong but very unacceptable competitive fantasies toward them. With the realization that she unconsciously felt that she was destroying her sisters by having a happy married life, she saw why she was trying to destroy Frank, her husband, instead. Janet was so worried about losing her sisters' love if she had a man, that without consciously realizing it she was sabotaging her marriage. Said Janet, "I guess Frank's love is easier to lose than my sisters'."

LATENCY "POWER STRUGGLES" IN MARRIAGE

During latency, when oedipal fantasies are frightening, there is a tendency on the part of many youngsters to regress to pregenital preoccupations, particularly to anal matters. Children at this time like to indulge in "bathroom talk" and use words like "shit," "piss," and "asshole." Rather than deal with incestuous fantasies and oedipal competition which creates so much anxiety for them, they return to the life of the anal period. One of the features of the anal period, we recall, is power struggles between the child and his parents as to whom is the boss. These power struggles are recapitulated in marriage.

In contrast to those individuals who are fixated at the anal stage of development, husbands and wives who are involved in "latency power struggles" are regressing from the anxiety that love, tenderness, and eroticism evokes. Rather than make love—which is dangerous to them—they prefer to make war.

Latency power-strugglers often describe a very pleasant and enjoyable courtship and cannot understand why their relationship deteriorated as soon as they got married. They are unaware of the fact that the commitment that is inherent in a marriage is repulsive to them for many reasons. First, they are frightened of the intimacy and closeness which marriage implies. Second, because they have moved away from tenderness and eroticism, they perceive marriage as a situation in which they are being constantly controlled and overpowered. Finally, they are very upset about feeling so weak next to their mate, to whom, at one time, they had felt like an equal; yet they do not realize that the reason they feel so vulnerable is because they have unconsciously made themselves children and made their mates parents.

Usually latency power-strugglers seek conjoint marriage counseling. However, their motives for doing so are not always apparent. What the clinician should realize when conjoint marriage counseling is proposed by these clients is that unconsciously these people want to fight some more; if they or their mates are seen alone, they lose this opportunity. Concomitant with this desire is often another one—to present their fight to a neutral and understanding parental figure with the hope that he will help them resolve their marital conflicts.

In working conjointly with the clients that we are discussing, it is important to help them become aware of the gratification and the protection that they derive from their squabbles. Unless they can face this, limited growth takes place.

Gene and Joan O., a couple in their early thirties, came for marriage counseling to Mr. I. because they were battling verbally and physically during the entire course of their seven-year marriage. They could not agree on anything, felt controlled by one another, and derived almost "no satisfaction" from one another.

In their first interview with Mr. I., the O.'s spent only about two minutes before a battle between them started. Gene said, "We're here because we fight all the time." Joan responded, "Yes, as soon as we sit down, he says something negative." She turned to Gene and said, "You don't say, we've come here to learn to get along better and the reason you don't say it is because *you* want to fight." When Gene was silent, Joan looked at Mr. I. and said, "Doesn't his silence mean he agrees with me? He wants to fight!" Gene then said, "You are trying to get him to side with you. Isn't she trying to do that, Mr. I?" Before Mr. I. could respond, Joan angrily snarled, "You know damn well that's what you want, you bastard!"

Toward the end of their session, the O.'s agreed with Mr. I. that it might be a good idea to return for more discussions, but they used the next six or seven weekly sessions of their conjoint therapy to battle intensely. During the middle of their seventh session Mr. I. had a chance to comment and stated, "You people obviously find fighting to be a way of life for you. What do you suppose you get out of it?" There was a long silence. Then Gene said, "It's a funny thing. We didn't fight when we were living together unmarried. Something happened when we put on the rings." Joan, for the first time in their therapy, agreed with Gene and said thoughtfully, "You are right, Gene. I don't know what happened when we got married."

Mr. I. encouraged the couple to think more about what getting married meant to them. They concurred that on getting married they had both lost interest in sex and much of their love had turned to hatred. Further reflection yielded much data. It turned out that both Gene and Joan were products of broken homes. They had both witnessed a great deal of strife between their respective parents. Each of them realized that, indeed, fighting had been a way of life for their parents and that this was something which they had "unconsciously copied." Gene was able to remark during their eleventh session, "I guess I want to be the same as my old man—always keeping my dukes up and always ready for the battle." Joan then said, "I guess I kind of admired my mother who wouldn't take shit from my father."

As Gene and Joan explored their identification with their parents, they began to consider the fact that love in marriage was something neither had witnessed. "It's something foreign to me," remarked Joan. Gene said he felt the same way. When Gene and Joan were asked by Mr. I. what frightened them about loving one another, neither of them could answer the question. Instead, each began to accuse the other of not being able to tolerate their warm feelings. The battles reemerged with each telling the other that he or she was "all shit," "a lot of junk," and "sexless." Inasmuch as the insults continued unabated for five or six sessions, Mr. I. intervened and said, "During the last several weeks you have both been preventing the other from loving you!" After some silence Gene said, "I'm ready to be loved," and Joan said, "So am I." A long silence ensued and then the couple argued about who was going to initiate the loving. Each felt "put down" if he or she "went first." Each was able to acknowledge that initiating lovemaking or even expressing loving feelings induced a powerless feeling, and each felt like a child "giving in" to a more powerful parent. Gene was able to say that when he initiated either making love or verbalizing loving feelings he felt as if he were "in the position of a little child being commanded to do something—like doing homework, washing the dishes, or shitting on a pot." Joan laughed but pointed out that she felt the same way.

As the O.'s talked in their conjoint sessions about their fears and anxieties regarding intimacy, they reported that they were fighting less at home and having sex a little bit more. Nonetheless, they both acknowledged after six months of treatment that they were each struggling with anxiety over intimacy.

When Gene and Joan could face their fears around sexual and emotional closeness, they were both able to confront repressed oedipal fantasies. Joan talked about "being a sexual woman is something frightening." She commented that she had had sexual fantasies toward her father when she was a young girl but she had felt that these fantasies were very danger-ous. Exploration revealed that inasmuch as her father hated her mother, she would have felt too much like a destroyer of her mother if she had been amorous with her father. Gene remarked that he had felt the same way with his parents when he was a boy.

In a session after a year-and-a-half of treatment had elapsed, Gene said to Mr. I., "Every time I'm near her, I hear the voice of my mother and I cringe." Joan replied, "But I'm not your mother and you are not my son." Gene became reflective and began to realize that it had never dawned on him that it was up to him as to how much Joan would be a mother figure for him. He always felt that it was something imposed on him. Joan was able to acknowledge similar distortions.

The more Joan and Gene faced the facts that they were turning one another into parental figures and then feeling vulnerable and guilty, the better they communicated, enjoyed sex, felt more loving and reduced their hatred.

Sometimes in the counseling situation, latency power-strugglers can col-lude and try to fight with the therapist. When the therapist is clear that he is being utilized as a scapegoat, he can confront the couple with this fact and study with them what gratification and protection they derive from blasting him. Usually it is the couple's way of not facing their own hostility toward one another. Of course, by maintaining a fight, the couple also defends against a bigger and more ominous fear—that of closeness and intimacy.

LEAVE ME ALONE

As we have suggested several times, the average environment expects a great deal from the latency child (Hartmann, 1964). Most children are required to adapt to the many requirements of a school situation from the rather free life of prelatency. The child must internalize a host of *new* rules and regulations; he must learn to share with more youngsters than ever before; he is asked to acquire new cognitive and social skills, and in several ways is asked to be a "little adult." Tremendous respect is due the child who meets the many demands society places upon him during the latency period (Josselyn, 1948).

According to some researchers (English and Pearson, 1945), the en-vironment should provide experiences that allow the child to relapse into play and to do what he wants to do—in effect giving the child a "vaca-tion" so that he can build up a reserve with which to face the demands of the social world. Unfortunately, the same institutions which are designed to provide fun and to provide the sublimatory expression of instinctual drives actually require tremendous effort from the child in controlling those drives. Many camps, little leagues, schools, and community centers tend to overlook how much pressure they place on latency children to work hard and produce and how little emphasis they put on helping these children to relax and enjoy themselves.

When the latency child has had a great deal of pressure to produce placed on him by parents, schoolteachers, community center workers, and so on, he builds up a tremendous amount of resentment toward anybody who wants something from him. This resentment is then taken into his marital relationship where he invariably experiences his mate as somebody who is pressuring him to produce. Sex is viewed not as an experience that will provide mutual pleasure, but as a command performance in which he is supposed to "put out" and satisfy his mate. If the mate is hurt, upset, or unhappy, listening to her is experienced as another chore and realistic domestic chores are seen as heavy burdens. All this spouse wants, after a while, is to be left alone. Being in contact with his mate always means that he is placed in a situation where he is working hard for a parental figure.

Usually the spouse who consciously wants to be left alone is married to someone who does put many demands on him. The reason a demanding mate has been chosen by him is because he is in reality a guilt-ridden person with a punitive superego who unconsciously wants a boss against whom he can rebel. If he did not have such a demanding mate, he would constantly be tormented by guilt and feel very depressed. With a nagging mate he can discharge his enormous resentment.

The spouse who wants to be left alone rarely seeks marriage counseling. He sees it as another burden to take on—and he is sure it has nothing in it for him. He is convinced that the marriage counselor's office is a place for him to be chastised and criticized. If anybody benefits from counseling, it will be his mate and/or the therapist—not he. Consequently, in working with this spouse it is very important not to try to convince him to come into treatment. If he does not want treatment his wish should be respected. Otherwise he becomes a very resistant client. If he truly believes that the therapist is not going to pressure him to become a client, he may become one. However, if he thinks the therapist has some investment in turning him into a client, he will insist on being left alone.

Herman P., age 35, was pressured by his wife, Nancy, to see her marriage counselor because she could not tolerate his constant resentment of her. He seemed to be against everything she was for, and he also seemed to oppose anything she wanted for herself.

After resisting his wife's "pestering" him for many months, Herman finally relented and made an appointment to have an interview with her therapist. During the course of the interview when the therapist told him that he needed treatment Herman said, "Nobody is going to tell me what I need," and walked out on the therapist.

Two years later when Herman was again persuaded to see a therapist, he saw Dr. H., a male therapist. Upon realizing that Herman was not really very motivated to pursue treatment out of an inner conviction of his own, Dr. H. shared this observation with Herman and told him, "I get the impression that you feel pressured to be in counseling and that it's not really something you want for yourself." Herman brightened up and remarked, "You are right on target!" He brought out how much he resented Nancy's constant demands and that "marriage counseling is another one of them." Herman said, "For once I'll do what I want. I'm not going into this counseling. If I ever want it for myself, I'll be back."

A month later Herman returned to see Dr. H. He told Dr. H. that for about two weeks after he saw him, he felt "on top of the world." However, his elated feeling turned into depression and now he was convinced that he needed treatment.

The initial experience with Dr. H. that Herman had in which he felt elated after his first interview with him and then became depressed was utilized by Dr. H. in further work with Herman. Herman and Dr. H. learned that the former felt very pleased after the first interview because he experienced Dr. H. as somebody who was helping him to defy Nancy; this gave him a feeling of liberation. However, exploration revealed that Herman felt so guilty for defying Nancy that he had to punish himself and, therefore, he became depressed. This pattern of defiance and then wanting punishment for it was something that Herman had been doing throughout his entire marriage and throughout a good part of his life.

As a child Herman was pressured to do outstandingly well in everything he undertook. It was only when he got into treatment with Dr. H. that he was able to recognize how much resentment he felt about "putting out for the whole world" and doing it almost all of his life. In his therapy Herman was able to relive and then resolve many of his marital conflicts and his other interpersonal difficulties. When he saw that Dr. H. did not pressure him to work hard and did not punish him if he "felt like being left alone," Herman began to recognize how much he was using Nancy as both a mother and a father whom he had to obey. He also saw that he hated her for it. He was also able to realize that many of his arguments with Nancy could be avoided if he didn't view her as such a punishing parental figure.

The more Herman could face his own wish to be obedient and then fight being compliant, the more his relationship with Nancy improved. Because she became less of a superego figure to him, he began to be with her more and enjoy it.

Unresolved latency problems contribute toward many marital difficulties. Just as latency requires the child to develop more frustration tolerance, more empathy with others, and more capacity to delay gratification, marriage requires these ego functions to work. If the husband or wife has not diminished some of his or her narcissism, grandiosity, and omnipotence, he or she will be a very difficult mate with whom to live and love.

CHAPTER 10

Treating the Romantic Spouse

Prior to Freud's *Three Essays on The Theory of Sexuality* (1905), adolescence was viewed as the beginning of an individual's sexual life. However, since the time Freud discovered infantile sexuality, adolescence has been conceptualized differently. It is now considered to be a period of final transformation, a bridge between diffuse infantile sexuality and genitally centered adult sexuality (A. Freud, 1958).

In a paper called "Some Problems of Adolescence," the psychoanalyst Ernest Jones (1922, pp. 398–399) pointed out that

> adolescence recapitulates infancy, and that the precise way in which a given person will pass through the necessary stages of development in adolescence is to a very great extent determined by the form of his infantile development . . . The individual recapitulates and expands in the second decennium of life the development he passed through during the first five years.

In *The Ego and the Mechanisms of Defense,* Anna Freud (1946) pointed out that the *Sturm und Drang* of adolescence should be expected. Oedipal and other childish fantasies are revived in intense form; under the impact of anxiety the teenager wants to regress. However, the wish to regress and be a young child again conflicts with the adolescent's desires to be independent and emancipated from his parents. This emotional seesaw that young people experience—wanting cuddling, hugging, and dependency gratification—threatens the adolescent's wish for autonomy. Consequently, many adolescents are extremely moody because they cannot tolerate either dependence or independence and go back and forth, not satisfied with either.

When the conflict of independence versus dependence is not resolved during the teenage years, the struggle manifests itself in marriage. Many spouses want to be hugged, cuddled, and loved but feel contemptible when they show these desires. Therefore they try to be independent of their mates, but are left feeling unfulfilled and ungratified. Usually these spouses project their conflicts onto their mates, much like teenagers project their struggles onto their parents. Many adolescents, when they find their dependency yearnings unacceptable, point out that their parents are too controlling and too intrusive. Yet these same young people also aver that their parents do not give them appropriate advice, sufficient material goods, and enough privileges. By the same token, spouses who have unresolved adolescent problems accuse their mates of not giving them enough space, but at the same time they maintain that their mates do not give them enough support and empathy either.

Adolescents tend to show considerable volatility of feeling. They love passionately and hate intensely. They are capable of keen interest in one subject but can be equally bored with another one. Each emotion fills the teenager totally, but none for long. Allied to this intensity of feeling is the adolescent's strong desire for frequent and immediate gratification. He wants what he wants when he wants it, but he has poor frustration tolerance. Because it is unlikely that he is aware of the consequences of his actions, he can make rash judgments and poor decisions. He frequently suspends such ego functions as judgment and reality testing and fails to show any self-awareness or self-criticism. Often regressing to an infantile state of narcissism, the adolescent can appear to be insensitive and indifferent to the needs and wishes of others (Fountain, 1961). Adolescence, therefore, can be described as an "interruption of peaceful growth, and the upholding of a steady equilibrium during the adolescent process is in itself abnormal" (A. Freud, 1958, p. 275).

Many spouses who visit marriage counselors appear like passionate adolescents. These are the emotional men and women who yearn for a deep and close relationship with their mates but are furious with them for not reciprocating enough. They believe romance is and should be available all the time in their marriages and they want therapeutic help so that their deep wishes can be realized.

A close-to-universal phenomenon that teenagers demonstrate in coping with their sexuality is what Alexander and Ross (1952) term "bribing the superego." Adolescents pet above the waist but not below; they do not neck on the first date, but do so on the second date, and they do not have sexual intercourse until they agree "to go steady." These compromises are arranged to appease the superego and to expiate guilt. Frequently these "bribes" are carried into other dimensions of their interpersonal lives. They can masturbate after they have studied energetically; they can take some "pot" after they have performed "a good deed," and they can gorge themselves with food after they have fasted for a couple of days.

Placating the superego is something that is frequently observed in many marriages. One or both spouses feel extremely ambivalent about enjoying sexual pleasure—or enjoying pleasure in general. One way of coping with this ambivalence is to avoid pleasure after having some. Sometimes two partners can do this at the same time; more often they make each other a superego and expect punishment and rejection from the mate after they have partaken in a joyful experience. A phenomenon to which we alluded in earlier chapters is the one in which a spouse provokes a fight, gets punished, and only then feels the freedom to enjoy himself. Or, a spouse can be the recipient of pleasure from his mate and then destroy it by unconsciously arranging to be rejected or hurt afterwards.

When dependency needs are strong but unacceptable, when sexual desires are intense but frightening, and when wishes to be strong and capable are powerful but activate anxiety, the adolescent can "drop out," "tune out," or "act out." In many ways, teenagers in asserting their identities loudly proclaim, "I rebel, therefore I am!" (Blos, 1967; Erikson, 1956).

Rebellion during adolescence is an overdetermined symptom. Rather than acknowledge passive and dependent desires, the teenager says to his parents, "Who needs you?" Rather than owning his sexual desires toward the opposite sex, the adolescent states, "The hell with sex!" In renouncing his loving and sexual wishes toward both boys or girls, he yells, "A plague on both your houses."

Erik Erikson (1950) has referred to a form of behavior that is quite common during adolescence with the term "negative identity." By this term, Erikson is referring to the kind of action in which the teenager sensitizes himself to what he thinks parents, teachers, and "significant others" want from him—and then he does the opposite. If he thinks his parents want him to be religious, he becomes an agnostic. If he thinks he is expected to dress fashionably, he wears old clothes. If he thinks he should be a liberal, he becomes a reactionary.

Some husbands and wives cope with the *Sturm und Drang* of marriage by acquiring a negative identity. They sensitize themselves to what they think their mates want and then do the opposite. If the mate prefers sex at night, they insist on it during the day. If the mate prefers small groups, they look to huge assemblies. If the mate votes Democratic, they vote Republican. Like the adolescent with a negative identity, these spouses acquire a sense of power and a feeling of security through their spiteful behavior.

Although sexual pleasure may be regarded unquestionably as a constructive form of pleasure and a basic directing force of mental life, it can also serve as a defense to obscure anxieties and terrors that are not always visible to the client or to the practitioner (Coen, 1981). This is particularly true among many adolescents who use sexuality to cover up intolerable feelings of anger, depression, separation anxiety, a weak self-image, or a weak body-image. Husbands and wives can use sex compulsively to ward off anxiety. If two partners feel anxious at the same time and both want to use sex to diminish their discomfort, then this form of defense will not necessarily create marital conflicts. However, the way it usually works out is that one partner wants to use sex to ward off anxiety and the other partner feels used. Then both partners feel misunderstood and marital tension mounts.

Because adolescents have to cope with the resurgence of infantile wishes and therefore are bombarded by oral fantasies to incorporate, anal desires to smear, oedipal wishes to compete, incestuous yearnings, homosexual tendencies, and murderous thoughts, they often feel they are "going crazy." Due to their powerful narcissism, frequent lack of relatedness, and at times impeded ego functions, teenagers have often reminded some clinicians of adult schizophrenics (Spotnitz, 1961). Indeed, the original Greek term for schizophrenia, *dementia praecox,* means "the disease of adolescence."

Many spouses feel that their mates are driving them crazy. Like teenagers, these spouses do not know what to do with their dependency wishes, aggressive desires, sexual fantasies, and soon, and like the adolescent who appears schizophrenic, they withdraw for long periods of time, talk to themselves, and refuse to relate.

Let us now examine in more detail some of the marital problems that emerge from unresolved conflicts at adolescence and discuss some of the therapeutic principles that are important in clinical work with husbands and wives who show these problems.

THE EMANCIPATED SPOUSE

In this day and age feeling emancipated is important to many people. The quest for autonomy, individuality, and independence seems ubiquitous. Many of the men and women who live together but are not formally married frequently talk about their need for space and their resentment toward anyone who interferes with their own unique modus vivendi (De Burger, 1978; Hunt, 1974).

As we discussed in earlier chapters, the wedding ceremony often connotes to the partners a severing of their independence and a shackling of their bodies and souls. Consequently, many husbands and wives constantly fight with each other to avoid feeling controlled, dominated, and intruded upon. They are trying to protect their seemingly threatened autonomy under the guise of asserting themselves.

When husbands and wives who want to feel emancipated enter marriage counseling they seem, at first blush, eminently reasonable. They talk about wanting their own friends, their own hobbies, their own ideas, and their own privacy. They can also convincingly document how their partners are unenlightened, unsophisticated, and unliberated. These clients believe that they are mature adults who have a clear idea about how to govern their lives. Their only problem, they contend, is their mates who resist adhering to a live-and-let-live philosophy.

What is extremely important in work with the spouse who champions the "Emancipation Proclamation" is to recognize that he is a very ambivalent individual. Like the adolescent who wants to deny his own dependency and passivity and blames his parents for trying to control him, the spouse that we are discussing denies his own dependency strivings and projects the problem onto his mate. As far as he is concerned it is the mate—like the parents of his past—who are interfering with his pursuit of autonomy.

Just as the adolescent who is angry about being dominated does not recognize that he is allocating a great deal of power to his parents, the spouse who feels controlled is unaware of the fact that he is giving a lot of power to his mate. Both are unconsciously keeping themselves children, are placing themselves in a submissive position, and are then yelling at those whom they have empowered. Many of the spouses who are angry about being dominated and have fantasies of breaking up their marriages are really like teenagers who want to run away from home because they feel so misunderstood and mistreated. Both fail to understand that many of the power struggles in which they find themselves are of their own making. If they did not unconsciously want to be controlled, they would not feel so controlled. Again, we can note the validity of the notion that behind every chronic marital complaint is an unconscious wish. In this case, it is the unconscious wish to be dominated.

There are a few transference and countertransference problems that frequently emerge in working with the spouse who complains that his autonomy is being denied in his marriage. Because this spouse is really ambivalent about his quest, he tries to enlist the counselor's support and validation. Then he can go home with more confidence and tell the mate that she is interfering with his life. If the counselor gets seduced into enacting this role, all he will accomplish is an intensification of the client's marital squabbles and nothing much will really be accomplished. The danger of becoming prey to this type of countertransference reaction is particularly strong when counseling wives. Many wives can legitimately point to how they have been realistically oppressed in a patriarchal society and can accurately document how male chauvinism has victimized them unfairly (Hite, 1976). However, behind these correct statements and understandable protests is ambivalence. Many of these women are really protesting too much. They are not in tune with the parts of themselves that unconsciously view their wishes for separation and autonomy as hostile acts, and they often are frightened to acknowledge their own passivity and dependency.

When husbands and wives chronically complain about how their autonomy is squelched but are afraid to assert themselves and/or are reluctant to consider leaving their marriages, the counselor should take note. He needs to help these people get in better touch with how adolescent they are and how much they are recapitulating their earlier power struggles with their own parents.

The spouse who strives for autonomy but can never successfully achieve it in marriage because he is really ambivalent about it is usually ambivalent about treatment. If this client does not try to enlist the therapist's support in challenging the mate, he may very well begin to view the therapist as the oppressor. He may start to perceive the therapist's office as a place he *must* come and he can experience the therapist as somebody who is trying to control him. Often, he will ask the therapist to justify why he "has to be" in therapy and he may also question the rationale of the therapist's treatment procedures. It is very important for the therapist *not* to answer this client's questions and *not* to explain the necessity or advisability of counseling. If the therapist succumbs to the client's pressure, a therapeutic impasse can develop for several reasons. Firstly, the client's ambivalence goes unexplored and it will continue to govern his behavior in and out of marriage. Secondly, the client's passivity and dependence are partially gratified when he receives answers to questions. Consequently, he never gets to appreciate the fact that it is his own passive and dependent wishes which account for his inability to be autonomous. Finally, the client never will be able to acknowledge his own role in his marital tensions and in his other interpersonal difficulties if responded to in this manner.

Elaine A., age 35, sought marriage counseling from Dr. B., a male therapist, because she felt very angry with her husband, Steven, almost all of the time. She felt that during their 10-year marriage he was always invading her privacy, resenting her friends, not supporting her independent ideas, and being too much of "a clinging vine."

Elaine, who was an only child, described her mother as very domineering and intrusive. "She was a woman who controlled my life and always insisted on knowing where I was. She never left me alone," declared Elaine in her first interview. Elaine's father was described as a passive man who did not have too much to do with his daughter. Said Elaine, "He always seemed to be catering to my mother."

Sheltered during childhood, Elaine was "able to emancipate myself" when she went to college. Rather than obey the "strict dictates" of her mother, Elaine was sexually promiscuous, politically rebellious, and "loved arguments" throughout her college years. Although she derived a lot of satisfaction from her activities during that time, she frequently "saw the face of my mother haunting me when I did things I knew she did not approve of." Elaine likened herself to Marjorie Morningstar, the main character in Herman Wouk's novel, who rebelled against her parents' admonitions for many years but ended up conforming to them. Elaine regarded her own marriage to Steve as marrying "the nice guy my mother wanted."

During her first few months of twice-a-week treatment Elaine complained a great deal about Steve. She talked some more about his never letting her go out alone with her friends, not appreciating her private intellectual interests, and never being able "to have my own space." The only place she felt comfortable was at her job where she was a business manager. "There," Elaine pointed out, "I'm the boss and Steve can't tell me what to do."

When Dr. B. spent most of his time silently listening to Elaine during her first few months of treatment and only occasionally asking some questions, Elaine began to become quite restless. She started to ask Dr. B. his opinions and wanted to know whether she was correct in her assessments about "Steve's infantilism" and "his demandingness." Dr. B. did not answer Elaine's questions but asked her what her doubts were when she asked them. At first Elaine tried to explore her doubts, but she became increasingly anxious and felt that she could not come up with thoughts of her own. She tried to enlist Dr. B.'s support again and when it was not forthcoming she became very irritated with him. She accused him of being "a male chauvinist," a "controlling bastard," and "an oppressor." However, when she began to have fantasies of leaving treatment, she became very frightened. She thought that Dr. B. would punish her for her independence and she knew that she would "fall apart" if she tried "to spite" him.

As Elaine was helped to see how terrified she was of being independent of Dr. B., she started to realize that, for her, independence was a hostile, rebellious act. In her seventh month of treatment she had dreams in which she was decapitating Dr. B., maiming Steve, and throwing rocks at her mother. She began to realize that the main reason she could not be autonomous was that she unconsciously wanted to murder those from whom she wanted to be emancipated.

When Elaine could more objectively understand what was operating within herself that prevented her from feeling and acting autonomously, she became more comfortable with her assertiveness and her life with Steve became more tolerable. However, when she began to discuss her sex life in treatment, many conflicts emerged. She felt used, derogated, and demeaned when having sex with Steve and felt as if she were being ordered to bed. She described Steve as "a hungry pig" who was inconsiderate of her.

Exploration of Elaine's sexual conflicts revealed that she was projecting her own "hunger" onto him. She found her own "insatiable thirst" for sex repugnant and was able to see that in many ways she was making Steve both her own id as well as her mother whom she wanted to devour. These fantasies became clarified through an examination of her transference fantasies toward Dr. B. At times she experienced the therapy as Dr. B. ordering her to "put out" and referred to him as "a hungry pig." Later she was able to talk about fantasies of merging with him and "being one" with him. As Elaine became more accepting of her dependency and less frightened of her aggression, her marriage improved a great deal. Counseling for Steve was necessary because he found it difficult to accept Elaine's therapeutic gains with equanimity.

The marital relationship, as we have reiterated, is a system. Two actors are in constant interaction, striving to maintain a homeostatic balance (Bertalanffy, 1973). The sadist "needs" a masochist and vice versa; the dominant spouse "needs" a submissive mate and vice versa, and the alcoholic "needs" a partner who will tell him to stop drinking but who will concomitantly subtly sabotage her commands. Therefore, it should not surprise us that the spouse who wants emancipation but is afraid to pursue autonomy is usually married to a mate who gives some credence to the spouse's complaints.

If a wife, such as Elaine A. in the above example, is essentially ambivalent about achieving autonomy, she is probably going to be married to a husband who fosters her ambivalence. Her husband will probably be a jealous man who cannot easily accept her having a private life. He will resent her friends, criticize her independent thoughts, and try to squelch her independence. If his wife enters therapy he will try to sabotage it and, at times, he may be successful. Occasionally he will accept his wife's advice and come for therapy and if he feels very desperate, he may seek treatment on his own.

Les C., upon the advice of his wife, Norma, went into counseling with Ms. D. Les, a 35-year-old man, had been married for 11 years. He described the first six or seven years of his marriage as "comfortable," but during the last three years he felt that "all hell has broken loose." He told his therapist that Norma seemed to have withdrawn from him and he was very upset by it. He found Norma "to be in a different world" and he felt very depressed that she did not want to be with him as much as she used to. Angrily Les told Ms. D., "Now she wants her own friends, her own recreation, her own ideas, and her own everything. I feel so unimportant, so taken for granted—it's just plain awful."

During the first two months of treatment Ms. D. quietly listened to Les's complaints with only occasional comments; Les became quite anxious. He began to have less and less to say and seemed to be getting more and more depressed. When these reactions were explored with him, Les was eventually able to tell Ms. D. that he had been wanting to hear more from her and "to know what's going on in your mind." In his third month of treatment Les said, "When I don't know what you are thinking, I begin to wonder whether or not you dislike me."

Les was experiencing in his transference relationship with Ms. D. almost the identical doubts that he experienced in his marriage, and Ms. D. pointed this out to him by saying, "Perhaps when Norma doesn't share all her thoughts with you just as I don't, you feel that she dislikes you, like I do." Les responded to Ms. D.'s interpretation with a great deal of emotion and spent several sessions relating to it. He pointed out that if Norma really loved him she wouldn't be interested in so many things besides him. He also noted that her enthusiasm toward others was much greater than it was toward him. Stated Les, "If Norma or you really valued me, you wouldn't keep so much distance from me."

It became apparent to Ms. D. that Les felt that if he could not merge with his wife or with his therapist and form a symbiosis he felt rejected, depressed, and became very demanding. It also became obvious to her that Les's demandingness and intrusiveness only alienated Norma further. When she removed herself further, Les became even more anxious and the vicious cycle repeated itself over and over again. Inasmuch as Les's behavior seemed so very childlike, Ms. D. tried to examine with him the historical roots of this behavior.

Les described the relationship with his mother as one that was very close because his father was quite sickly most of the time, and Les's mother, according to him, "needed a confidante." While Les enjoyed the closeness to his mother as a child, on becoming a teenager he began to resent her "intrusiveness and controlling manner." He started to rebel by not telling her where he was going when he left the house, disagreeing with many of her religious and political values, and not being as solicitous of her. Les's mother found his attempts to emancipate himself from her as "horrendous" and told him that his behavior was "killing" her.

When Les realized that he viewed his own independence and autonomy as destructive acts that "killed" his mother, he was able to see how much he was projecting his own destructive wishes onto Norma. As Les stated in his sixth month of counseling, "I was out to tell the old lady to go to hell when I was trying to be independent. I guess I believe that Norma is telling me to go to hell each time she goes to her women's consciousness raising group or reads without telling me about it."

As Les got more in touch with his strong hostile feelings toward his mother for being "so damn demanding," it struck him in one session how much he was behaving just like her with Norma. This piece of understanding embarrassed him a great deal and he castigated himself for a few sessions. However, when Ms. D. asked him why he was beating himself so much, he was able to recognize how much he would rather beat himself than examine his own hostility, particularly murderous fantasies toward his mother.

Many of Les's symbiotic wishes covered his murderous feelings. When he became less frightened of these feelings he did not need to be as symbiotic with Norma, nor did he need as much of a symbiosis with Ms. D. He began to have interests and hobbies of his own, joined a men's club, and became much more autonomous.

On witnessing Les's declining intrusiveness and demandingness, Norma was initially pleased. However, she became very critical of Les's independent behavior after a while. She referred to Les's men friends as dopes, his hobbies as juvenile, and his interests as dull. When her anger seemed to mount and mount, Les was able to persuade her to seek treatment. In her treatment she learned that her own compulsive need for autonomy covered her own unacceptable symbiotic cravings. She further discovered that when Les became more autonomous, she resented it because she was so worried about losing him. In effect, she interpreted his independence the same way he had interpreted her's—as angry rejection.

When Norma faced her own symbiotic wishes, she became less hostile toward Les. After each of the C.'s had three years of individual treatment, the marriage became much more liveable and, at times, quite enjoyable.

It is important in therapeutic work with the spouse who is striving for emancipation but feels frustrated by his controlling and uncooperative partner that the clinician recognize that this spouse really has many conflicts. Underneath his pleas and complaints he is a very dependent person who would rather complain about his dependent spouse who will not let him grow than face his own dependency strivings. If given the opportunity to be autonomous and independent, this spouse, without treatment, would become very anxious and would somehow wreck it. As we have seen repeatedly in many of our previous case illustrations, the dynamics of two marital partners are usually quite similar. The spouse who is striving for autonomy but never achieves it has many fears. He is afraid of and denies his own dependency. He unconsciously views assertion, independence, and autonomy as destructive acts. His mate usually suffers from similar fears.

THE PASSIONATE SPOUSE

During the course of their careers all marriage counselors are confronted with the passionate spouse many times. This is the intense, emotional individual who in very colorful and dramatic language points out that he or she is full of love and passion, is very interested in sex, and is capable of leading a full life. There is only one obstacle that prevents this spouse from doing so—the mate.

The passionate spouse tearfully tells the counselor how his attempts at lovemaking are rebuffed by the partner, how his compliments are ridiculed, and how his enthusiasm is squelched. The passionate spouse cannot understand how such an interesting, dynamic, lovable, sexual person like himself can be so scorned by the partner.

This spouse tells the marriage counselor repeatedly how he has sensitized himself to every one of the mate's likes and has worked hard to avoid displeasing her. Yet, whatever he does is never appreciated. The mate does not seem interested in sex. The mate does not want to communicate. The mate does not like feeling anything. The mate wants to be left alone.

What is extremely important for the therapist to keep in mind in the treatment of the passionate spouse is that despite the fact that he appears very likeable, very interesting, very stimulating, and very convincing, he suffers from a profound problem. This spouse, although full of yearnings, does not feel that his desires should be gratified. Actually, he feels very guilty about his sexual wishes, his desires for attachment, and his deep appetite. If he were not so guilty about his passion and if he were not so questioning about his sexual desires he would not have married such a detached, withdrawn mate and would not stay married to her.

The passionate spouse who complains about his dispassionate partner really wants (although it is an unconscious want) to be deprived. Like the teenager who cannot cope with his burgeoning sexuality and unconsciously seeks out a parental figure to condemn him for it because of the intense guilt he experiences, the passionate spouse unconsciously wants to be rebuffed. Otherwise, he would feel like an anxious criminal. That is why the passionate spouse never seems to succeed in getting the intimate relationship he says he desires. He does not get gratified because he unconsciously wants to be ignored.

The passionate spouse, like the passionate but ungratified teenager, usually has many oedipal problems. This individual has many erotic fantasies toward the parent of the opposite sex but feels guilty about them. Usually the parent of the same sex has been experienced by him as very threatening; consequently, each time he wants to be gratified, he also wants to be punished. He is reminiscent of the adolescent who wants constant sexual gratification but also wants his face slapped when he asserts what he wishes.

The passionate spouse, when he has the opportunity of examining the dynamics of his marriage, usually reveals that he has married an individual who is a composite of both his mother and father. For example, if the passionate spouse is a woman, her husband is experienced as the attractive but distant father with whom she would like to become sexually and emotionally intimate and, concomitantly, the mother who forbids it. Every time she is with her marital partner she feels both stimulated and rebuffed. As a result, she is in constant turmoil.

Invariably the passionate spouse relives her teenage conflict in the transference relationship with her therapist. She pleads for advice, tries valiantly to induce sympathy, and constantly wants feedback. If the practitioner gratifies her wishes and gives advice, she becomes insatiable because she does not really feel she has a right to be gratified. Therefore, it is very inadvisable for the therapist to fall into the trap of trying to be "a giving parental figure." If he does, treatment becomes a prolonged failure because this spouse is being given the very thing for which she feels guilty.

Arlene E., age 37, was in treatment with Dr. F., a male therapist. She had been married for nine years to Ronald and pointed out in her first consultation interview with Dr. F. that Ronald had been withdrawn, unresponsive, and hostile ever since they got married. Although he seemed reasonably responsive with their two children, he never gave her "the time of day."

In reviewing her history Arlene described her father as a likeable man "who was not particularly emotional." She experienced her mother as a "tight-fisted" woman who also was not very emotionally responsive. Arlene felt close to an older brother, three years her senior, who gave her "some guidance and support" but often seemed to be too preoccupied with his own interests and his own friends.

In her treatment Dr. F. was very supportive of Arlene. He told her that inasmuch as she had a depriving background it was difficult for her to think that she had the right to receive. Arlene corroborated Dr. F.'s interpretation and felt grateful to him for his "sensitivity." She used his interpretation to feel even more deprived in her marriage and presented more and more evidence of how Ronald was "an emotional cripple." Dr. F. agreed with her assessments of Ronald and even shared with her that he suffered from "a preoedipal disorder" and that he was quite depressed.

As treatment went on with Arlene and Dr. F. agreeing that Ronald was emotionally disturbed while Arlene had so much to give and had come a long way in her treatment, her marriage got worse and worse. Eventually Dr. F. proposed that Arlene come into conjoint treatment with Ronald and he would see them together. For a long time Ronald resisted coming into treatment, but after Arlene persisted he did consent to do so.

In the conjoint treatment, Ronald felt as if he were "ganged up on" by Dr. F. and Arlene and refused to reveal himself. Attempts by Arlene and Dr. F. "to get him to show himself" were met with defensive remarks and attacks. Eventually Ronald dropped out of treatment and a year later left Arlene. Arlene became enraged with Dr. F. after the divorce and quit treatment with Dr. F. It took her several years with a different therapist to resolve some of her conflicts.

It is rarely helpful in the treatment of a spouse to diagnose and/or be critical of the mate. While the client might receive some gratification from this type of therapeutic response, it only leads to marital disaster and to a therapeutic impasse. The spouse never gets to examine his childish rage, his unresolved sexual conflicts, and his dependency. Instead, he goes into further battle with the mate, and alienates the mate even more. Inevitably, the client feels betrayed by the therapist and "divorces" him.

Particularly for the passionate spouse—but also for other clients in marriage counseling—it is necessary for the therapist to take a neutral position on the marital conflicts. By doing so the client is placed in the appropriate position of being able to examine his own contributions to the marriage and to face his own neurotic conflicts as they are expressed in the transference relationship with the counselor. As we have repeatedly implied, there is no such thing as a healthy, passionate spouse married to an unhealthy, dispassionate one. The passionate spouse has selected a withdrawn mate because this spouse is a guilt-ridden person who unconsciously wants to be deprived. Unless this spouse can see and feel his or her unresolved teenage conflicts, no resolution of the marital conflicts can take place.

Frank G., age 31, went into marriage counseling with Dr. H., a woman. He had been married to Pam for six years and the couple had a girl of three. The reason Frank wanted treatment was that he felt Pam was uninterested in sex, emotionally withdrawn, unavailable for communication, unsupportive, and critical of his relationship with their daughter.

When Dr. H. did not join Frank in his criticisms of Pam, nor condemn him for them either, Frank became more and more withdrawn in the therapy, was silent on many occasions, and canceled several sessions. In investigating his transferential responses, Frank told Dr. H. that he was withdrawing from her because he was "convinced" that she did not like him. Exploration of his conviction yielded a great deal about his relationships with his parents. He told Dr. H. that he often wanted his mother's love which, at times, was available, but more often he felt shunned by her. He described his father as "a rather aloof man."

As Frank described his early life to Dr. H. he began to have several transferential dreams which revealed his powerful oedipal conflicts. In one of his dreams he "was trying to make it sexually" with Dr. H. but her husband started to yell at him and hurt him. In another dream, as he approached Dr. H. she initially responded, only to end up laughing at him. Frank was able by the seventh month of his twice-a-week treatment to see how he was recapitulating his oedipal conflicts in his marriage. Instead of seeing Pam as an ogre he began to realize that in many ways he had "made her my conscience." Said Frank insightfully, "If I make her my mother who I want to screw, then I'm going to have to get her to reject me."

The more Frank studied his oedipal conflicts in the transference relationship with Dr. H., the less disparaging he was of Pam. Responding to his less critical attitude, Pam became more interested in Frank emotionally and sexually. In this case she did not need therapy for herself in order to cope with her mate's gains.

Sometimes successful therapy with the passionate spouse can lead to divorce, although this is not the usual outcome. However, if the passionate spouse does overcome his or her neurotic conflicts and the mate strongly resists treatment, divorce may be a consequence of the treatment.

Gertrude I., age 27, was married to Harry, age 50. She had been a student of Harry's at college and after a "mad, passionate love affair," they married. Harry was in his third marriage when he met Gertrude. She knew he was "a father figure" and found him to be very "irresistible." Gertrude also felt sorry for this "attractive man who was so brilliant but felt so unloved." She "rescued" him from his "horrible fate" by showing him a lot of love and during their six-month courtship "life was blissful."

After a year of marriage, Harry became very withdrawn and depressed. Gertrude "tried everything" to get him out of his moods but "nothing helped." She tried to persuade him to get treatment but he refused. Feeling very discouraged and despondent, she entered therapy with Ms. J.

In her treatment Gertrude was able to discover that she really "had a thing" with her own father and was able to recall many incidents where father and daughter spent time with each other having philosophical discussions about everything from sex to politics. Although she found her time spent with "my Daddy" as "very thrilling," she often felt guilty about "usurping my mother's position."

As Gertrude talked about her competition with her own mother, she began to compete quite actively with Ms. J. She told Ms. J. that she, Gertrude, could be a better therapist, a better wife, and a better lover than Ms. J. was. When Ms. J. did not compete with Gertrude, the latter was enabled to examine her own oedipal conflicts in detail. As she did so she began to see how she had made Harry her forbidden father and how much she unconsciously wanted to be punished for having him. When she shared her insights with Harry, he became infuriated and he seemed to distort her attempts to communicate positively with him. He said that he felt used by her and that she was immature. He became more and more withdrawn from her. Eventually Gertrude left Harry and was able to have a much happier marriage with another man. Her second marriage was less colored by adolescent fantasies and therefore it became more fulfilling.

BRIBING THE SUPEREGO

When a teenager has many intense sexual and aggressive fantasies that cause anxiety, he erects powerful controls to hold down his impulses and to reduce his anxiety. As we described earlier in this chapter, many teenagers find themselves making all kinds of neurotic compromises. They may eat a lot after a fast, have sexual orgies after abstinence, or sleep for days after working hard. If this "bribing of the superego" is not resolved during adolescence, the conflict will express itself in marriage.

The spouse who bribes the superego is one who retains all of his adolescent ardor but feels that every time he is gratified he must pay a price. Usually this spouse is unaware of the fact that his fights with his mate, his periodic depressions, his feeling of unfulfillment in the marriage, and his conviction that he is deprived are all punishments which he is heaping on himself. This is the spouse who goes on a vacation with his partner, has some joyful moments, but later thinks about all the pleasures he did not have. Or this spouse may go on a vacation, have a good time on it, and then find himself fighting with his mate after they have returned home. Another way that this conflict is expressed is for this spouse to alternate between having joyful and unpleasant times on the vacation. As one wife put it, "On Monday we were euphoric and on Tuesday we were miserable. Wednesday was great and Thursday was a terror!"

One of the issues that can be misunderstood in the treatment of the spouse who bribes the superego is that this client, for a seemingly unknown reason, at some point begins to devalue the treatment. Usually the therapist is baffled because this client can spend several sessions talking about how his marriage is getting better and how the therapist is very helpful only to follow these optimistic statements by pointing out how terribly misunderstood he feels in his treatment and his marriage. Equally baffling is when this client is full of doom and gloom for many sessions, and then, one day for apparently no explicable reason, comes in for his appointment and says enthusiastically, "All is well with the world. I love you and I love my mate!"

The alternation of moods in this client usually has very little to do with the therapist's activity or inactivity. What these alternations have to do with is the fact that the client must punish himself when he derives pleasure from the therapy and the therapist. If his self-esteem rises from the non-judgmental, accepting attitude of the therapist, he experiences his good feeling as something akin to forbidden sex. Then he has to devalue the treatment and suffer for a while. After he has had enough suffering he can again use the therapy constructively.

If the therapist can help the client gain some awareness of how he has to bribe his superego in both his marriage and therapy, he can then work on taming the power of his punitive superego. This is usually accomplished by the therapist's consistent acceptance of the client's expression of id impulses. As he sees that the therapist is not as cruel as his own superego, the client can better accept himself and enjoy his id wishes more (Fine, 1982).

Bill K., age 32, went into marriage counseling because he was very unhappy most of the time, particularly in his seven-year marriage to Margie. Bill told his therapist, Mr. L., that he, Bill, was a very "phlegmatic" fellow and was always finding himself vacillating in his moods. He could be happy one day and miserable the next. Bill could not find any particular reason to account for his constant mood changes but he was very angry at Margie who seemed to find him "hard to take." Quoting Margie, Bill said, "You are always going up and down. I can never depend on you."

Describing his family, Bill pointed out that he was an only child of "very moody" parents. Quite early in his twice-weekly treatment he realized that he had never known where he stood with his parents and the family atmosphere probably influenced him greatly. Stated Bill, "If I came home from school, I never knew if my mother would be loving or whether she would be snarling. I never knew if my father would want to play ball or whether he would be critical. I guess I became like them."

As Bill brought out a great deal of anger toward his parents in his first few months of treatment, he started to feel better. Margie commented that he was more "even" and she could enjoy him more. Margie's comments reinforced the positive feeling that Bill was having and for several weeks he felt euphoric. One day in his fourth month of treatment, after having a session with Mr. L. in which he was feeling very warmly toward both Margie and Mr. L., Bill told Mr. L. that he was feeling very depressed and had even had some suicidal thoughts. He had been impotent with Margie when they had sex the night before and he could not find any reason to account for "my disgusting feeling." Mr. L. was baffled by Bill's inexplicable shift in mood and felt helpless about doing anything for him. Bill seemed to sense Mr. L.'s feeling of impotence and told Mr. L. that he got the impression that he was ready to give up on him.

On studying his own countertransference reactions, Mr. L. began to recognize that what he was feeling was similar to what Margie experienced—a feeling of helplessness next to Bill. Mr. L. began to wonder if Bill was unconsciously trying to drive a wedge between the two of them and that perhaps there was something about the good feeling that Bill was experiencing that bothered the client. Therefore, Mr. L. asked Bill, "I wonder how you've been feeling about the positive changes occurring in you and in your marriage?" To Mr. L.'s surprise, Bill asked, "What positive changes? Things have been going horribly for me for years and this therapy has not helped me one iota."

After Mr. L. recovered from his own feeling of surprise he began to realize that Bill had to wipe out any reminder that he was feeling better. Mr. L. realized further that Bill truly was feeling miserable and that the happy feeling that Bill was experiencing was terrifying to him. As Mr. L. was attempting to figure out how to help Bill face his wish to destroy his own pleasure, again to Mr. L.'s surprise, Bill came in to a session 10 days later and told Mr. L. that he was feeling great. When Mr. L. asked Bill how he accounted for his shift in mood, Bill again denied any shift and told Mr. L. that he had been feeling quite good for some time. Again, Mr. L. was a bit surprised, but less so than the previous time. He began to realize that Bill's alternation in moods was so completely unconscious that he really did disown his role in them.

During the fifth month of treatment while Mr. L. was wondering if he had a case of organic or constitutional manic-depressive psychosis on his hands, Bill brought in a dream. In the dream, Mr. L. was complimenting Bill for his therapeutic progress and Bill was snarling at him. Work on this dream was extremely helpful for Bill and the work also strengthened Mr. L.'s optimism. Bill was able to see from his associations to the dream that he had to undo Mr. L.'s attempts to support him. He also could see how he was treating Mr. L. the same way his father had responded to him—by snarling. Eventually Bill could consciously recognize that if he received warmth or caring from somebody, he had to knock it down.

Exploration of Bill's need to repudiate another person's offer of warmth revealed that he was reliving a part of his relationship with his parents. As Bill said in his eleventh month of treatment, "I am so angry at my parents for not giving to me consistently that when I get warmth from them or from anybody else I can't accept it."

When Bill recognized how angry and revengeful he had been for many years, he began to castigate himself unmercifully. Mr. L. pointed out that he was punishing himself for all of his aggression and that he seemed to prefer punishing himself for his rage over understanding it. With this interpretation Bill began to talk about bribing his superego during his teenage years. He recalled how much of the pleasure he received from masturbating, having sex with girls, and eating lots of food was his way of telling his parents "to go screw themselves." He also recalled how he felt very guilty and depressed after having these pleasures but did not realize then that he was really more guilty about his defiance than anything else.

As Bill saw how much he equated getting pleasure with acting out rebelliously, he began to enjoy his id wishes much more. He told Mr. L. that it was possible to have sex without being in a fight with his parents and that he could have fun with Margie without fighting with Mr. L. or anybody else.

Bill continued to feel good about himself and about his marriage for several months. However, when Mr. L. and Bill talked about termination, Bill's improved emotional status declined. Therapist and client were able to discover that there was muffled rage on Bill's part toward Mr. L. It became apparent that Bill was still involved in an oedipal battle with Mr. L. and that a treatment success in Bill's mind was only a success for Mr. L. in which the latter would feel triumphant and Bill would feel like a loser.

As Bill talked about his competition with Mr. L., he recalled some memories from his teenage years when he wanted "to show up" his father and prevent his father from succeeding. When he recognized that he was carrying on a futile battle with his father in the present with Mr. L., Bill slowly began to feel more fondness toward him. He also resumed a good relationship with Margie, although Margie did go into treatment near the end of Bill's therapy. She was eventually able to accommodate to Bill's more "even moods" on a consistent basis.

As we suggested earlier in this chapter, when couples bribe their superegos at the same time and for the same reasons they can maintain some form of a balance in their marriage. There are some couples who have an unconscious agreement that sex is dirty, though pleasureful, and assertiveness is destructive, though gratifying. These are the couples who compulsively bathe and shower before and after sex, and tell each other repeatedly how much they love each other before and after every disagreement. However, their mutual adjustment is usually quite precarious and sooner or later they find themselves in conflict. One member of the dyad eventually gets irritated with the other's habitual rituals, while the other partner becomes frightened when his mate does not readily join him in some ritual designed to placate the superego and reduce guilt.

More often than not the member of this dyad who seeks out treatment is the one who complains that his partner's rituals are driving him crazy. He avers that he is the more liberated member of the marital union and that his partner is inhibiting him. However, he fails to recognize that he has unconsciously projected his own punitive superego onto his partner and that the partner's rituals protect him. If the partner relinquishes the ritual about which he protests, he becomes quite anxious.

Martin M., age 28, had been in treatment with Dr. N., a female therapist. One of his marital complaints was that his wife, Maria, would not have fellatio with him. The couple had four or five arguments a week in which Martin would demand fellatio and Maria would defiantly reject him. Martin would call Maria "an inhibited and uptight person" and Maria would label Martin "a stupid pervert." The battles were intense and long.

After Martin explored in therapy some of the reasons for his persistent rage, he reported to Dr. N. in his sixth month of treatment that he was not going to fight with Maria any more. He reasoned that it really didn't make him feel any better and it certainly was not making his wife more sexually responsive. Therefore, instead of pleading and arguing with Maria, Martin decided to wine and dine her and buy her expensive gifts. Maria responded positively to Martin's endearing gestures and decided that she would attempt to have fellatio with him. The couple enjoyed the experience very much. However, while Martin and Maria were relaxing and feeling warmly toward each other after sex, the telephone rang. Martin picked up the phone and the call was for Maria. Spontaneously Martin blurted out while handing Maria the phone, "Here, cock-sucker!"

When Martin and Dr. N. studied the former's response when the phone rang, Martin was able to get in touch with the fact that he, himself, had many sexual inhibitions and unconsciously felt that fellatio was something forbidden. As Martin and Dr. N. examined the client's sexual inhibitions in more detail, Martin's need for a prohibitive wife became clearer to him. When he accepted his own id wishes with more equanimity, he felt more empathy toward and less criticism of Maria.

SEXUALIZATION AS A DEFENSE

Earlier in this chapter we discussed how adolescents can use sex compulsively in order to cover up intolerable feelings of anger, depression, separation anxiety, or a weak self-image (Coen, 1981). If their underlying problems are not resolved, they grow up to use sex as a defense in marriage.

Many spouses who enter marriage counseling because they feel their partners are sexually inhibited and therefore depriving them of legitimate gratification are unaware of how or why they use sex compulsively. All they know is that their mates are unaccommodating, unfulfilling, and ungratifying. They are sure that they are the ones who are liberated, healthy, and exempt from neurotic conflicts. When they seek out the counselor they rarely ask for help for themselves. It is their pristine, up-tight, constricted mate who needs help and/or should be gotten rid of.

Particularly in this day and age when sexual liberation is championed and sexual constraint is repudiated, the spouse under discussion can easily be misunderstood by the clinician. It seems on the surface that this spouse "has it together." He talks about wanting joy and is against boredom and ritual. He champions pleasure and is against pain. He is for gladness and against sadness. Yet, the clinician always has to ask himself, "Why is this seemingly healthy and happy person married to someone who is so up-tight? Why did this individual choose his partner if she is against everything he is for?"

As the clinician asks himself the aforementioned questions, he again becomes aware of the fact that this spouse's complaints, like all spouses' marital complaints, shield wishes. Behind his protests and complaints this spouse has some awareness that his sexual habits are similar to an addiction and, like an alcoholic or a gambler, part of him wants to be controlled by his mate.

If the therapist investigates this spouse's sexual experiences, he learns a number of things which, when eventually understood by the client, can make life happier for him. First, upon investigation, the therapist learns that although this spouse always wants more and more sex, he very rarely achieves true pleasure from it. His orgasms are partial and he does not feel the contentment and relaxation that accrues from a successful sexual experience. It is because he does not achieve full release of tensions from sex that he wants more and more of it. He reasons that if he keeps on trying, somehow he'll be able to relax and feel better.

When the therapist also investigates what the client is feeling prior to wanting sex, he usually learns that the client is feeling depressed, tortured, and agonized. Sex, like an alcoholic beverage, is sought as a lift to cope with troublesome feelings. Inasmuch as the troublesome feelings are not obliterated after a sexual experience, the client persists in wanting more sex with the hope that eventually he will feel better.

Because the client who uses sex compulsively induces a feeling in his mate that she is being demeaned and exploited, the mate begins to resist sex more and more. Then the client feels more deprived and angrier and craves for sex even more. It is usually when his mate is angrily resisting his sexual demands that he seeks therapeutic help.

When this client seeks therapeutic help he is not consciously aware of his turning sex into an addiction. On the contrary, he tells the therapist that his mate is unreceptive sexually and he cannot understand why she is so inhibited. Usually he wants some kind of magical solution from the therapist—one that will provide him with a mate who gratifies his sexual needs immediately.

Shirley O., age 32, was in marriage counseling with Ms. P. She sought Ms. P.'s help because, ever since she got married three years before her initial consultation, she had been sexually dissatisfied. She referred to her husband, Nat, as "uptight," "sexually inhibited," and "unromantic." According to her own assessment Shirley, in contrast to Nat, was "loose," "sexually free," and "a loving person."

During the first few sessions with Ms. P., Shirley discussed her premarital and her married life. By her tenth session, she realized that while she never clearly articulated it to herself or to another person, she always felt "an inner emptiness," and "a low grade depression" most of the time. In talking about her parents and younger brother, her family members appeared to be very isolated, emotionally constricted people who shared little with each other and were by themselves a great deal of the time.

Although Shirley began to feel less anxiety and less distress by talking to Ms. P. about her unhappy family and married life, her "good feeling," was very short-lived. She began to feel that Ms. P., while an "interesting person" and "a concerned person," did not seem to be "emotionally spontaneous" nor "emotionally responsive." By her third month of twice-weekly therapy Shirley was making the same accusations of Ms. P. that she had been making of Nat. Without any prompting from Ms. P., Shirley was able to sense how similarly she experienced Nat and Ms. P. However, she did not see that she had anything to do with this. She was "just unfortunate to have an up-tight husband and an up-tight therapist."

As Shirley began to vent considerable rage toward Ms. P. for being so "sterile," so "proper," and so "asexual," she also felt very frustrated with her therapist for not "fighting back." She again likened Ms. P.'s "noncombativeness" to her husband's unresponsiveness. Shirley complained, "Even in an argument you both are difficult." Again she felt very sorry for herself for being the victim of such a horrible fate.

During Shirley's fifth month of therapy, she had a dream which helped clarify her own role in her interpersonal problems. In the dream, Shirley saw a little girl who was very depressed and Shirley was giving the little girl warm caresses as well as a breast to suck on. Associations to the dream revealed that Shirley was the depressed little girl who wanted to be loved. She began to recall feeling very depressed as a child and "would have loved somebody to lean on." The hostility that she had been feeling toward Nat and Ms. P. was the same hostility she had toward her parents whom she felt were extremely "unresponsive," "cold," and "unloving." Shirley recalled how she "compulsively masturbated" during her latency and teenage years "to ward off feeling depressed." As she shared some of her depressed feelings with her therapist she cried a great deal, discharged much anger, and felt better. However, just as it occurred at the beginning of treatment after being emotionally spontaneous she again began to feel deprived by Nat and Ms. P. When this was investigated in therapy Shirley was able to see how much she was convinced that Ms. P. and Nat were angry at her for showing them her needs. Dependency, anger, and wishes for intimacy were, in Shirley's mind, taboo and she projected her guilt onto Nat and Ms. P. as if they were her forbidding parents.

When Shirley recognized that she was very critical of herself for "being needy" and for "wanting an empathic ear," her sexual compulsiveness diminished and her relationship with Nat improved. However, after she had been in treatment for a year-and-a-half, she brought "a confession" into one of her sessions. What Shirley confessed was that when she had sex with Nat she often had sadistic fantasies of which she was quite frightened. Therapy revealed that she was unconsciously making Nat her mother and father and "beating them up for not loving me enough." When Shirley recognized that she was still conducting a futile battle with her parents, she mastered her sadistic fantasies better, and started to have a more spontaneous sexual and emotional relationship with Nat. When Nat saw changes in Shirley he welcomed them for a while. However, since he could no longer fight her sexual compulsiveness—inasmuch as it did not exist anymore—he had to face his own sexual anxieties and needed treatment himself in order to do so.

Just as the spouse with a sexual addiction initially likes to believe that he has no conflicts of his own but is just unfortunate to be married to an emotionally constricted person, his mate reasons similarly. She believes that she has an addict on her hands and that is her sole problem. However, she feels intruded upon and nagged. She rarely recognizes that she is projecting her own unacceptable sexual wishes onto her partner and by opposing him, she opposes what she regards as sinful within herself.

Evelyn R., age 30, came for marriage counseling with Mr. S. Married to Wayne for three years, she found his powerful sexual appetite very difficult to cope with. Wayne wanted to have sex three or four times a day and this was "way beyond the call of duty." Evelyn told Mr. S. that she tried to talk to Wayne several times about the problem but was unsuccessful. On occasion she tried to comply with his wishes, but this made her resentful. By the time she came for treatment she had become very depressed.

During her first six or seven sessions with Mr. S., Evelyn talked animatedly and intensely. She seemed to feel less anxious and appeared more relaxed after doing so. However, by the tenth interview she became quite silent and withdrawn. Although it took some time to understand, it eventually became clear that Evelyn was feeling "under pressure" to "put out" for Mr. S. She experienced him as a teacher giving her an exam, and she had to have the answers. Slowly she began to see how she transferred on to Mr. S. the same feelings she experienced with Wayne—she had to "put out" and resented it.

The resentment that Evelyn felt toward Wayne and Mr. S. derived from her relationship with her "very rigid, authoritarian parents" who "intimidated" her and "made her feel very compliant." When this perception was investigated further in her therapy, Evelyn was able to see how much she squelched most of her emotions, particularly her sexual desires. She viewed sex as something exclusively for her partner, much the same way she viewed life with her parents—it was solely for their pleasure, not hers.

As Evelyn voiced some of her resentments toward Mr. S. for being "so controlling" and saw that he did not retaliate, she began to feel quite warmly toward him. This led to her having some conviction that she was a sexual person in her own right and "not just a receptacle for Wayne."

When Evelyn became more spontaneous emotionally and sexually, Wayne became very frightened. This led to him becoming totally impotent. Eventually he went into treatment which helped their marriage a great deal.

THE UNEMPLOYED SPOUSE

When the adolescent suffers from problems regarding his ego identity, that is, not knowing whether he is an adult or child with neither role being too comfortable for him, he can express his conflicts in schoolwork and through resisting other tasks. Although swamping of the ego by excitation that goes undischarged can obviously interfere with memory, concentration, and other ego functions, many educational and work problems have additional etiological sources.

Inasmuch as the adolescent often experiences the role of student or worker as submitting to an arbitrary authority, he frequently has to spite the authority by not producing. Often the ineffective student or dropout is not incapacitated physically or intellectually, but is full of resentment toward those whom he feels make demands on him (English and Pearson, 1945). Furthermore, the assumption of an aggressive and independent role which is part of the working and learning process may be too frightening to the teenager. Independence may mean to the teenager that he has to carry too many burdens all alone and that there is no support or reciprocity in the environment. When independence activates anxiety and aggressiveness stimulates dread, the adolescent may regress to a state of infantile dependence in which he rejects the notion of being responsible for himself and for others.

As we have alluded to earlier in this chapter and in Chapter 3, another source of conflict in the inability to assume a work or learning role are unresolved oedipal conflicts. The teenager may feel that to be an equal or to surpass the parent of the same sex is to win an oedipal victory and therefore is equivalent to murder. Inhibiting his aggression, the adolescent regresses to a passive state and becomes unwilling to assert any ambitiousness.

Hence, work and educational problems may be the result of two different sources. The teenager may feel like a dependent child with the authority figure and hate him, or he may feel too much like a triumphant adult and fear him.

Although a spouse's ability to sustain himself on a job is a function of economic, social, and other factors, one variable that is frequently operative is the lack of resolution of adolescent conflicts. The ineffectual worker or absentee worker, like the adolescent, is often full of anger toward those who are making demands on him. He is unable to assume the role of responsible breadwinner because he feels he is either winning a murderous battle and/or he resents his dependency on his boss.

Very often the spouse whose work is unsteady is a very dependent, irritable marital partner. On one hand he feels embarrassed about his working habits; on the other hand he would like his partner to take over for him but is frightened to acknowledge this. For a long time he will avoid the idea of getting therapeutic help when it is suggested to him. If he does succumb to the notion, he resents being in therapy because he tends to view the therapist as another taskmaster who should be defeated.

In working with the spouse under discussion, it is important for the therapist to avoid being drawn into a power struggle which this client is prone to set up. Rather, the therapist, as with most clients, should quietly listen and help the client see how and why he wants to battle and how and why he wants to avoid taking responsibility.

Leo T., age 33, after resisting his wife Bertha's strong wish that he get therapeutic help, finally relented and went into treatment with Ms. V., a social worker at a social agency. Leo had been married for 10 years but had worked sporadically for about five of them. When Leo did work as a salesman, he argued with bosses and customers and would invariably get himself fired. He would go for long periods of time not even attempting to work and while unemployed would be very demanding of his wife and his two children.

On entering counseling, Leo told Ms. V. that he was coming to her under a threat. His wife insisted on it, but he knew it would not do him any good. However, Bertha herself was getting very depressed and angry, and recently she had threatened divorce twice and suicide once. This was of concern to Leo.

Relating to Leo's reluctance to be a client, Ms. V. asked him what it was about coming to see her for help that bothered him so much. Leo took a number of interviews to tell Ms. V. how much he "hated being ordered around," how much he "hated somebody telling (him) what to do," and how much he would "rather be alone" and solve his own problems by himself. On sensing that Leo was reacting to her in the same way he responded to bosses, Ms. V. said, "I guess you are very resentful about being bossed around and coming to see me puts you in a very uncomfortable position." Leo told Ms. V. that she was "on target" and stated with much anger, "I don't take crap from anyone and I won't from you either." Despite Leo's protests, he continued to see Ms. V. regularly on a weekly basis and continued to discharge considerable resentment toward most authorities.

Although Leo constantly brought out his distrust of Ms. V., it was obvious from his occasional smiles and laughter that he was getting some satisfaction from his work with her. Soon after a session in which he told Ms. V. that "talking helped," he began to cancel some appointments and to come late for others. He started to question this "whole business of counseling." When Ms. V. pointed out that he started to dislike coming to see her after he told her that "talking helped," Leo responded by saying, "Yeah, you trapped me, I told you I don't like to depend on anybody and you have ignored that." On Ms. V.'s recognizing with Leo how betrayed he felt, Leo was able to spend many sessions talking about "being made to feel like a little boy" at work, in his marriage, and with Ms. V. It reminded him of his teenage years when he felt that his teachers, parents, and other adults "were trying to be bosses and trying to make me feel inferior."

As Ms. V. and Leo worked on his notion that everybody treated him as if he were a little boy, during his seventh month of treatment he shared with Ms. V. a rather persistent fantasy that he had had ever since he was about 15 years old. The fantasy started off with his being 10 feet tall and with each step he took, he would get several inches shorter until he became a midget or a baby. Examination of this fantasy helped Leo realize how much he was afraid to be potent—he had to cut down his height and turn himself into a baby.

Discussion of his fantasy helped Leo a great deal. He was able to see that because he was so frightened to be a man, unconsciously he actually arranged to be a child—even though he resented being a child very much. As Leo was able to face the fact that it was in many ways he, himself, who unconsciously wanted to be a child, he became less irritable, more tender with his wife, and more potent with her sexually. However, he needed several months of therapeutic work to understand better his fear of his own potency. The fantasy of being 10 feet tall was explored further. When he saw himself as a man, he had wishes to be taller and tougher than everybody else and he was convinced his potency invited people to attack him. As he accepted his oedipal wishes with less anxiety, he returned to work and achieved a much better marital relationship with Bertha.

Very often mates of unemployed spouses become clients. Like most mates in most unhappy marriages they are unaware of how they contribute to the very issue that disturbs them—their marital partner's unemployment. The idea that they derive unconscious pleasure from their partner's dysfunctional behavior is something that is quite remote to them. In working with these mates, the counselor should try to help them get in touch with the unconscious gratification that they receive from their partner's maladaptive functioning.

Mildred V., age 40, sought help from a social agency because her husband, Hyman, was consistently unemployed. During their 15 years of marriage Hyman worked for less than five. Although he was a trained accountant he consistently found his work boring and quit jobs after a few months of employment. Mildred told her therapist, Mr. W., that she had the feeling that Hyman liked being unemployed and though she and her two children tried to persuade him to go back to work, "it never worked." Mildred was feeling depressed and helpless and she was also concerned that her children were suffering a great deal as they witnessed their parents arguing and appearing very unhappy.

In working with Mildred, Mr. W. noticed that she rarely answered his questions but, instead, often changed the subject that was under discussion. He also noticed that when he talked she interrupted him and rarely let him finish a sentence. As Mr. W. studied his countertransference reactions, he realized how very impotent he felt with Mildred. He also realized that he was losing interest in working with her. The more Mr. W. thought about his reactions to Mildred the more he realized that what he was feeling was probably quite similar to what her husband, Hyman, felt— impotent and wishing not to work. "Perhaps," Mr. W. thought to himself, "Mildred unconsciously *wants* her husband and me to be impotent and unemployed."

When Mildred continued to ignore Mr. W.'s interventions, Mr. W. eventually asked her what she felt when she did so. Mildred denied that she was ignoring Mr. W. She told him, however, that his questions and statements had no meaning to her. She thought about what he had to say but since he "didn't come up with anything worthwhile," she couldn't be very responsive. To this Mr. W. said, "It sounds like you have an impotent therapist who can't come up with anything worthwhile. I guess that explains why you can't be very responsive to me."

On hearing Mr. W.'s remarks, Mildred became quite embarrassed. She told him that he sounded like he "was trying to make it" with her and that wasn't part of his job. When Mr. W. commented, "I guess I don't know how to work correctly. I also guess I have poor work habits," Mildred asked, "Are you trying to tell me that I treat you and Hyman the same way?" Mr. W. asked Mildred what she thought of that idea, and Mildred, for the first time in her therapy (which was now in its fifth month), became very thoughtful. She said that maybe she was "subtly keeping Hyman down" by nagging and pestering him, and maybe she was "frightened of a guy who had balls."

In examining her fear of a potent man Mildred had many memories of her mother demeaning and denigrating her father. She began to see how she identified with her mother in wanting to castrate men. She later realized that to have a potent man in her life was to surpass her mother; this idea filled her with so much guilt that she concluded it was much safer to have a man who gave her very little.

As Mildred became more sensitized to her own role in Hyman's difficulties, she became more empathic and more loving toward him. She acknowledged in a talk with him that she had been nagging and pestering him in a way which was not helpful to him or to their marriage. When Hyman saw Mildred's change of attitude and realized that it occurred as a result of her treatment, he went into treatment for himself. It took him two more years before he could stay on a job without feeling bored, but it would have taken much longer if Mildred had not received treatment. Without her treatment, she would have continued to subtly encourage Hyman's being unemployed.

THE SPOUSE WITH BODILY ACHES

Particularly during adolescence when the young person is trying to cope with many intense impulses is he likely to somaticize his problems. Because the growing organism is a system comprising biological, psychological, and social subsystems, any alteration in one part will affect another (Bertalanffy, 1973). It is well known to even the casual observer that undischarged quantities of anger can lead to a migraine headache or to insomnia; unfulfilled dependency wishes that are unacceptable to the person can lead to an ulcer, and undischarged aggression and frustrated libidinal longings can induce heart conditions. Note in common parlance statements like "That was a heartbreaker"; "He gives me a headache"; "I could not stomach that."

Many spouses handle the tensions of their marriages by developing heart conditions, migraine headaches, ulcers, or other psychosomatic problems. They are so frightened to feel their feelings and even more terrified to express them that only through their bodies can they seem to show their conflicts. By unconsciously arranging to handle their tensions through their bodies, they escape facing their marital conflicts and also receive sympathy from their mates while they suffer. When they see that suffering "pays off," they continue to suffer more.

Some authors contend that psychosomatic illnesses are merely expressions of dammed-up excitation and tension and do not express a unique set of psychodynamic conflicts. Glover (1949), for example, believes that psychosomatic disorders have in themselves no psychic content and consequently do not present stereotyped patterns of conflict. He explains the particular zone of the body that is dysfunctional as a constitutional vulnerable area. Fenichel (1945), on the other hand, has concluded that the particular body zone selected reflects a unique psychological conflict. Bronchial asthma, for example, according to Fenichel, is particularly a passive-receptive longing for the mother which is expressed in pathological changes of the breathing function. The asthmatic seizure is, first of all, an anxiety equivalent. It is a cry for help directed toward the mother, whom the client tries to introject by respiration in order to be permanently protected. Similarly, Fenichel and others with an orientation similar to his explain dermatitis as crying out through the skin.

The clinician working with clients who have psychosomatic problems cannot fail to note the diminution of symptoms when the client is given the opportunity to verbalize what his "grinding stomach" or "heavy heart" is saying. No doubt, the somatic distress is a reflection of psychic tension attaching itself to a weak constitutional zone, but the clinician is also impressed with the phenomenon just described; namely, that when the heart or stomach is given a chance to speak about a unique conflict the pains tend to diminish.

Tom Y., age 35, sought treatment from Dr. Z., a male therapist. Married for over seven years with one seven-year-old son, Tom had many psychosomatic problems. He had acute migraine headaches, constant heart palpitations, insomnia, and backaches. As far as Tom was concerned, his job, his marriage, and his life, in general, were "in good shape." Consequently, he found it difficult to accept his physician's referral for psychotherapy because he saw "nothing wrong."

As Dr. Z. listened to Tom he observed that the client made every effort to deny psychological problems and feelings. The only area that appeared available for discussion was his muffled resentment about being referred for treatment. Therefore Dr. Z. said to Tom, "I get the feeling you would rather not be here, talking to a psychologist." Tom responded by saying that Dr. Z. was a well meaning person who was trying to help. He just couldn't accept the fact that he had psychological problems. When Dr. Z. asked, "So how do you feel talking to somebody whom you don't need?", Tom asked, "Are you trying to say I'm angry?" Showing some mild resentment, he said, "Well I'm not angry!" After a silence, Tom said, "Your silence does bother me, a bit. Please say something!" Here Dr. Z. asked, "What are you feeling right now?" and Tom answered, "Nothing!" Dr. Z. then wondered out loud if perhaps Tom was the sort of guy who kept his feelings inside himself and because he bottled them up, they expressed themselves through throbbing headaches and throbbing heart palpitations. Tom said that his wife told him the same thing. He had never thought about that idea too much.

Tom consented to the idea of having a few more interviews with Dr. Z. He persisted in denying he had any problems until his seventh session when he came into Dr. Z.'s office with heart palpitations that were intense and painful. After Tom spent about 20 minutes describing his symptoms, Dr. Z. asked, "What do you suppose you are feeling today when you come and see me?" Spontaneously, Tom blurted out, "When I see how hard you are working you remind me of my wife, Becky. You are trying to help me, but you can't, and it *breaks my heart!*" On repeating Tom's statement, *"Breaks your heart,"* Tom laughed but went on to talk about how badly he felt about rejecting his wife's help and rejecting Dr. Z.'s help. As he verbalized his sad feelings, he noticed that his heart palpitations diminished; however, he was quick to point out that talking did not help.

Although Tom persisted in devaluing treatment, he continued to come for his appointments, suggesting thereby that his contact with Dr. Z. had some meaning to him. As he worked overtime to deny his feelings, he frequently came into sessions with somatic symptoms. On one occasion when he had migraine headaches Dr. Z. asked him what thoughts he was holding back that were painful to talk about, and slowly Tom faced some anger toward Dr. Z. and Becky. Each time he had a somatic symptom in his sessions and was encouraged to look at the thoughts and feelings he was holding back, Tom saw that verbalizing his feelings helped his symptoms to diminish.

Eventually Tom could talk about his history. He was able to see that his early family life was one that "rewarded" him for keeping feelings and thoughts to himself. While at first it was difficult for him to acknowledge how furious he felt for being squelched by his parents, he eventually faced how terrified he was to "really tell my parents how I felt."

In talking about his family life further, Tom, during his eighth month of weekly treatment, pointed out that he didn't realize that one of the things that attracted him to his wife was the fact that she "could emote easily." Tom further reflected, "I guess I had to keep that a secret because I've also been threatened by it."

As Tom allowed himself to feel freer to acknowledge his feelings, his somatic problems disappeared. His marriage became more enjoyable and his total life became more fulfilling. Becky also received some counseling when Tom's "new emotional life" frightened her.

As consistently suggested throughout this text, the mate of a client who manifests neurotic problems derives some satisfaction from the partner's distress. Mates of the psychosomatic client, like mates of the unemployed client, usually need help in coming to grips with the contribution they make to their partner's distress.

To summarize: A repressed attitude, feeling, or thought which is rooted in unconscious instinctual conflicts causes a certain behavior. This behavior in turn causes somatic changes in the tissues. As Fenichel points out, "The changes are not directly psychogenic; but the person's behavior, which initiated the changes was psychogenic; the attitude was intended to relieve the internal pressure; the somatic symptom, which was the consequence of the attitude, was not sought by the person, either consciously or unconsciously" (Fenichel, 1945, pp. 239–240). The client's mate, albeit unconsciously, invariably aids and abets the persistence of the partner's psychosomatic problems (Ackerman, 1958) and usually needs help in coming face-to-face with his or her own contributions to it.

CHAPTER 11

The Mature Spouse—
an Epilogue

Although there are many books and articles focusing on marital therapy, there are relatively few written attempts by clinicians to conceptualize marriage (Paolino and McCrady, 1978). As Prochaska and Prochaska stated, "Most therapists are about as poorly prepared for marital therapy as most spouses are for marriage" (1978, p. 1). In a survey of 85 percent of the 102 Ph.D. programs in clinical psychology approved by the American Psychological Association, only 7 percent were found to have seminars that gave substantial coverage to marriage counseling. Of 76 percent of the 21 APA approved Ph.D. programs in counseling psychology, only 18 percent listed seminars covering marital therapy. Likewise, of 52 percent of the 82 accredited schools of social work studied, only 19 percent had courses concentrating on marriage or marital therapy (Parloff, 1976). Although more attention has been given in recent years by clinicians and academicians to marriage and to marital therapy, and despite the fact that marriage is a very old institution and marriage counseling is a very ancient practice, conceptualizing marital interaction and marital treatment by helping professionals is a very recent development.

As we indicated in Chapter 1, there has been no time in the history of mankind and no society in the evolution of human civilization where the majority of married individuals have been happy with their mates. While current trends indicate that the divorce rate is higher than ever before in history and climbing at an unprecedented pace, it does not necessarily follow that married people are more miserable than ever before. It may be that married couples are just more willing to acknowledge it. Indeed, Lederer and Jackson (1968), in *The Mirages of Marriage,* stated that 80 percent of the hundreds of couples they interviewed reported that they had seriously considered divorce at one time or another. It is doubtful that if this study had been made in the 1930s or 1940s the respondents could have acknowledged their marital unhappiness with as much candor.

As clinicians and researchers have investigated marital interaction, many of them have questioned the viability of the marriage institution itself. They have not taken the position that we have espoused in this text; namely, that happy people can have happy marriages. Rather, they have been critical of the traditional form of marriage which they have described as rigid, institutionalized, formal, authoritarian, and patriarchal. For example, David and Vera Mace (1974) believe that the rising divorce rates portend the breakdown of traditional marriage and that serial monogamy has risen as a major alternative to what they consider the anachronistic and destructive institution known as the traditional monogamous marriage. Ziskin and Ziskin (1973) in *The Extramarital Arrangement* have argued that marriages can continue to grow with new vitality only when couples can agree to enter into an extramarital sexual arrangement. Of the 124 couples they interviewed, a majority of them declared that when they involved themselves in extramarital affairs by mutual consent they found that their marriages were not only happier, but that their sex lives with one another were enhanced.

Dr. Helen Kaplan, a sex therapist who uses techniques from behavior therapy, has taken a very strong stance against the traditional monogamous marriage. She has stated (1974, p. 520):

> The destructive effects of the conventional marriage model become clearly apparent when one works with couples. The roots of a person's unhappiness are often not to be found in the individual's pathology but rather in the model, which by its demands, constricts, defeats, controls, alienates and then gags and blindfolds its victims so they can have no redress. Thus they are hopelessly trapped and cannot even identify the source of their anguish.

Many therapists and researchers, as is frequently the case, hold sentiments of the wider society. In Chapter 1 I referred to a statement of the comedian Groucho Marx which has become very popular: "Marriage is an excellent institution, providing you like to live in an institution." The writer Tom Wolfe (1976) characterized our current era as the "me decade" in which individuals seem to care only about themselves. He points out that at the turn of the century the philosopher Nietzsche predicted that when people realized that God had died they would need to create a new Superman. Superman is now called the Self and it is not difficult to observe that in current American society the Self is very sacred. We live in a time which is often dubbed "The Age of Narcissism" and we are helped to be "Our Own Best Friend." In previous decades people were willing to die for a cause or sacrifice for another person. Today many individuals want to live for themselves, exclusively (Wheelis, 1958).

While recognizing that surviving in a monogamous marriage poses many difficulties for its participants, I believe that the foregoing pages demonstrate that when individuals have essentially resolved childhood conflicts and have mastered psychosocial tasks (Erikson, 1950), they are able to enjoy the pleasures and cope with the frustrations that are inherent in marriage. I tried to document that for any given husband and wife the marital relationship is inextricably bound to the parent-child relationship in their families of origin and that no comprehensive discussion of marital interaction can avoid the subject of parent-child interaction (Meissner, 1978). A major thesis of this book is that the success of marriage counseling is very much contingent on the therapist and the client helping the latter to become sensitive to the fact that he is recapitulating unconscious neurotic childhood conflicts in his marriage. I further contended that every chronic marital complaint that a spouse has regarding his mate emanates from unconscious wishes. These unconscious childish wishes, which interfere with interaction in marriage, can frequently be mastered in the therapeutic relationship if the therapist neutrally and benignly listens, rather than takes sides in the marital fracases. I believe this book also demonstrates that if the therapist is relatively free from countertransference problems of his own, the client will see in the treatment encounter that he writes his own unhappy marital script. He will observe this when he notes over and over again how his marital conflicts with his mate do become interpersonal conflicts in his transference relationship with the therapist.

When two individuals fall in love and get married, they bring with them much psychological baggage. Each of them "brings the psychological heritage that has characterized his/her unique psychological development so that each contributes to the composition of the marital dyad, in respective and proportional ways, elements of his/her own inner psychic constitution" (Meissner, 1978, p. 26).

Jane Howard in her book *Families* points out that every human being's functioning in marriage is dependent in so many ways on his own experience in his own family. She poignantly states (1978, p. 33):

> Every human being who has ever drawn breath has been part of at least one family. Families breed us, name us, succor us, embarrass us, annoy us, drive us toward adventures as foreign to them as we can imagine.

Parents are a given and we cannot wish them away. They form the core of our sense of self, they influence our ego identities, they help or hinder in the mastery of our ego functions, they strongly influence our choice of mate, and they serve, for better or for worse, as models for our own interactions in our own marriage.

Inasmuch as this book strongly contends that marital interaction is a function of one's psychic development, I have attempted to demonstrate through case vignettes that there is a marked tendency for partners of relatively equivalent degrees of maturity or immaturity to be attracted to each other. While this phenomenon has not been studied intensively, our many cases illustrate that it is extremely unlikely for there to be too many happy, mature husbands married to unhappy, immature wives or vice versa. Rather, as discussed in Chapter 4, married individuals unconsciously try to protect and gratify each other's neuroses; if one attempts to modify the neurotic marital equilibrium, the other tries to sabotage it. This is why studies of marriage counseling frequently find that when one member of the dyad becomes more mature and therefore more loving, the other tends to become more anxious, and often needs therapy for him- or herself.

DEFINING MATURITY

What is a mature spouse? This is a question that has not been faced by many marriage counselors or clinicians. Yet, in our work with clients we should have some idea, or perhaps some "ideal," of maturity in mind. If counseling or psychotherapy has been successful in helping the client resolve some maturational tasks, then it is reasonable to expect the client to manifest maturer behavior. But what is "maturer behavior"? What is "maturity"?

Dictionary definitions attempt to answer the questions we have posed by stating that to "mature" is "to ripen" or "to develop." However, the psychotherapist would or should ask, "Ripen into what?" When Sigmund Freud was asked these questions, that is, what he thought a mature person should be able to do well, he answered, "Lieben und arbeiten" ("to love and to work").

While Freud's response is perhaps too general and somewhat vague, further amplification of his curt description might be able to help us arrive at a definition of maturity that would be available for practitioners of marriage counseling. Erik Erikson (1950), in considering in more detail what Freud meant by "love and work," concluded that the prototype of mature love is the mutual orgasm. In the mutual orgasm, according to Erikson, there is a "supreme experience" of the mutual regulation of two human beings which breaks the point off the hostilities caused "by the oppositeness of male and female and fact and fancy." In relating to both "love and work," Erikson concluded that the mature person should be able to enjoy a mutuality of orgasm with a loved partner of the other sex with whom one is able and willing to share a mutual trust and with whom one is able and willing "to regulate the cycle of work, procreation, and recreation," so as to "secure to the offspring," too, a satisfactory development.

Although Erikson has utilized the mutual "orgasm" as a prototype of mature love, it would appear that mutuality would be one dimension of a mature and loving relationship. When there is mutuality in a marriage, both individuals derive pleasure in giving and taking from the other. They empathize with one another without considering it an ignoble task or an ominous burden. They trust one another but can maintain a certain privacy from the other. They are sexually attracted to one another but can fuse tender and erotic feelings when with one another.

The amplification of Freud's "love and work" prescription is of course an ideal to achieve and no two human beings can mutually love and work creatively without periodic regressions. As a matter of fact, maturity would seem to imply that an individual is capable of accepting—without too much guilt or shame—his own imperfections. Furthermore, the mature person should be able not only to accept his own lack of omnipotence but also be able to accept imperfections in his mate and in others. He therefore does not have powerful residues of anger toward his parents and toward significant others for not being able to be perfect parents. The mature person has the capacity to forgive others in the present and the past for not gratifying his wishes the way he believes they should have been gratified.

While the mature person should be able to give and take love, identify with his partner's needs and enjoy his counterpart's doing likewise, he is able to have enough of a self-image and sufficient autonomy that the lack of love at a particular time or the lack of validation at another, does not destroy him. Love and work do not have a compulsive quality for the mature person. He can spontaneously participate in both but not need either for purposes of proving himself to himself.

Implied in the ability to "love and work" is a "strong ego." If ego functions such as judgment, perception, reality testing, impulse control, and object relations are operating well, then we can fairly safely say that the individual has resolved to a large extent the maturational tasks that we have alluded to throughout this text.

Although enjoying a wide range of feelings and experiences, the mature person knows when to defer his gratification. He can trust his environment where it can be trusted and has sufficient reality testing to know when to be cautious. Maturity, as already implied, involves the capacity to be relatively autonomous, to feel independent without resenting it and without being shameful or doubtful about one's strengths.

Mature individuals can enjoy their sexual roles, take initiative as men or women with their partners without thinking or wishing that they are supplanting somebody else. They have a sense of their own identities and are capable of feeling and being intimate. They enjoy giving to and receiving from another person.

THE MATURE SPOUSE AND PSYCHOSEXUAL DEVELOPMENT

Just as the emotionally healthy child in growing up moves from *attachment* to the mother to *admiration* of both parents followed by *sexual enjoyment* at adolescence which leads him toward an *intimate* relationship primarily with one person of the opposite sex and later followed by *devotion* to children (Fine, 1975), the mature spouse should feel and demonstrate these five ingredients in his love relationship with his mate.

The mature spouse should be able to feel attached to his mate and enjoy her attachment to him without worrying that he will be swallowed up or that he will be overwhelmed by the partner. The mature spouse can depend on and trust his mate and can be relied on without feeling anxiety. He has overcome his wishes for a symbiosis with his mate so that he can tolerate independence from her and frustration by her. He is not threatened by her independence and is not frightened to frustrate her occasionally.

Cooperation with the mate is something that the mature spouse is quite capable of achieving inasmuch as he is not involved in power struggles. He is not worried about how much power or lack of power he has, because to him his mate is his equal and one who complements him and supplements him. He is free to admire his mate, identify with her achievements and empathize with her pains. He has enough sense of his own sexual identity that he does not have to compete with the mate nor feel threatened by her successes.

The mature spouse, having overcome oedipal conflicts, can enjoy his erotic feelings toward his mate and concomitantly feel tender toward her. He is capable of a sustained monogamous marriage because he is not making his mate an incestuous object whom he fears or a conquest about which he feels guilty. His sexual life with his mate is consistently enjoyable because he does not have to regress to homosexual preoccupations or to other pregenital fantasies. The mature spouse, having resolved much of his hatred, is not dominated by a punitive superego. Consequently, he does not have to arrange for his mate to criticize or punish him constantly. He has no need for a punitive, tyrannical parental figure. If the mate needs to criticize or be punitive, the mature spouse does not need to retaliate.

Feeling no fear of intimacy, mature spouses can share their feelings and thoughts with their mates and do not feel uncomfortable about expressing their doubts, anxieties, and fears to them. They can also listen to their mates discuss issues that involve their own vulnerabilities, and they do not feel oppressed by such discussions. Mature spouses enjoy sharing a child or children with their mates. They do not compete with them for their children's attention or affection, but are capable of enjoying and sharing the children. Mature spouses are dedicated parents and are usually married to mates who are also dedicated parents.

THE MATURE SPOUSE AND THE ANALYTIC IDEAL

The mature spouse has been able to tame his hatred and wants to love most of the time (Fine, 1982). He is able to communicate a wide range of feelings to his mate and is stimulated by conversations with her. The mature spouse has a stable role in the family and in the social order. He enjoys considerable pleasure, particularly sexual pleasure, and does not have to arrange to suffer pain. The mature spouse is often a creative person who is free from neurotic symptoms.

Usually, if not always, the mature spouse is married to a mature individual who loves rather than hates and also communicates a wide variety of feelings, enjoys sex, and so on. The two feel a strong sense of mutuality in their relationship and both derive much pleasure from their marriage.

As we stated in Chapter 1, few people are capable of achieving something akin to the analytic ideal without going through psychotherapy. Most people are dominated by hatred rather than love, suffer from neurotic symptoms, feel unhappy in their marriages and in their families, and do not feel particularly creative. Many people have sexual problems and need to escape from the intimacy of marriage. It is only through psychotherapy that they can resolve their hatreds, recognize that their marital complaints are unconscious wishes, and that the type of marital unhappiness they experience is something that is in many ways self-created.

Through psychotherapy men and women can learn to be dependent on each other without wanting a merger. They can learn to accept frustration without feeling sadistic or masochistic, and they can learn to enjoy sex without being bombarded with competitive or incestuous fantasies. Psychotherapy, based on the principles we have reviewed and elaborated upon in this book, can help a spouse become a happier human being who will want to devote himself to another happy human being.

As constantly reiterated here, a happy marriage consists of two happy human beings. Most of those who argue against the institution of marriage (Kaplan, 1974; Mace and Mace, 1974) fail to recognize that many people who get married are psychologically still children seeking gratification of childish wishes—to merge, to dominate, to rescue, to be demeaned, to compete, and so on. Because unresolved childish wishes create anxiety, many married people must defend themselves against intimacy because it conjures up wishes that they cannot tolerate. In practically every case, the unhappy spouse is an unhappy person who has not resolved psychosexual tasks and has failed to mature. However, he is usually the last person to recognize that he has failed to overcome childish wishes and childish attitudes. Either he believes his spouse is causing his unhappiness or he believes the institution of marriage is much too oppressive.

The fate of an unhappy marriage is decided long before the marriage occurs. The human psyche is formed in early childhood and the result is enshrined in the person without his conscious knowledge. Marital partners do many things to ward off the anxiety that childish wishes create—withdraw, fight verbally and/or physically, murder, divorce, or have extramarital affairs. It often takes clients many years of treatment before they can accept the emotional truth about their neuroses. It is extremely difficult for them to face the fact that their marital arguments and marital discontents are part and parcel of their neuroses. Spouses cringe when they hear that their marital frustrations are due to unresolved oedipal conflicts, forbidden homosexual desires, or unacceptable dependency wishes. Most of them fail to appreciate that if they label their mates sadistic, they are probably masochistic—and vice versa.

Most of the people (professionals, laymen, and clients) who rebel against marriage are unhappy people who understandably rationalize their complaints and their objections. They are uninformed about the psychological forces that make them unhappy. They need therapy so that they can mature and lead more pleasureful lives and have more fulfilling marriages.

Bibliography

Ables, B. 1977. *Therapy for Couples*. San Francisco: Jossey-Bass.

Abraham, K. 1927. *Selected Papers of Karl Abraham*. London: Institute of Psychoanalysis and Hogarth Press.

Ackerman, N. 1958. *The Psychodynamics of Family Life*. New York: Basic Books.

Alexander, F. and Ross, H. 1952. *Dynamic Psychiatry*. Chicago: University of Chicago Press.

Austin, L. 1958. "Dynamics and Treatment of the Client with Anxiety Hysteria." In *Ego Psychology and Dynamic Casework*, ed. H. Parad. New York: Family Service Association of America.

Bach, G. 1969. *The Intimate Enemy: How to Fight Fair in Love and Marriage*. New York: Avon.

Balint, M. 1961. *Psychotherapeutic Techniques in Medicine*. London: Tavistock Publications.

Barbara, D. 1958. *The Art of Listening*. Springfield, Ill.: Charles C. Thomas.

Barker, R. 1984. *Treating Couples in Crisis*. New York: Free Press.

Bartusis, M. 1978. *Every Other Man*. New York: Dutton.

Benedict, R. 1958. "Continuities and Discontinuities in Cultural Conditioning." In *Social Perspectives on Behavior*, eds. H. Stein and R. Cloward. Glencoe, Ill.: Free Press.

Bergler, E. 1978. *Divorce Won't Help*. New York: Liveright.

Bergler, E. 1969. *Selected Papers of Edmund Bergler*. New York: Grune & Stratton.

Bergler, E. 1963. "Marriage and Divorce." In *A Handbook of Psychoanalysis*, eds. H. Herma and G. Kurth. Cleveland, Ohio: World.

Bernard, J. 1972. *The Future of Marriage*. New York: World.

Bertalanffy, L. von. 1973. *General System Theory*. New York: Braziller.

Block, J. 1978. *The Other Man, The Other Woman*. New York: Grosset & Dunlap.

Blos, P. 1967. "The Second Individuation Process of Adolescence." In *The Psychoanalytic Study of the Child*, Vol. 22, ed. K. Eissler. New York: International Universities Press.

Bowen, M. 1966. "The Use of Family Theory in Clinical Practice." *Comprehensive Psychiatry*, Vol. 7, pp. 345–374.

Bowlby, J. 1969. *Attachment and Love*. New York: Basic Books.

Brenner, C. 1955. *An Elementary Textbook of Psychoanalysis*. New York: International Universities Press.

Brody, J. and Osborne, G. 1980. *The Twenty Year Phenomenon*. New York: Simon & Schuster.

Brozan, N. 1982. "Lark–Owl Marriages." *The New York Times,* January 24, 1982, p. 48.

Burgess, E. and Locke, H. 1960. *The Family.* New York: American.

Bychowski, G. 1956. "Interaction Between Psychotic Partners: Schizophrenic Partners." In *Neurotic Interaction in Marriage,* ed. V. Eisenstein. New York: Basic Books.

Cleckley, H. 1959. "Psychopathic States." In *American Handbook of Psychiatry,* Vol. 1, ed. S. Arieti. New York: Basic Books.

Coen, S. 1981. "Sexualization as a Predominant Mode of Defense." *Journal of the American Psychoanalytic Association,* Vol. 29, No. 4, pp. 893–920.

Cookerly, J. 1973. "The Outcome of the Six Major Forms of Marriage Counseling Compared: A Pilot Study." *Journal of Marriage and the Family,* Vol. 35, pp. 608–611.

Coombs, R. 1966. "Value Consensus and Partner Satisfaction Among Dating Couples." *Journal of Marriage and the Family,* Vol. 28, pp. 165–173.

De Burger, J. 1978. *Marriage Today.* Cambridge, Mass.: Schenkman.

DeMause, L. 1981. *Foundations of Psychohistory.* New York: Creative Roots Press.

Demos, J. 1976. "Myths and Realities in the History of American Family Life." In *Contemporary Marriage: Structure, Dynamics, and Therapy,* eds. H. Grunebaum and J. Christ. Boston: Little, Brown.

Dicks, H. 1967. *Marital Tensions.* New York: Basic Books.

Dickes, R. 1979. "The New Sexuality: Impact on Psychiatric Education." In *On Sexuality,* eds. T. Karasu and C. Socarides. New York: International Universities Press.

Durant, W. 1935. *Our Oriental Heritage.* New York: Simon & Schuster.

Durbin, K. 1977. "On Sexual Jealousy." In *Jealousy,* eds. G. Clanton and L. Smith. Englewood Cliffs, N.J.: Prentice-Hall.

Duvall, E. 1977. *Marriage and Family Development,* 5th ed. Philadelphia: Lippincott.

Duvall, E. 1971. *Family Development.* Philadelphia: Lippincott.

Eckland, B. 1968. "Theories of Mate–Selection." *Eugenics Quarterly,* Vol. 15, pp. 71–78.

Eisenstein, V. 1956. "Sexual Problems in Marriage." In *Neurotic Interaction in Marriage,* ed. V. Eisenstein. New York: Basic Books.

Ellis, H. 1907. *Studies in the Psychology of Sex.* New York: Random House.

English, O. and Pearson, G. 1945. *Emotional Problems of Living.* New York: Norton.

Erikson, E. 1950. *Childhood and Society.* New York: W. W. Norton.

Erikson, E. 1956. "The Problem of Ego Identity." *Journal of the American Psychoanalytic Association,* Vol. 4, pp. 56–121.

Esman, A. 1979. "Adolescence and the New Sexuality." In *On Sexuality,* eds. T. Karasu and C. Socarides. New York: International Universities Press.

Evans, R. 1964. *Conversations with Carl Jung.* Princeton, N.J.: Van Nostrand Reinhold.

Eysenk, H. 1952. "The Effects of Psychotherapy: An Evaluation." *Journal of Consulting Psychology,* Vol. 16, pp. 319–323.

Fenichel, O. 1945. *The Psychoanalytic Theory of Neurosis*. New York: Norton.

Fine, R. 1985. *The Meaning of Love in Human Experience*. New York: John Wiley & Sons.

Fine, R. 1982. *The Healing of the Mind*, 2nd Edition. New York: Free Press.

Fine, R. 1981. *The Psychoanalytic Vision*. New York: Free Press.

Fine, R. 1975. *Psychoanalytic Psychology*. New York: Jason Aronson.

Fine, R. 1974. "The History of Psychotherapy—From Magic to Social Reform." *Book Forum*, Vol. 1, No. 2, pp. 156–163.

Fine, R. 1972. "The Age of Awareness." *Psychoanalytic Review*, Vol. 59, No. 1, pp. 55–71.

Fine, R. 1968. "Interpretation: The Patient's Response." In *Uses of Interpretation in Treatment: Technique and Art*, ed. E. Hammer. New York: Grune & Stratton.

Ford, C. and Beach, F. 1951. *Patterns of Sexual Behavior*. New York: Harper & Row.

Fountain, G. 1961. "Adolescent into Adult: An Inquiry." *Journal of the American Psychoanalytic Association*, Vol. 9, pp. 417–433.

Freedman, A., Kaplan, H., and Sadock, B. 1976. *Modern Synopsis of Psychiatry*, Vol. 2. Baltimore: Williams & Wilkins.

Freeman, D. 1981. *Marital Crisis and Short-Term Counseling*. New York: Free Press.

Freeman, L. and Roy, J. 1976. *Betrayal*. New York: Stein & Day.

Freud, A. 1965. *Normality and Pathology in Childhood: Assessment of Development*. New York: International Universities Press.

Freud, A. 1958. "Adolescence." In *The Psychoanalytic Study of the Child*, Vol. 13, ed. K. Eissler. New York: International Universities Press.

Freud, A. 1946. *The Ego and the Mechanisms of Defense*. New York: International Universities Press.

Freud, S. 1939. *An Outline of Psychoanalysis*. Standard Edition, Vol. 23. London: Hogarth Press.

Freud, S. 1938. *The Basic Writings of Sigmund Freud*. New York: Random House (Modern Library).

Freud, S. 1932. *The Anatomy of the Mental Personality*. Standard Edition, Vol. 22. London: Hogarth Press.

Freud, S. 1926. *Inhibitions, Symptoms and Anxiety*. Standard Edition, Vol. 20. London: Hogarth Press.

Freud, S. 1925. *Negation*. Standard Edition, Vol. 20. London: Hogarth Press.

Freud, S. 1916. *Some Character Types Met With in Psychoanalytic Work*. Standard Edition, Vol. 16. London: Hogarth Press.

Freud, S. 1914. "On Narcissism." Standard Edition, Vol. 14. London: Hogarth Press.

Freud, S. 1910. *Wild Psychoanalysis*. Standard Edition, Vol. 11. London: Hogarth Press.

Freud, S. 1909. *Notes Upon a Case of Obsessional Neurosis*. Standard Edition, Vol. 10. London: Hogarth Press.

Freud, S. 1905. *Three Essays on the Theory of Sexuality*. Standard Edition, Vol. 7. London: Hogarth Press.

Garrett, A. 1951. *Interviewing: Its Principles and Methods.* New York: Family Service Association of America.

Gaylin, W. 1976. *Caring.* New York: Alfred A. Knopf.

Glick, P. 1975. "A Demographer Looks at American Families." *Journal of Marriage and the Family,* Vol. 37, pp. 15–26.

Glick, P. 1957. *American Families.* New York: John Wiley & Sons.

Glover, E. 1949. *Psychoanalysis.* London: Staples Press.

Green, A. 1958. "The Middle–Class Male Child and Neurosis." In *Social Perspectives on Behavior,* eds. H. Stein and R. Cloward. Glencoe, Ill: Free Press.

Greenson, R. 1967. *The Technique and Practice of Psychoanalysis.* New York: International Universities Press.

Grunebaum, H. and Christ, J. 1976. *Contemporary Marriage: Structure, Dynamics and Therapy.* Boston: Little, Brown.

Grunebaum, H., Christ, J., and Neiberg, N. 1969. "Diagnosis and Treatment Planning for Couples." *International Journal of Group Psychotherapy,* Vol. 19, pp. 185–202.

Gurman, A. 1978. "Contemporary Marital Therapies: A Critique and Comparative Analysis of Psychoanalytic, Behavioral, and System Theory Approaches." In *Marriage and Marital Therapy,* eds. T. Paolino and B. McCrady. New York: Brunner/Mazel.

Hamilton, G. 1951. *Theory and Practice of Social Casework.* New York: Columbia University Press.

Hartmann, H. 1964. *Essays on Ego Psychology.* New York: International Universities Press.

Hendin, H. 1975. *The Age of Sensation.* New York: Norton.

Henton, J., Russell R., and Koval, J. 1983. "Spouse Perception of Midlife Career Change." *American Personnel and Guidance Journal,* Vol. 61, No. 5, pp. 287–291.

Hepworth, D. 1979. "Early Removal of Resistance in Task-Centered Casework." *Social Casework,* Vol. 69, No. 7, pp. 317–322.

Hill, R. 1970. *Family Development in Three Generations.* New York: Schenkman.

Hite, S. 1976. *The Hite Report.* New York: Macmillan.

Howard, J. 1978. *Families.* New York: Simon & Schuster.

Hudson, J. and Henze, L. 1977. "Campus Values in Mate Selection: A Replication." In *Marriage Today,* ed. J. De Burger. Cambridge, Mass.: Schenkman.

Humphrey, F. 1975. "Changing Roles for Women: Implications for Marriage Counselors." *Journal of Marriage and Family Counseling,* Vol. 1, No. 3, pp. 219–228.

Hunt, M. 1977. "Is Marriage in Trouble?" In *Marriage Today,* ed. J. De Burger. Cambridge, Mass.: Schenkman.

Hunt, M. 1974. *Sexual Behavior in the 1970's.* New York: Dell.

Hunt, M. 1969. *The Affair.* Bergenfield, N.J.: New American Library.

Hunt, M. 1959. *The Natural History of Love.* New York: Alfred H. Knopf.

Jackson, D. 1965. "The Study of the Family." *Family Process,* Vol. 4, pp. 1–20.

Jacobson, E. 1956. "Interaction Between Psychotic Partners: Manic-Depressive Partners." In *Neurotic Interaction in Marriage,* ed. V. Eisenstein. New York: Basic Books.

Johnson, J. 1979. "Nixon's Use of Metaphor: The Real Nixon Tapes." *Psychoanalytic Review,* Vol. 66, No. 2.

Jones, E. 1953. *The Life and Work of Sigmund Freud,* Vol. 1. New York: Basic Books.

Jones, E. 1922. "Some Problems of Adolescence." In *Papers on Psychoanalysis,* ed. E. Jones. London: Bailliere, Tindall and Cox.

Jong, E. 1973. *Fear of Flying.* New York: Holt, Rinehart, & Winston.

Josselyn, I. 1948. *Psychosocial Development of Children.* New York: Family Service Association of America.

Kadushin, A. 1972. *The Social Work Interview.* New York: Columbia University Press.

Kaplan, H. 1974. *The New Sex Therapy.* New York: Brunner/Mazel.

Karasu, T. and Socarides, C. 1979. *On Sexuality.* New York: International Universities Press.

Kernberg, O. 1972. *Psychotherapy and Psychoanalysis. Final Report.* Topeka, Kansas: Bulletin of the Menninger Clinic.

Kirkpatrick, C. 1977. "The Family in Transition: Impact of the Scientific Revolution." In *Marriage Today,* 2 ed. J. De Burger. Cambridge, Mass.: Schenkman.

Klein, M. 1957. *Envy and Gratitude.* New York: Basic Books.

Klimek, D. 1979. *Beneath Mate Selection in Marriage.* New York: Van Nostrand Reinhold.

Koch, L. and Koch, J. 1976. *The Marriage Savers.* New York: Coward, McCann, & Geoghegan.

Kubie, L. 1956. "Psychoanalysis and Marriage: Practical and Theoretical Issues." In *Neurotic Interaction in Marriage,* ed. V. Eisenstein. New York: Basic Books.

Langley, R. and Levy, R. 1977. *Wife Beating: The Silent Crisis.* New York: Dutton.

Langs, R. 1981. *Resistances and Interventions.* New York: Jason Aronson.

Lederer, W. and Jackson, D. 1968. *The Mirages of Marriage.* New York: Norton.

Leighton, A. 1963. *The Character of Danger.* New York: Basic Books.

LeMasters, E. 1965. "Parenthood as Crisis." In *Crisis Intervention,* ed. H. Parad. New York: Family Service Association of America.

Levinson, D. 1978. *The Seasons of a Man's Life.* New York: Alfred A. Knopf.

Licht, H. 1932. *Sexual Life in Ancient Greece.* London: Abbey Library.

Linton, R. 1936. *The Study of Man.* New York: Appleton–Century.

Litz, T. 1968. "The Effects of Children on Marriage." In *The Marriage Relationship,* ed. S. Rosenbaum. New York: Basic Books.

Lloyd, R. and Paulson, I. 1972. "Projective Identification in the Marital Relationship as a Resistance in Psychotherapy." *Archives of General Psychiatry,* Vol. 27, pp. 410–413.

Lutz, W. 1964. "Marital Incompatibility." In *Social Work and Social Problems,* ed. N. Cohen. New York: National Association of Social Workers.

Lynch, J. 1977. *The Broken Heart.* New York: Basic Books.

Mace, D. and Mace, V. 1974. *We Can Have Better Marriages.* Nashville: Abingdon.

Mahler, M. 1968. *On Human Symbiosis and the Vicissitudes of Individuation.* New York: International Universities Press.

Malinowski, M. 1963. "Marriage." *Encyclopedia Britannica.*

Malinowski, M. 1922. *Argonauts of the Western Pacific.* New York: Dutton.

Marasse, H. and M. Hart. 1975. "The Oedipal Period." In *Personality Development and Deviation,* ed. G. Weideman. New York: International Universities Press.

Martin, P. 1976. *A Marital Therapy Manual.* New York: Brunner/Mazel.

Mason, A. 1977. "Paranoid and Depressive Positions in Marital Relations." *Modern Psychoanalysis,* Vol. 2, No. 1, pp. 43–54.

Masters, W. and Johnson, V. 1970. *Human Sexual Inadequacy.* Boston: Little, Brown.

Maugham, S. 1954. *Of Human Bondage.* Garden City, N.Y.: Doubleday.

Mead, M. 1967. "Sexual Freedom and Cultural Change." Paper delivered at Forum, "The Pill and the Puritan Ethic," San Francisco State College, February 10, 1967.

Meissner, W. 1978. "The Conceptualization of Marriage and Family Dynamics from a Psychoanalytic Perspective." In *Marriage and Marital Therapy,* eds. T. Paolino and B. McCrady. New York: Brunner/Mazel.

Meltzoff, J. and Kornreich, M. 1970. *Research in Psychotherapy.* New York: Atherton Press.

Miller, A. 1964. *After the Fall.* New York: Viking Press.

Mittelmann, B. 1956. "Analysis of Reciprocal Neurotic Patterns in Family Relationships." In *Neurotic Interaction in Marriage,* ed. V. Eisenstein. New York: Basic Books.

Montagu, A. 1956. "Marriage—A Cultural Perspective." In *Neurotic Interaction in Marriage,* ed. V. Eisenstein. New York: Basic Books.

Murdock, G. 1949. *Social Structure.* New York: Macmillan.

Neiberg, N. 1976. "The Group Psychotherapy of Married Couples." In *Contemporary Marriage: Structure, Dynamics and Therapy,* eds. H. Grunebaum and J. Christ. Boston: Little, Brown.

Neubauer, P. 1960. "The One–Parent Child and His Oedipal Development." In *The Psychoanalytic Study of the Child,* Vol. 15, ed. K. Eissler. New York: International Universities Press.

New York Times, November 18, 1973.

Nixon, R. 1962. *Six Crises.* New York: Doubleday.

O'Neill, N. and O'Neill, G. 1972. *Open Marriage.* New York: M. Evans.

Paolino, T. and McCrady, B. 1978. *Marriage and Marital Therapy.* New York: Brunner/Mazel.

Parad, H. 1965. *Crisis Intervention.* New York: Family Service Association of America.

Parloff, M. 1976. "The Narcissism of Small Differences—and Some Big Ones." *International Journal of Group Psychotherapy,* Vol. 26, pp. 311–319.

Peele, F. 1975. *Love and Addiction.* New York: New American Library.

Perlman, H. 1968. *Persona: Social Role and Personality.* Chicago: University of Chicago Press.

Perlman, H. 1957. *Social Casework: A Problem Solving Process.* Chicago: University of Chicago Press.

Pietropinto, A. and Simenauer, J. 1979. *Husbands and Wives: A Nationwide Survey of Marriage.* New York: Times Books.

Reid, W. and Shyne, A. 1969. *Brief and Extended Casework.* New York: Columbia University Press.

Reik, T. 1941. *Masochism in Modern Man.* New York: Grove Press.

Reiss, I. 1973. *Heterosexual Relationships: Inside and Outside of Marriage.* Morristown, N.J.: General Learning Press.

Rennie, T. 1962. *Mental Health in the Metropolis.* New York: Dell.

Rodgers, R. 1973. *Family Interaction and Transaction: The Developmental Approach.* Englewood Cliffs, N.J.: Prentice-Hall.

Rodgers, R. 1964. "Toward a Theory of Family Development." *Journal of Marriage and the Family,* Vol. 26, August 1964.

Rogers, C. 1951. *Client-Centered Therapy.* Boston: Houghton Mifflin.

Roheim, G. 1952. *The Gates of the Dream.* New York: International Universities Press.

Russel, B. 1929. *Marriage and Morals.* New York: Liveright.

Sager, C. 1966. "The Development of Marriage Therapy: An Historical Review." *American Journal of Orthopsychiatry.* Vol. 36, pp. 458–467.

Sapirstein, M. 1948. *Emotional Security.* New York: Crown.

Sarnoff, C. 1976. *Latency.* New York: Jason Aronson.

Segraves, R. 1982. *Marital Therapy: A Combined Psychodynamic–Behavioral Approach.* New York: Plenum.

Serban, G. 1981. Interview in *Frontiers of Psychiatry,* Vol. 11, No. 9, October 15, 1981.

Sheehy, G. 1976. *Passages.* New York: Dutton.

Siporin, M. 1975. *Introduction to Social Work Practice.* New York: Macmillan.

Skynner, A. 1976. *Systems of Family and Marital Psychotherapy.* New York: Brunner/Mazel.

Smith J. and Smith, L. 1974. *Beyond Monogamy.* Baltimore: Johns Hopkins University Press.

Socarides, C. 1977. "On Vengeance: The Desire to 'Get Even'." In *The World of Emotions.* New York: International Universities Press.

Sorokin, P. 1931. *A Systematic Source Book in Rural Sociology,* Vol. 2. Minneapolis: University of Minnesota Press.

Spitz, R. 1965. *The First Year of Life.* New York: International Universities Press.

Spotnitz, H. 1961. "Adolescence and Schizophrenia: Problems in Differentiation." In *Adolescents: Psychoanalytic Approach to Problems and Therapy,* eds. S. Lorand and H. Schneer. New York: Haber.

Spotnitz, H. and Freeman, L. 1964. *The Wandering Husband.* Englewood Cliffs, N.J.: Prentice-Hall.

Spotnitz, H. and Meadow, P. 1976. *Treatment of the Narcissistic Neuroses.* New York: Manhattan Center for Advanced Psychoanalytic Studies.

Srole, L. 1962. *Mental Health in the Metropolis: The Midtown Manhattan Study.* New York: McGraw Hill.

Stein, H. and Cloward, R. 1958. *Social Perspectives on Behavior.* Glencoe, Ill.: Free Press.

Stein, M. 1956. "The Unconscious Meaning of the Marital Bond." In *Neurotic Interaction in Marriage.* ed. V. Eisenstein. New York: Basic Books.

Stern, M. and Stern, A. 1981. *Sex in the U.S.S.R.* New York: Times Books.

Stoller, R. 1975. *Perversion: The Erotic Form of Hatred.* New York: Pantheon Books.

Strean, H. 1985. *Resolving Resistances in Psychotherapy.* New York: John Wiley & Sons.

Strean, H. 1983. *The Sexual Dimension: A Guide for the Helping Professional.* New York: Free Press.

Strean, H. 1980. *The Extramarital Affair.* New York: Free Press.

Strean, H. 1979. *Psychoanalytic Theory and Social Work Practice.* New York: Free Press.

Strean, H. 1978. *Clinical Social Work.* New York: Free Press.

Sullivan, H. 1972. *Personal Psychopathology.* New York: Norton.

Sullivan, H. 1953. *The Interpersonal Theory of Psychiatry.* New York: Norton.

Tennov, D. 1979. *Love and Limerence.* New York: Stein & Day.

Truax, C. 1973. "Effective Ingredients in Psychotherapy." In *Creative Developments in Psychotherapy,* Vol. 1, Eds. A. Mahrer and L. Pearson. New York: Jason Aronson.

Vangaard, T. 1972. *Phallas.* New York: International Universities Press.

Waelder, R. 1941. "The Scientific Approach to Casework with Special Emphasis on Psychoanalysis." *Journal of Social Casework,* Vol. 22.

Weideman, G. 1975. *Personality Development and Deviation.* New York: International Universities Press.

Wheelis, A. 1958. *The Quest for Identity.* New York: Norton.

Willi, J. 1976. "The Hysterical Marriage." In *Contemporary Marriage: Structure, Dynamics and Therapy,* eds. H. Grunebaum and J. Christ. Boston: Little, Brown.

Williams, F. 1968. "Family Therapy." In *Modern Psychoanalysis,* ed. J. Marmor. New York: Basic Books.

Wolfe, T. 1976. *Mauve Gloves and Madmen, Clutter and Vine, and Other Stories, Sketches and Essays.* New York: Farrar, Straus & Giroux.

Zilbach, J. 1968. "Family Development." In *Modern Psychoanalysis,* ed. J. Marmor. New York: Basic Books.

Ziskin, J. and Ziskin, M. 1973. *The Extramarital Arrangement.* London: Abelard-Schuman.

Author Index

Subject Index